VIOLENCE TAKING PLACE

Cultural Memory
in
the
Present

Mieke Bal and Hent de Vries, Editors

VIOLENCE TAKING PLACE

The Architecture of the Kosovo Conflict

Andrew Herscher

STANFORD UNIVERSITY PRESS

STANFORD, CALIFORNIA

Stanford University Press
Stanford, California

This book has been published with the assistance of the University of Michigan's
Office of the Vice President for Research, Taubman College of Architecture and
Urban Planning, and Department of Slavic Languages and Literatures.

Printed in the United States of America

Library of Congress Cataloging-in-Publication Data

Herscher, Andrew, 1961-
  Violence taking place : the architecture of the Kosovo conflict / Andrew Herscher.
    p. cm.--(Cultural memory in the present)
  Includes bibliographical references and index.
  ISBN 978-0-8047-6935-8 (cloth : alk. paper)--ISBN 978-0-8047-6936-5 (pbk.
)
  1. Kosovo War, 1998-1999--Destruction and pillage. 2. Buildings--War damage--
Kosovo (Republic) 3. Architecture and society--Kosovo (Republic) 4. Architecture
and war--Kosovo (Republic) I. Title. II. Series: Cultural memory in the present.
  DR2087.6.A74H47 2010
  949.7103'15--dc22   2009052311

Typeset by Bruce Lundquist in 11/13.5 Adobe Garamond

Contents

Acknowledgments

This book was conceived, researched, discussed, and written in many places, where I have benefited from the assistance of many people and the support of many institutions.

I am extraordinarily grateful for the discussions I have had with and help I have received from many people in and around Kosovo, especially Yelena Baldanova, Rao Biyyala, Amra Hadjimuhamedović, Arber Hadri, Ylber Hysa, Father Sava Janjić, Garentina Kraja, Haxhi Mehmetaj, Engjellushe Morina, Jolyon Naegele, Dick Sandberg, Edi Shukriu, Shqipe Spahiu, and Flora Topanica. Gjejlane Hoxha was particularly generous with her time and assistance. In Prishtina, the Department of Cultural Heritage in the Ministry of Culture, Youth, and Sports, Cultural Heritage Without Borders, and the Kosovo and Prishtina Institutes for the Protection of Monuments each supported my work in crucial ways. I am thankful for receiving permission from Bishop Artemije of the Serbian Orthodox Eparchy of Raško-Prizren to republish photographs from the Eparchy's press department.

My initial research in Kosovo was undertaken under the auspices of the International Criminal Tribunal for the Former Yugoslavia (ICTY) and was supported by a grant from the Packard Humanities Institute. I undertook further research on material gathered by the ICTY at the Open Society Archive at the Central European University in Budapest, with the assistance of a research support grant from that archive.

I have benefited from participating in three interdisciplinary humanities institutes during the time I was thinking about and writing this book: the 2002 seminar "The Near in Blood, the Nearer Bloody: Inter-Ethnic Civil War / Cultural Genocide / Cultural Resistance," at the Leslie Center for the Humanities at Dartmouth College; the 2003 seminar "Violence," at the Illinois Program for Research in the Humanities; and the 2007 fellows seminar at the Institute for the Humanities at the University of Michigan. I thank, in particular, Lynda Boose and Annabelle Winograd at Dartmouth,

Matti Bunzl at Illinois, and Daniel Herwitz at Michigan for the collegial and intellectually rich environments they each crafted and nurtured. The 2003 summer course at the Central European University, "Violence and Culture: Rethinking Ethnic, Religious, and Nationalist Conflict in the Post Cold War Context," was also invaluable for focusing my thinking; I am especially grateful for the conversation with Allen Feldman that began during that course.

I have enormously benefited from the readings of parts, and sometimes wholes, of this book by Matt Biro, Ross Chambers, Alison Goebel, Daniel Herwitz, Wendy Hesford, Katherine Ibbett, Keith Mitnick, Brendan Moran, Alona Nitzan-Shiftan, Mireille Roddier, and Maria Todorova; each has generously contributed reactions and suggestions. Malkit Shoshan's encouragement came at a moment when it was especially needed. The encouragement, advice, critique, and example of Dan Monk have been particularly important to me; without his involvement, this book would have been a far different and, I think, much lesser thing entirely.

At the University of Michigan, the support of Tom Buresh, chair of the Architecture Program in the Taubman College of Architecture and Urban Planning, and Herb Eagle, chair of the Department of Slavic Languages and Literatures, has been essential to the completion of this book. I also thank the Taubman College and the Department of Slavic Languages and Literatures for their contributions to the publication subvention that has facilitated the production of this book.

At Stanford University Press, the steadfast belief of Emily-Jane Cohen in this, my first book, has been a source of wonderment and a cause for huge thanks.

And at home, Akiko accompanied me throughout the writing of this book; her reassurance, support, and love also enabled this writing to take place.

Note on Place Names

As there cannot be a "proper" name for violence, so, too, can there be no "proper" name for a place—a name adequate to all of a place's constituencies and representations, adequate through history and ongoing time, adequate to a place in its own supposed self-presence. If violence is a form of nomination, then nomination is a form of violence—and yet places are and must be named. In Kosovo, all places, including Kosovo itself, have Albanian and Serbian names, and sometimes names in other languages, as well. In this book, I use the Serbian name *Kosovo* (Albanian *Kosova*), which is conventional in English. I provide both Albanian and Serbian names for villages, towns, and cities when these places are first mentioned. Thereafter, I use Serbian names when discussing sites primarily identified with Serbs, Byzantine or Serbian Orthodox monuments, or when quoting from Serbian sources; Albanian names when discussing sites primarily identified with Albanians, Ottoman or Islamic monuments, or when quoting from Albanian sources; and whatever name is given when quoting from sources in other languages. The International Criminal Tribunal for the Former Yugoslavia and NATO tended to use Serbian names for places and I follow this usage when discussing places in the context of the activities of these organizations. When none of the preceding applies, I use Albanian names for places, a usage which is emerging as conventional in English. I do not make recourse to convention as a form of propriety—a source of proper place names—but, rather, as a form of place-holding, one that hopefully allows attention to fall on places as well as just their names.

VIOLENCE TAKING PLACE

Introduction:
Violence Taking Place

It was the fall of 1999. Almost three months before, Slobodan Milošević had agreed to withdraw Serb forces from Kosovo if NATO stopped its bombing campaign against Serbia. I waited for hours to cross the Macedonian border into Kosovo. Around eight hundred thousand Kosovar Albanians—almost half of Kosovo's population—had fled or been expelled from their homes during the previous two years of conflict between Serbia and the Kosovo Liberation Army. Most had quickly returned after the war, but I was waiting among others—returning emigrants, visiting relatives, incoming aid workers—thronging to cross Kosovo's recently opened borders. I was coming to Kosovo to survey the state of architectural heritage after the just concluded conflict. A colleague and I were working on behalf of the International Criminal Tribunal for the Former Yugoslavia, which at the time was researching indictments for war crimes in Kosovo. According to media reports and interviews with refugees, Serb military and paramilitary had inflicted catastrophic damage on architecture during their counterinsurgency campaign against the Kosovo Liberation Army. If this architecture was included within what the tribunal termed "Kosovo's cultural and religious heritage," its deliberate destruction comprised a war crime for the tribunal, a form of the crime of persecution. I was an architect with some work experience on Ottoman-era architecture in Bosnia, both before and after the Bosnian War, and a doctoral student in architectural history. Putting my dissertation on hold, I was going to find out what had been destroyed, how it had been destroyed, and who was responsible for this destruction: questions that at the time seemed wholly sufficient to frame an account of the role of architecture in the Kosovo conflict.

Throughout Kosovo, architecture registered ample and vivid evidence of violence: facades stippled by the spray of bullets, black aureoles of smoke around gaping holes where doors or windows once were, and piles of rubble that were no longer identifiable as architecture at all. In some towns, entire blocks were in ruins. In other towns, destruction yielded even less: at the center of Vushtrri/Vučitrn, for example, there was an expanse of bare earth, vacant except for some scattered stones, bricks, and the octagonal foundation of, we eventually discovered, the minaret of a bulldozed mosque. Some small villages were completely uninhabited, with some or all of their houses burned, stray dogs wandering the streets, and fruit trees in abandoned gardens rustling in the wind. In one destroyed village, we encountered an elderly Albanian couple living in a shed behind their burned house. The husband put two pieces of wood on the grass for us to sit on while his wife prepared tiny glasses of tea for us. The man told us about the burning of the village, but it was impossible for me to comprehend what had happened, what had been experienced, what had been lost. We gave the couple two hundred deutsch marks when we left. Our gesture was at once typical and symptomatic. It was but one of many attempts, each that seemed inadequate in its own way, to respond to what we experienced as massive social suffering. It was also a response based on my felt interpellation as a "relief worker" who could provide such things as financial aid or redress, access to the postwar NGO industry, justice, or sometimes just empathetic listening.

The survey for the tribunal, of course, was our primary instrument of relief, but as the survey continued, my understanding of it became increasingly complicated. I wanted to assist in the prosecution of perpetrators of violence, but who or what did these perpetrators represent—a state, a political elite, an ideology, "history" itself? I wanted to assist the victims of violence, but how to locate individual situations of suffering with respect to cover terms like "ethnic violence" or "ethnic cleansing"? How to differentiate the violence of war, which I was documenting, from the violence of postwar "peace," which was unfolding in many dimensions, including the architectural, in the very midst of this documentation? What relation did violence against architecture bear to violence against the people who built, inhabited, or identified with that architecture? Is architecture always innocent? Is destruction always violent? Is passing judgment on violence—part of my work for the tribunal—an effective form of resistance to violence? Framing these and related questions, I came to regard my work for the tribunal as only preliminary, and to project my response to violence in Kosovo onto many other forms, architectural, institutional, and narrative. The latter form includes this book, in which I explore the intersection of architecture with violence, identity, agency, and history in modern and contemporary Kosovo.

Constructing Destruction

Bullet-sprayed facades, ruined city blocks, burned houses, uninhabited villages: I have only begun to set the stage for this story and have already recruited destroyed architecture to represent abstract conditions in vivid, material form—a typical and symptomatic gesture toward destruction, and precisely the one around which this book will revolve. Indeed, the destruction I surveyed in 1999 would be referred to in just this way when the report I eventually coauthored was entered as evidence in the trial of Slobodan Milošević in 2002.[1] In the Milošević trial, destruction was at once a war crime and a representation of the various forces and causes behind that crime. Destruction was therefore traced back to a single author, Milošević himself; destruction was confined to the formal, if illegal operations of a state; destruction was regarded as politically rational, an instrument knowingly applied as a means to achieve a specified end; and destruction was thought to embody a political power that preexisted and stood separate from its applications, a power that was understood to distribute itself continuously across space, from a central point of authority to peripheral sites of violence. Destruction, that is, served to make manifest a host of otherwise inchoate presences, from the authority of Milošević, through the political agency of his regime, to the power of the state.

Milošević, it was clear, bore political responsibility for war crimes, in Kosovo as in Bosnia and Croatia. Yet, the narrative of destruction that emerged in his trial, just like narratives of destruction in many other discursive contexts, was based on a decisive yet unmentioned exclusion of destruction from the problematic of architecture. Consider the fundamentally different ways in which architecture (whether imagined or realized) and destruction are usually understood. Architectural discourse has produced sophisticated interpretive techniques to register the material and semantic autonomies of architectural constructions, to accommodate the capacity of architecture not only to reproduce already existing contextual realities in another form, but also to produce new realities, to act upon and even transform its putative contexts: in short, to problematize reflexive assumptions about architecture's relationship to the presences of which it might be taken as mere product, effect, expression, or mediation.[2]

When architecture is destroyed, however, it is typically regarded as just such a product, effect, expression, or mediation. Destruction usually displaces architecture from architectural discourse, if not the domain of "culture" more generally, and positions it in the domain of "violence," and so, in typical formulations, in radically different disciplinary sites and epistemological frameworks. The underlying assumption, characteristic in humanist discourse, is that "culture" and "violence" stand in unmediated opposition to one another, that violence is always absent from or aberrant in fully "cultural" formations. This assumption sponsors not only opposing valuations of culture and violence but also opposing epistemologies: while cultural phenomena are posited as complex and necessary to interpret, violence is apprehended as obvious and apparent. As such, violence is typically reduced to either a rational or irrational act, either an instrument to achieve a specified end or an exit from instrumental logic altogether. As a rational instrument, an act of violence is presumed to be already interpreted; as an irrational irruption, an act of violence is presumed to be uninterpretable. What often passes for the "interpretation" of violence is thus contextualization, the rendering of an act of violence as a mediation of preexisting and self-constituting contextual formations of antagonism, authorization, or legitimization. As Gyanendra Pandey describes this dynamic, "historical discourse has been able to capture the moment of physical or psychological violation only with great difficulty. The history of extreme violence is, therefore, almost always about context—about everything that happens around violence."[3]

Like other cultural forms, violence is a kind of inscription, an investment of material with identity and meaning that is irreducible to the intention of an author, the determination of a context, or the explanation of an interpreter.[4] In the case of architecture, however, only design is usually recognized as inscription; destruction tends to transform architecture from *inscription* to *transcription*, from the production of identity and meaning to their mere circulation—a transformation in architecture's fundamental mode of existence. In the predominant forms of disciplinary labor, then, architecture invites critical interpretation, just as other cultural forms do—until it is destroyed. Destruction, by contrast, prompts contextualization as a mere surface expression of supposedly "deeper" social, political or, economic conditions—themselves the typical sites of scholarly labor and academic knowledge production on violence, and, not at all incidentally, of state management and control of violence.[5]

Such was the case with the report I coauthored for the tribunal. What was destroyed? When was it destroyed? And who destroyed it? Those were the questions that organized our report and that neatly fit our description of wartime violence against architecture into the tribunal's prosecutorial narrative. This was a narrative that paid far less attention to acts of violence against architecture than to their context of authorization, the chain of command connecting Milošević—the supposed point of origin of those acts—to forces on the ground in Kosovo. And such is also the case in most historical discourse about the post-Yugoslav wars. The title of one of the most thorough surveys of this discourse—"Who's to Blame, and for What? Rival Accounts of the War," by Sabrina Ramet—succinctly expresses the prevailing focus on naming and judging the authorizing agencies of violence over and against describing the violence that these agencies supposedly authorized.[6] Whether these agencies comprise states, actual or imaginary communities, ideological formations, or historical dynamics, it is as if, in most accounts of the post-Yugoslav wars, the wars' violence was immediately apparent, and as if the interpretive problem was therefore to assess responsibility—political, historical, or ethical—for this violence. With respect to architecture, just like other targets of violence, this protocol of historical representation moves interpretive attention away from the architectural articulation of violence to violence's supposed agents, causes, or originary conditions. The destroyed facades, houses, and villages that I mentioned in passing at the beginning of this introduction tend to *only* get mentioned in passing.

Moreover, even when histories of political violence do attend to architecture, the epiphenomenal status of architecture tends to be maintained, if not further reified. In almost all historical accounts of destruction in the former Yugoslavia, the seemingly automatic assumption is that architecture is targeted as a representation of the actual, intended, or final destination of violence. This representation is often posited as a "sign," so that violence against architecture targets "signs of the culture of the 'enemy'"; it is also often posited as a "symbol," so that violence against architecture targets "symbols of other nations."[7] This representational status is often reiterated in the guise of correcting it, of presenting a "historically accurate" represen- tation as a replacement for the merely ideological ones staged by history's protagonists: "It is not only that the shrines represent the religious 'other' but, more importantly, that they embody five centuries of religious plural- ism and accommodation."[8] And histories of conflict also project this rep- resentational status back into history itself, so that it becomes the original intention of architecture's authors or patrons: "(s)acred landmarks, as bor- der guards and visible material cultural markers, were built for millennia by various empires, native regimes, and foreign invaders."[9] What remains unquestioned, in other words, is that architecture represents something else, a presence—culture, nation, community, history—that exists prior to and exterior from its architectural signification or symbolization.

At the same time, however, even as historiography *differentiates* ar- chitecture, as representation, from the seemingly autonomous presences that stand as origins, grounds, or causes of history, it also poses violence against architecture as an *identification* of those presences with their archi- tectural representation. This representation exposes otherwise unavailable presences to violence; it allows cultures, nations, communities, or history to be attacked through their architectural "signs" or "symbols." In one typ- ical formulation, "the link between erasing any physical reminder of a peo- ple and its collective memory and the killing of the people themselves is ineluctable."[10] As a "reminder," architecture is differentiated from a com- plete and stable presence, here termed "a people," but, as a target of vio- lence, architecture is identified with that presence, so that a people can be attacked via its architectural reminders. A people is presumed to be merely represented by architecture, although the destruction of this architecture is presumed to destroy the people who are represented.

This paradoxical status of architecture in political violence, both dif- ferentiated from and identified with what it represents, renders architec- ture to be what Jacques Derrida has termed "supplemental." On one level, the supplement is a superfluous addition to an already complete presence. It "adds itself, it is a surplus, a plentitude enriching another plentitude": the conceptualization of architecture as a sign or symbol of a culture, com- munity, nation, or history assumes each of the latter as such a plentitude.[11]

But, Derrida points out, the supplement is also a compensation for that seeming plentitude's incompleteness. The supplement "adds only to replace. . . . If it represents and makes an image, it is by the anterior default of a presence. . . . It is not simply added to the positivity of a presence . . . its place is assigned in the structure by the mark of an emptiness."[12] This emptiness is what summons architectural signification or symbolization in the first place. It is, for Derrida, originary. No presence exists prior to or separate from its representation. The illusion of representation, writes Derrida, is that it "creates nothing," that it re-presents "a present that would exist elsewhere and prior to it . . . a present whose plenitude would be older than it, absent from it, and rightfully capable of doing without it."[13] This plenitude is the object of an architectural representation that does not simply *add* to this object but *completes* it. Architecture thus comprises one form of the "supplementary mediations that produce the sense of the very thing that they defer: the impression of the thing itself, of immediate presence, or originary perception."[14]

In this book, then, rather than searching for the historical causes, origins, or contexts behind or prior to violence against architecture—the typical destinations of interpretive labor—I focus on where *violence takes place*: the particular sites, both spatial and discursive, where violence is inflicted and where the subjects and objects of violence are articulated. I do not include destruction, therefore, in already established narratives of political identity and agency as simply another field on which those phenomena are mediated, expressed, or effectuated. I seek to register the emergence of power, agency, and identity from violence, rather than to rely upon power, agency, and identity as self-constituting and free-standing historical constructs. I posit destruction, that is, as a form of construction, irreducible to its supposed contexts and productive of the very identities and agencies that supposedly bear on it as causes: a supplement to the presences usually cited as causal in accounts of political violence in the former Yugoslavia.

Violence, Theoretically

The understanding of violence as both materially and culturally destructive has, for the most part, displaced violence against architecture from architectural history. Yet conceptualizations of the cultural productivity of violence have been adumbrated in artistic and architectural discourse. Foremost here are the aesthetics of the early twentieth-century avant-gardes, for whom violence was a resource for cultural production, and culture, in turn, a resource to apprehend violence.[15] Italian Futurism was here in the lead: F. T. Marinetti's call to "the good incendiaries with charred fingers" to burn down museums and libraries; Luigi Russolo's evocation of modern warfare's "infinitely sensual, significant, and expressive" noises; and Giovanni Papini's prediction of a new art produced by those "refreshed by destruction" each posed violence as a constituent element of modern culture.

In their attempts to engage violence, the avant-gardes glorified, celebrated, and aestheticized war, destruction, and injury—but these were not simply ideological misrecognitions. These glorifications, celebrations, and aestheticizations were acknowledgments of existing conditions as well as performances of transgressive cultural ideologies. The avant-gardes did not merely proclaim the beauty of war; they revealed the beauty that bore upon those who imagined war, designed war, narrated war, beheld war, and in some cases carried war out. The avant-gardes, that is, acknowledged symbolic and expressive dimensions of violence that were—and still are— denied by moralizing and rationalizing discourses. The theoretical frame was Nietzschean: the aesthetic was a negotiation with and by power, and violence was not a regrettable interruption of social life but rather an indispensable form of social transformation.

Concepts of ecstatic, revolutionary, or messianic violence in the almost contemporaneous writings of Antonin Artaud, Georges Bataille, and Walter Benjamin similarly recovered aspects of violence neglected by or suppressed in predominant articulations, authorizations, and legitimizations of violence. And, in muted form, similar concepts of violence were brokered elsewhere in modernist aesthetics. The Formalist concept of art as "defamiliarization," for example, suggests that destruction, as well as construction, possesses cultural agency and semantic capacity. Here, destruction is not a simple removal or erasure of its target from social space, but a transformation of that target's social status and meaning and, with it, of the social itself. Material destruction is cultural production: this seeming paradox was crucial to the critical force of avant-garde and modernist aesthetics, but it also attests to the symbolic and practical efficacy of violence more generally.

The cultural productivity of violence has framed recent revisionist art histories of vandalism and iconoclasm.[16] This productivity has also suggested a new disciplinary labor for histories concerned with architecture.[17] The themes around which such histories have been organized—the constitutive relation of imagined or built objects to their social, political, and historical surroundings, the representational vocations to which architecture is assigned, the signifying potential of architectural form—are as relevant in the case of destruction as in that of construction. Political conflicts conducted, narrated, or imagined by destruction, that is, have a particularly *architectural history* that solicits representation as such.

The theoretical catalog that I draw upon to represent this history to some extent emerged in dialogue with the avatars of avant-garde and modernist aesthetics and, thus, the violence that preoccupied them.[18] Indeed, that Derrida's writing, in particular, was partly constituted in relation to and conversation with Nietzsche, Artaud, Bataille, Benjamin, and others invested in the apprehension of violence testifies to the particular significance of violence in that writing, as well as in poststructuralism more generally. The poststructuralist critique of structuralism was oriented, in part, to the latter's violence, its liquidation of negativity and difference, its legislation of change as chance, if not disaster. "The structuralist consciousness is a catastrophic consciousness," writes Derrida, "simultaneously destroyed and destructive, *destructuring*."[19] But this observation is exterior to structuralism, outside of or beyond it; the cognition of this catastrophic consciousness, of the violence that structuralism not only displaced or repressed but also inflicted, is, perhaps definitively, poststructuralist.

So, too, consciousness of the violence of cognition may be poststructuralist. Derrida evoked this violence through a figuration of the structures of structuralism as ruins: "The relief and design of structures appears more clearly when content, which is the living energy of meaning, is neutralized. Somewhat like the architecture of an uninhabited or deserted city, reduced to its skeleton by some catastrophe of nature or art. A city no longer inhabited, not simply left behind, but haunted by meaning and culture."[20]

This is a critique of structuralism as a species of destruction, yet it is also an apprehension of the semantic and cultural productivity of destruction. The "meaning" and "culture" that haunt a destroyed city are, in this sense, not so much residues of destruction as enmeshed with, summoned through, and supplemented by that destruction.

Humanist thought, by contrast, posits "meaning" and "culture" as exterior to violence, exposed to violence only as its target or dichotomous opposite. Violence is excluded from humanist thought through teleological schemes of nonviolence, which pass by such names as culture, politics, and history. The elimination of violence typically marks the end of culture, politics, and history, both in terms of their final determination and their temporal destination. It also shapes the status of violence as an object of thought, an object always subordinate to and disruptive of a primary, seemingly autonomous concept. Yet the normative disqualification of violence stands in opposition to violence's constitutive qualifications of culture, politics, and history, qualifications that are encoded in the very attempt to marginalize violence as merely "empirical" and therefore detached from the ideal orientations and ends of human(e) praxis.[21] Poststructuralism's interpellation by violence thus opens onto an interpellation of violence by poststructuralism, an apprehension of violence within reconstituted concepts of culture, politics, and history.[22]

From Archives to Traces

The materials that I rely on in this book are a diverse set of archival records, media accounts, human rights reports, oral histories, and my own documentation of wartime and postwar spatial situations. Each of these materials reveals specific aspects of violence against architecture in Kosovo. These materials are heterogeneous and fragmentary. I collected them in an attempt to register the available discursive representations of violent destruction—that is, destruction defined as violent by some interpretive community—in modern and contemporary Kosovo.

One risk of such a collection strategy is that the indeterminate definition of the sources under study would prompt reflexive confirmation of my own theoretical preconceptions—that I would find only what I was looking for. The necessity of this strategy, however, was founded in the status of the formal archive as a wholly inadequate repository of information on violence against architecture in Kosovo. This inadequacy has two dimensions. First, violence against architecture in Kosovo has at times included violence against archives. Along with other cultural institutions, archives were sometimes specifically targeted for destruction; this destruction, then, was a phenomenon that destroyed its own archival prehistory.

Jalal Toufic describes two sorts of catastrophes, one sort that is recorded in archives and another sort, termed by Toufic the "surpassing catastrophe," that involves even the destruction of archives.[23] The 1998–99 counter-insurgency campaign conducted by Serb forces in Kosovo comprised such a catastrophe, as its targets included the buildings and collections of various state archives, libraries, and museums; and Islamic libraries, theological schools, and Sufi lodges.[24] Some archives and collections were also removed from Kosovo into Serbia proper; in 1999, for example, the archives of the Institute for the Protection of Monuments of Kosovo were taken from the institute's building in Prishtina/Priština by staff from the Yugoslav Ministry of Interior; as of the writing of this book, these materials remain in the ministry's possession.

Second, there is also a violence *within* the archive, a violence that is more pronounced when the subject at hand is violence. The archive is a construction of the state, dedicated to subjects and objects of concern to the state. The archive's view is the view from the center, from the authority of the state or other sovereign institution; from this vantage point, nonstate violence is almost always disruptive, aberrant, and necessary to control, while state violence is a counterviolence, invoked at the last instance to restore order. Subaltern studies have opened up new possibilities to read through state-sanctioned accounts of violence to construct or reveal the hidden agencies of the dominated.[25] At the same time, historical and cultural studies have opened up the study of other forms of cultural memory and alternative sites of historical materialization—sites that, unlike the archive of documents, are not founded and managed by the state and are thus untethered to imperatives of state self-definition and legitimation.[26]

In this book, I both consider and complement material on violence against architecture collected by the Serbian state, the Serbian Orthodox Church, and the Islamic Community of Kosovo. In so doing, I register violent spatial production in Kosovo in architectural and urban artifacts, visual and textual representations, and social practices, each recovered from the heterogeneous set of materials described above. Here, then, the historical form of violence against architecture is comprised of what Derrida has called a "text": "a relational network of instituted traces" in which written language is conjoined with and perforce complicated by inscriptions of other types.[27]

Architecture of the Book

In this book, I insert the 1998–99 conflict between Serbia and the Kosovo Liberation Army into a genealogy of anticipated, threatened, inflicted, and remembered violence against architecture in Kosovo. This genealogy stretches from the late 1940s and the advent of socialist modernization in Yugoslavia to the first decade of the twenty-first century and the development of Kosovo's postwar "reconstruction." Tracking violence against architecture in each of these periods, "war" becomes but one moment of political violence that assumes different names, targets, and visibilities in various historical contexts.

The book is divided into three parts. Chronologically, the parts correspond to the conventional periodization of Yugoslavia's modern and contemporary history: socialist modernization, late- and post-socialist conflict; and postconflict reconstruction. In empirical historiography, these periods are usually the sources of failures or contradictions, either contingent or structural, that drive history; the failures of modernization determine ethnic conflict and violence, the contradictions of ethnic conflict and violence determine postconflict reconstruction, and so on. Where empirical histories point to change, I point, instead, to a condition of repetition. This condition is architectural: it is the recurring positioning of architecture as a nexus between a posited alterity and present actuality. In the moments I study here, these alterities were posited as abject, endangered or dangerous, or unjust; their elimination thus entailed the elimination of their architectural supplements. I stage history, then, as the repeated summoning of architecture to simultaneously represent and annihilate rejected presences—a history of the negation and assimilation of alterity.

In his poem "Spomenik" (Monument), Vladislav Petković Dis dreamed of a monument:

It has a long life,
Today it descends into new legends,
To prepare our descendents for the next monument.[28]

Dis was writing in 1913, just after Serbia wrested possession of Kosovo from the Ottoman empire and installed an obelisk on the site of the famous medieval battle in which Serbia was thought to have lost Kosovo. His dream has sometimes been interpreted as a fantasy of Serbia's perpetual return to

Kosovo; I pose it as a historical premonition—itself sign of a history that suppresses historicity—an anticipation of a history of repeated attempts to make alterity manifest in architecture.

Part I of this book explores the destruction of rejected architectural heritage in Kosovo's socialist modernization, focusing on Kosovo's capital city, Prishtina. Socialist modernization staged itself by contrast to a premodernity, prior to and inherited by it. This premodernity was made manifest in both treasured and debased versions, the latter, in Kosovo, fabricated primarily by Ottoman-era architecture. Modernization was carried out through the destruction of abject heritage, a destruction that was narrated by the socialist state as the destruction of premodernity itself. Yet heritage was not simply a contingent mediation of premodernity, one of its many forms of appearance, but an essential completion of premodernity, the form in which it was made manifest to the beneficiaries of modernization. Premodernity was thereby produced in the very process of destroying its architectural supplement; this was a historicization of destruction rather than a destruction of prehistory, a simultaneous summoning and expulsion of premodernity that took place, through the medium of architecture, in the name of political progress.

Part II investigates the destruction of endangered or dangerous architectural patrimony as a manifestation of ethnic alterity in late- and postsocialist conflict in Kosovo. In these conflicts, self-appointed representatives of Serbian ethnic communities consolidated the identity of these communities in response to violence against architecture claimed as patrimony or assigned as patrimony of ethnic others. One aspect of this consolidation involved the narration of late-socialist vandalism against Serbian Orthodox graves and cemeteries as "ethnic violence" carried out by Kosovar Albanians against Serbs; another involved the postsocialist destruction of Islamic buildings posed as Albanian patrimony by Serb military and paramilitary forces. In both cases, patrimony was apprehended as the primordial inheritance of an ethnic community. The apprehension of architecture as patrimony, however, took place within political conflict; the fabrication of architecture as patrimony thereby comprised an ethnicization of conflict rather than a form of ethnic conflict, an ethnicization conducted through the medium of architecture. The architectural mediation of ethnic identity was not, then, a symbolic representation of that identity as much as an architectural supplement of it—a supplement that installed ethnicity in political conflict.

Part III examines the destruction of architectural surrogates of un-avenged violence in postwar Kosovo. After the 1998–99 war, calls for retri-bution for prior violence inflicted by Serb forces against Kosovar Albanians circulated through Kosovar Albanian public culture. The postconflict de-struction of Serbian Orthodox churches and monasteries was narrated as a form of this retribution, with architecture becoming a surrogate for the agencies deemed responsible for the violence to be avenged—initially the Milošević regime and its military forces. The fabrication of architecture as a surrogate for unavenged violence, however, not only mediated an already constituted concept of violence but also ramified on that concept; the de-struction of churches and monasteries represented not only revenge for the violence of the 1998–99 war but also a continuous sequence of actual or imagined violent acts stretching back to the medieval construction of churches on crypto-Albanian religious sites. The destruction of architec-tural surrogates of violence thereby elicited a potentially endless justifica-tion for destruction rather than a politics of justice.

In these scenarios, violence takes place in three major senses. First, violence is instantiated in specific sites and situations, instantiations that in turn produce simulations and effects of power, authority, and legit-imization. Violence becomes, then, a supplement to what are convention-ally regarded as its sources, origins, or causes; it comprises "a subaltern instance which *takes-(the)-place.*"[29] Analysis of this supplement, which here comprises destruction, defamiliarizes narratives that posit violence as origi-nating in and distributed from a central locus, be that locus defined geo-graphically, institutionally, historically, or ideologically. Second, violence transforms place, thereby becoming what Henri Lefebvre calls a form of "spatial production."[30] Analysis of the violent transformation of place re-veals a general aspect of modernity that is repressed in historiography that presumes violence as aberrant, exceptional, or transitional. Third, violence targets architecture, one of the key figures of place in modernized contexts. Here, architectural damage and destruction are posed not as threats to or fractures of social order, but as attempts to impose novel forms of order through the production of place.

This analytical perspective situates *Violence Taking Place* within a set of recent studies of political conflict in the former Yugoslavia. These stud-ies refuse a priori distinctions between "politics" and "culture" and attend closely to the symbolic, expressive, or performative dimensions of "political" actions and events.[31] More particularly, this perspective prompts an examination of the sites and situations of violence against architecture via the interpretive protocols of architecture. The placement of architectural construction within the domain of these protocols and architectural destruction outside this domain has nothing to do with construction and destruction themselves and everything to do with the history of their study—and thus, with history more generally. A blurring of the discursive and disciplinary separations between construction and destruction, then, may comprise an opening toward or initiation of other histories.[32]

Mimesis as / of Violence

I conducted the research from which this book emerged in Kosovo from 1999 to 2004. This period, however, was not only the temporal frame for my research but also a historical moment I intervened in and, in microscopic ways, affected. My participation in postwar Kosovo is not explicitly foregrounded in what follows—but, at the same time, I also do not claim to write in a position removed from who and what I write about. My participation in Kosovo's history began in 1999, with my survey of wartime destruction for the International Criminal Tribunal. Encountering not only the catastrophic destruction of architecture but also the destruction of the institutions responsible for maintaining and reconstructing that architecture, I became involved in a number of ventures to "build capacity" in those institutions, as the process is known in reconstruction discourse. In 2000, I cofounded and codirected a nongovernmental organization, the Kosovo Cultural Heritage Project, which raised funds and organized the reconstruction of architectural heritage damaged during the war. In 2001, I joined the United Nations Interim Administration Mission in Kosovo, first as a cultural heritage officer and then as the international cohead of the Department of Culture. From 2002 to 2005 I worked on a national inventory of architectural heritage in Kosovo with the Ministry of Culture in Kosovo's Provisional Institutions of Self-Government. And in 2006 I advised representatives of Kosovo's provisional government on cultural heritage issues in United Nations–sponsored negotiations with Serbia over Kosovo's future status.

Through this work, I became involved in a number of political projects, most notably one aiming to render Kosovo independent from Serbia;

I not only observed the drive toward independence but I also participated, in ways both witting and unwitting, to further it. This sort of participation in a historical situation is often distinguished, either negatively (as the site of bias) or positively (as the site of close observation), from a distanced and dispassionate inspection of that situation. Timothy Garton Ash, for example, contrasts the interpretive positions of "the witness" and "the historian." While the historian can "gather all the witnesses' accounts and is generally unswayed by . . . first-hand experience," the witness can "see things that the historian will not find in any document," "a glance, a shrug, a chance remark" that may be more historically salient than, Garton Ash writes, "a hundred speeches."[33]

In Garton Ash's account, the distinction between "historian" and "witness" is organized around a number of unmediated oppositions: historical reading is a passive and objective practice, while historical witnessing is active and subjective; reading is focused on documents, while witnessing accommodates a wide spectrum of visual and textual evidence; and reading neither produces nor is produced by experience, while witnessing is itself an intensely experiential act. These oppositions suggest that, on one side or the other, protocols for the mimetic representation of history can be found—either the mimesis of the witness, up close and personal, or the mimesis of the historian, distant and objective.

Yet mimesis itself is a constituent feature of violence. Mimesis is another name for the process by which violence comes to represent imagined or imaginary communities, ideological positions, or political agencies— another name, that is, for the suppression of supplementarity. Mimesis has thereby underwritten the destruction of architecture in Kosovo, destruction that has been posed—by its authors, victims, and historians alike— as an instrument to destroy ethnic communities, cities, culture, cultural memory, multiculturalism, and an array of other targets. Each of these readings of destruction presupposes an architectural mimesis; destruction makes sense to the extent that such mimesis applies, to the extent that the authors, targets, and victims of destruction can be positioned as representative.

The history this book stages, by contrast, is that of failed mimesis, of repeated attempts to enact mimesis through destruction and to conceive destruction through mimesis. This is the history of a project to render architecture, through violence, a political resource and cultural medium—

an object of history. As such, this history suggests a reformulation of the relations usually subtended between history and architecture in empirical historiography that deals with architecture. In this historiography, architecture is typically posed as an effect, product, or representation of political power, agency, ideology, or identity—the typical sources of historical causality. These sources are presumed to occupy a different, more "present" ontological register than that of the "representations," architectural and otherwise, that supposedly manifest them.

But this positioning of architecture is, in effect, tautological; it begins from the position that architecture is epiphenomenal and mimetic, and then assimilates architecture into the narrative of whatever phenomenon is staged as causal. Architectural mimesis is not so much derived as assumed; architecture, if not culture more generally, is posited as a simple representation, so that the task of historical interpretation becomes the identification of that representation's authors, contents, and effects. In so doing, this historiography collaborates in the logic of the violence it seeks to analyze, a violence that authorizes and legitimizes itself by invoking the same presences as those invoked by its historiography. This historiography possesses, in other words, its own violence; it is part of an apparatus that renders violence a mere effect or product of something else—something that we may esteem or desire, something that we believe we may not be able to live without.

In this book, by contrast, I am concerned not only with who or what architecture represents, but also how it is that architecture becomes representational. Violence emerges as a simultaneous demand for and form of mimesis, a forcing of representation onto architectural material that is recalcitrant in its sheer particularity. The "burden of history," "surplus of history," or "abuse of history" that so many histories of Yugoslavia cite as causal of destruction here become, at least partly, architectural effects, derived from a historicization of violence achieved through the destruction of objects posited as "historical." To articulate an architectural history of destruction, then, is also to pose the object of architectural history not only as the history of architecture but also as the architecture of history: the ways in which architecture is enlisted as a supplement to history's assumed protagonists, structures, and dynamics.

It is not at all accidental that the subject of violence impels reflection on the architecture of history.[34] Architecture is insistently called upon to stand in for reality and assume historical significance precisely when that reality is apprehended as destabilized by violence. Violence intensifies architecture's historical significance and cultural meaning in the very process of destroying it. The historicization of architecture wrought by violence thereby calls specific attention to architecture as a representation of history. Accordingly, *Violence Taking Place* tells the story of architecture's participation in a series of particularly vivid and consequential mimetic acts. It is a story about architecture itself becoming a story: about power, about agency, about identity, about history. This story—what I am positing as history—relates the violence that must be inflicted on architecture to render it significant and signifying, to insert architecture into history.

The poststructuralist critique of representation also applies to the representation of this history—and, even more profoundly, to history itself *as* representation, as an order of causality, linearity, continuity, teleology, eschatology, determination or any of the a prioris by means of which the past is sensed, thought, and narrated. This critique thus problematizes history not only as a transcription of the past but also as an object of knowledge and an epistemological domain. For me, these problematizations do not yield a simple invalidation or rejection of history; rather, they imply a reinscription of history as a discursive site, textual field of dispersion, or even form of strategic counterviolence.[35]

They also imply a subject position that Dominick LaCapra has termed a "secondary witness." The relationship of this witness to her object of study parallels—though does not duplicate—that of the witness to the event. "Experience," LaCapra argues, "involves affect both in the observed and in the observer." For the observer, he continues, "the problem of experience should lead to the question of the role of empathy in historical understanding."[36] Empathy, then, becomes a kind of surrogate or virtual experience, centered not on identifying with or substituting for the experiences of others but rather on attending carefully to "the possibly split-off, affective dimension" of those experiences.[37]

In a sense, my passage from coauthor of a compilation of evidence for the International Criminal Tribunal to author of this book involved a passage—still, to be sure, in process—from a (seemingly) detached commentator to a secondary witness, to a position in which I could be troubled by, and could attempt to trouble, distinctions between the violence of war and the violence of "peace"; between the text of violence and the contexts that supposedly bear on that text; between the perpetrators of violence and the collectives they claim to represent; and between the intentions that precede violence and the effects that seem to follow from it. I understand secondary witnessing as involving an employment of mimesis against itself. While deploying the mimesis of both witnesses (myself and others) and historians, my abiding concern is to turn the mimetic representation of violence against mimetic violence—to historicize violence as inscription, representation, and cultural production. Of course, "violence taking place" also describes this book's effect on its object of study in the course of subsuming that object to a determinate order of thought. My hope, frankly, is that this is a counterviolence, a friction against the collapse of objects and representations that violence itself attempts and that histories of violence often ratify.

PART I

MODERNIZATION

1

A Relic of the Past, Fast Disappearing

Until the end of the Second World War, Prishtina was a typical Oriental town, with small one-story houses and narrow streets. Only after the Liberation has Prishtina passed through strong economic, cultural, and social development—and grown into a completely new modern town.

ESAD MEKULI AND DRAGAN ČUKIĆ, EDS., *Prishtina*

Anything about which one knows that one soon will not have it around becomes an image.

WALTER BENJAMIN, "The Paris of the Second Empire in Baudelaire"

War by Other Means

In the mid-1960s, the Yugoslav government published a number of books on the progress of socialist modernization in their country. Many books were published in 1965, the twentieth anniversary of the end of the Second World War. This was a war in which the Communist Party of Yugoslavia's Partisan forces, under the leadership of Josip Broz Tito, defeated Yugoslavia's German and Italian occupiers, along with their domestic allies. Soon after establishing Yugoslavia as a socialist state, with Tito as its president-for-life, the Communist Party set out on an ambitious program of modernization. Publishing the results of that program on and around the twentieth anniversary of the war's ending placed modernization in the history of war: in Yugoslav socialism, modernization was staged as a war of its own.

One such account of socialist modernization was *Kosovo i Metohija, 1943–1963* (Kosovo and Metohija, 1943–1963).[1] In socialist Yugoslavia, Kosovo was a province of Serbia, one of Yugoslavia's six constituent republics, just as it had been in prewar Yugoslavia and in Serbia before Yugoslavia's founding. *Kosovo i Metohija, 1943–1963* was published by Kosovo's provincial government for its constituents. The book's many photographs frequently visualized modernization with images of architecture. One photograph, from the city of Gjakova/Đakovica, showed, in the foreground, a half-destroyed group of mud-brick houses and, in the background, a tall, white apartment block (Figure 1.1). Architectural oppositions between the houses and the apartment block behind them are manifold—I have already emplotted some of them in my description of the photograph—and the caption of the photograph foregrounded several. These oppositions— modern versus historic, high versus low, concrete versus tiled—suggest, in turn, still another opposition, that between the intelligible (here, mod-

FIGURE 1.1   "Đakovica: Modern constructions rise more and more above the low tiled roofs." Photograph from Stanoje Aksić, ed., *Kosovo i Metohija, 1943–1963* (1963).

ernization) and the sensible (here, architecture). In this sense, the photograph represents the manifestation of modernization in, among other things, architecture.

The force of this representation was its status as documentation: a representation of a reality prior to and outside the scene of the photograph. Architecture, as well as the photograph that represented it, would be an apparent effect or product of modernization and therefore evidence of the latter's very existence. But the impossibility of modernization, whether as concept, ideology, or object, to manifest itself simply *as such* suggests that representation did not only reproduce an aspect of modernization but also produced its aspect—its otherwise absent or obscure appearance. Here, architecture, as well as its subsequent photographic representation, comprised a performance of modernization, a visualization of modernization that was inscribed in modernization's very concept. As such, photography and architecture are less ex post facto depictions of modernization than practices within modernization, reconciliations of concepts of modernization with material actuality that reciprocally form and transform both in that process.

In socialist Yugoslavia, the performance of modernization engaged architecture in two guises. In one guise, architecture was an object of construction, the "modern constructions" that manifested what modernization was; in another guise, architecture was an object of destruction, an abject heritage of premodernity that made manifest what modernization was not. Construction and destruction thereby comprised conjoined architectural supplements of modernization. Each supplement added onto modernization, comprising a mediation or effect of it, but at the same time, "this addition is a floating one because it comes to perform a vicarious function, to supplement a lack on the part of the signified."[2] This lack was the very incompleteness of modernization as a concept, the incompleteness that required this concept to be supplemented by architecture in the first place. The dichotomizing opposition of modern and historical architecture, staged in the photograph from Gjakova, thus led to the mutually constituting relation of modernization and architecture.

According to humanist theories of modernization, however, modernization—whether as historical process, economic mode of production, or cultural ideology—is taken to be separate from its "manifestations," architectural or otherwise. As simple mediations or effects, modernization's architectural manifestations can thereby be reduced to modernization-as-such. Humanist theorizations of modernization rely, in particular, upon an underlying historicism: history comprises time unfolding as progress, itself figured by such terms as *peace, prosperity, freedom, equality,* or *democracy.* Architecture thereby emerges as a manifestation of one or some of these figures. In capitalist contexts, modernist progress takes the form of "development," which is furthered by the "creative destruction" that opens up new opportunities for capital accumulation and sustains economic growth. In socialist contexts, like that of the former Yugoslavia, modernist progress took the form of "revolution" and destruction's creativity lay in its status as a motor of revolutionary change. In the *Communist Manifesto* Marx and Engels famously proclaimed that, in modernity, "all that is solid melts into air"—but the destruction that this transience implied was redemptive, a necessary phase in the social evolution that would lead to communism. In either case, however, construction and destruction are reduced to a mere acting-out of a progressive modernization that stands conceptually apart from its architectural mediation.

In this context, Walter Benjamin's account of Baron Haussmann's mid-nineteenth-century modernization of Paris is distinct in its refusal to recuperate modernist destruction. Haussmann's architectural modernization of Paris—one of the first great urban modernization projects—was posed by the French state as a necessary transformation of the city and of society itself. Benjamin quoted Maxime Du Camp on the perceived "uninhabitability" of pre-Haussmann Paris, in which "the people choked in the narrow, dirty, convoluted old streets, where they remained packed in."[3] Haussmann's broad boulevards were to bring light and air into previously dark and claustrophobic working-class neighborhoods, the slums of those neighborhoods were to be cleared, and the working class was to be provided with the civic amenities previously accessible only to the bourgeoisie.

Yet, for Benjamin, this all comprised "strategic beautification." While Haussmann relied upon the perceived reducibility of architectural transformation to social transformation, his modernization of Paris actually served, for Benjamin, as a substitute for and preemption of social change. Class antagonisms and social suffering were, for Benjamin, concealed rather than eliminated in Haussmanization, with the Parisian working class dispatched to the city's periphery and their former neighborhoods, though shot through with grand avenues, depleted of "their characteristic physiognomy."[4] Haussmann's modernization thereby secured Paris against the workers' uprisings that, for Benjamin, provided the sole chance for actual social change: its destruction did not reduce to modernization-as-progress but to a preventive war against organized labor.[5] Haussmannization, then, was war by other means, so that, for Benjamin, it was profoundly related to other forms of political violence. The end of the failed 1871 Paris commune in the "burning of Paris" was "a fitting conclusion to Haussmann's work of destruction."[6] And, as Susan Buck-Morss has observed, Benjamin also described the urban battlefields of cities in the Spanish Civil War by reference to the destructive technology developed in Haussmann's Paris. "Haussmann's activity," Benjamin wrote in 1935, "is today accomplished by very different means, as the Spanish Civil War demonstrates."[7]

The destruction that Haussmannization at once instrumentalized and obscured was, for Benjamin, the key to its violence. Yet Kosovo's modernization does not simply offer itself for reinscription in Benjamin's text as another instance of modernizing violence; it enables, rather, a historical relation to be drawn between itself and that text. Benjamin posed the conjunction of modernization and war as a critical insight, a revelation of a crucial aspect of modernization, but one concealed by its architectural constructions. To figure Haussmannization as war was thus to disclose its violence. But the figuration of modernization as war was explicit and operational *within* Kosovo's modernization. Just as Benjamin described Haussmann's boulevards "covered over with tarpaulins and revealed like monuments," so was the destruction of Kosovo's abject heritage the subject of visual and textual representations that revealed this destruction, too, as a monument of modernist progress.[8] Kosovo's modernization attempted to recuperate precisely the destruction that, according to Benjamin, was disavowed in Haussmannization. While Haussmann's constructions comprised ideological justifications for and physical concealments of the destruction that preceded and motivated them, the destruction in Kosovo's cities was specifically enfolded in a modernist narrative of war by other means: war was figured as both representation and instrument of historical progress. In Kosovo, this war was carried out against a debased heritage whose destruction manifested modernization. Supplemented, in the strict sense, by destruction, modernization made of Kosovo's history an architectural phenomenon and its politics an architectural praxis.

We Destroyed on Sundays

Yugoslavia's modernization after the Second World War was a form of reconstruction, a reaction to the war's thorough devastation; it was a form of socialism, a response to capitalist underdevelopment; a form of industrialization, an attempt to insert Yugoslavia into wider European and global economies; and a form of historical progress, a means of propelling Yugoslavia forward on the teleological trajectory that would led to communism. Each of these formulations invoked a prehistory, the premodern, against which modernization appeared. Though this premodernity was temporally "before" modernization, it emerged as a concept with, in, and by modernization. Modernization, therefore, involved the production of the premodernity that would be "discarded," "replaced," "abandoned," "overcome," or "destroyed"—to cite but a few names the process was given in socialist Yugoslavia—by modernization. Premodernity was just as much a product of modernization as the industrialization of production, the reconciliation of city and countryside, secularism, public education, social welfare, and other such goods that modernization claimed for itself. Modernization also was, that is, a form of historicism, stipulating both what was inside and outside of it according to a continuous and linear temporal trajectory.

Many empirical histories of socialist modernization stage their object against an inherited and objective premodernity, which is then emplotted as an obstacle to modernization.[9] With some of Yugoslavia's republics and provinces emerging from an "advanced" Austro-Hungarian empire (Croatia, Slovenia, Vojvodina), some from a "backward" Ottoman empire (Bosnia, Kosovo, Macedonia), and some from both empires (Serbia), many histories pose premodernity as the source of the "inequalities" in Yugoslavia that modernization had to overcome. Other histories pose premodernity as a "resistance" to modernization where premodernity existed "in surplus," as in places formerly under Ottoman rule. Still other histories pose premodernity as a cover term for other phenomena, such as Orientalism, Eurocentrism, or racism, which were themselves objectively present and causal on modernization. These histories therefore repeat, in the guise of analysis, a concept produced within modernization itself. They are histories of modernization that are themselves modernist. They fold premodernity's "origins," "signs," "symptoms," "products," and "failures" into the concept of premodernity, a second-order reification of a concept that was already reified in and by modernization.

One of the primary examples of the reification of premodernity in socialist Yugoslavia was architectural. This reification possessed a double aspect. One aspect was defined by "cultural monuments," or heritage that was named as such, valorized, studied, and protected. This process produced premodernity as an inheritance to be "preserved," with the very concept of preservation reproducing the ideology of prehistory as pre-existing modernization. In socialist Yugoslavia, Institutes for the Preservation of Cultural Monuments (Zavod za zaštitu spomenika kulture) were established in each republic to, in effect, produce heritage—a process enmeshed with the other productions of modernization. From 1946 to 1954, Kosovo lay under the responsibility of the Institute for the Preservation of Monuments of Serbia (Zavod za zaštitu spomenika Srbije).[10] In this period, the institute's efforts were concentrated on the Serbian Orthodox patriarchate at Peć, the Serbian Orthodox churches and monasteries at Gračanica and at Dečani, the Serbian Orthodox Church of the Holy Virgin of Ljeviš in Prizren, and the Sultan Murat Turbe in the Field of Kosovo battlefield. In 1954, an Institute for the Protection and Study of Cultural Monuments in Kosovo (Zavod za zaštitu i proučavanje spomenika kulture Autonomne Kosovsko-Metohijske Oblasti) was set up, but it by and large continued the focus on these monuments.

Kosovo was a province of the Ottoman empire for five centuries and its territory contained many examples of Ottoman architecture, yet only one Ottoman-era monument, the Sultan Murat Turbe, was classified as a "cultural monument" in this period; the other such monuments were drawn from the patrimony of the Serbian Orthodox Church. This catalog of heritage has subsequently been designated a manifestation of religious or ethnic ideology, which, on some level, it certainly was.[11] But this designation misses a larger point: that this ideology emerges historically as an after-effect, an origin that appears *after* the effect it supposedly causes. To regard ideology as determining the catalog of heritage, then, is to reproduce ideology on its own terms—to endow it with the same political agency as that claimed by heritage preservation, in relation to premodernity, in the context of modernization.

Premodernity was reified not only by preservation of its treasured signs, however, but also by the elimination of its obsolete components: an abject heritage whose purpose, in modernization, was to be destroyed.[12] This destruction was also institutionalized in socialist modernization. By the 1950s, this modernization was the responsibility of the Urban Planning Institute (Urbanistički zavod) in the capital cities of all republics. Before then, however, destruction was also planned and managed by local governments as part of urban modernization schemes. In Kosovo, beginning in the late 1940s, the destruction of abject heritage took place in each major city, most prominently in Kosovo's capital city of Prishtina.

The modernization of Prishtina was initiated with the destruction of the Ottoman-era bazaar (*čaršija*) at the center of the city: in 1947, the provincial government expropriated the buildings in the bazaar in the name of urban renewal and then demolished them.[13] The destruction of Ottoman-era bazaars was proposed at this time by municipal governments in other Yugoslav cities, especially in Bosnia; most notably, the largest such bazaar, the Baščaršija in Sarajevo, began to be demolished in the late 1940s. However, after some two hundred of the Baščaršija's buildings were destroyed, widespread protests led to the Baščaršija's preservation.[14]

Prishtina's bazaar was historically and formally quite similar to the Baščaršija, yet its destruction was not publically protested.[15] Laid out in the fifteenth century, Prishtina's bazaar was composed of some two hundred shops arranged around a mosque (*xhami* in Albanian, *džamija* in Serbian); these shops were owned by and operated by members of Prishtina's Albanian community. The shops were set within blocks, each devoted to a particular guild or craft. Across from the bazaar were a number of public buildings, such as mosques, an inn (*han*), and a bathhouse (*hamam*), and arrayed around these buildings were the city's residential neighborhoods (*mahalle*).[16]

Like other public works at the time in Yugoslavia, the destruction of Prishtina's bazaar was organized by labor brigades called Popular Fronts (*Fronti populluer* in Albanian, *Narodni front* in Serbian).[17] Though the labor of Popular Fronts was occasionally documented in Kosovo's two newspapers (*Rilindja*, in Albanian, and *Jedinstvo*, in Serbian), the destruction of the bazaar was not officially reported.[18] I thus searched for representations of this destruction through oral history, soliciting narratives from people who participated in Popular Front activities in Prishtina. In 2003–4, I met with four former members of Popular Front brigades: men, at that time in their seventies or eighties, who each still lived in the *mahalla* in which he grew up, next to the now long-gone bazaar. These men spoke of Popular Front organizers going door-to-door through the city's *mahalle* to sign up "volunteers" to fill work quotas.[19] One man described each *mahalla* in Prishtina as being assigned a certain part of the bazaar to destroy. Brigades labored on Sundays, so that their members did not have to leave their regular jobs— "We destroyed on Sundays and left work to be done for the next Sunday," explained another man. Still another described seeing shopkeepers "who did not have time to take the goods from their shops and were weeping."[20]

Carried out by the Popular Fronts, the destruction of the bazaar was staged as a communal effort, with urban space becoming an object of collective labor and socialist history. This labor and history were explained by the Popular Front slogan "Destroy the old, construct the new!" (*Uništite staro, izgradite novo!* in Serbian). This slogan explicitly figured modernization *as* destruction. Architecture, in the form of abject heritage, was appropriated as a manifestation of premodernity. What was destroyed was the past and what would be built was the future. Architecture thereby manifested time as historical progress; history was made visible in the form of a modern socialist city rising above its antiquated Ottoman predecessor.

In the first years of the present century, when I asked long-standing Prishtina residents for old photographs of the city, I was usually directed to Photo Ardi, a photography studio on the ground floor of Qafa, a 1960s-era shopping center. Qafa was located on the edge of the bazaar's former location, and just after the year 2000 there were still, scattered in the blocks around Qafa, the odd mud-brick house testifying to Prishtina's premodernized physiognomy. Photo Ardi had been in the same family's hands for two generations. The current owner pointed out to me the original location of the studio, across the street, in a building now gone. He also showed me many photographs, inherited from his father, of Prishtina before modernization. Some showed the city in the midst of modernization, including a few, probably taken by workers in the Popular Fronts, of the destruction of Prishtina's bazaar (Figures 1.2 and 1.3).

These photographs register the labor of destruction in two senses: first, the work of dismantling the bazaar's buildings and preparing its site for subsequent construction, but second, the work of inserting this destruction into history. The "past" targeted by destruction is, in these photographs, wood-frame buildings with mud-brick walls—objects whose particular significance as "premodern" was an effect of their modernist destruction as such.

FIGURE 1.2 Popular Front workers dismantling buildings in Prishtina's bazaar, 1947. Photograph from private collection.

FIGURE 1.3 Excavation of the Square of Brotherhood and Unity on site of demolished bazaar, Prishtina, early 1950s. Photograph from private collection.

The photographs show the Fronts at work in the abandoned bazaar, taking apart empty buildings and clearing building sites, the preparatory steps to the construction of new buildings. Figure 1.3 shows a bulldozer excavating the site that would become the Square of Brotherhood and Unity (Trg bratstva i jedinstva) in the center of New Prishtina; undestroyed buildings of the bazaar are visible in the lower right-hand corner of the photograph, and visible on the right is the Provincial Assembly of Kosovo (Skupština Kosova i Metohije), then under construction and soon to be renovated by one of Serbia's most significant modernist architects, Bogdan Bogdanović.

Circulating in domestic contexts, these photographs would likely have been narrated by their authors or their relatives, their meanings and effects thereby opened to the politics and poetics of diverse agencies. For almost ten years after the photographs were taken, the site of the destroyed bazaar remained empty, and the members of the Popular Front brigades spoke of the year-round dustiness of the city during that time, as well as of their continuing hope that the bazaar's shops would be replaced. At least in retrospect, the prolonged emptiness of the site of the bazaar shaped the meaning of its destruction; reflecting on the time lag between destruction and construction on the site, and perhaps on the subsequent history of destruction in Kosovo, as well, one member of a brigade told me that, "the aim was to destroy what was Albanian, not to build something new."

Building Something New

In the early 1950s, after the Urban Planning Institute of Serbia completed the master planning of Belgrade, it initiated the planning of Prishtina. Indeed, New Prishtina was a socialist *Gesamtkunstwerk*, an object of the collective labor of postwar Yugoslavia's leading urban planners, architects, and photographers. This labor, however, was focused on New Prishtina as an image as much as a socioeconomic instrument; while New Prishtina was staged as a modernist *component* of socialist modernization, one element of that modernization's ensemble of projects, it also functioned as a modernist *representation* of modernization, a visual conjuring of the socioeconomic conditions that modernization was intended to produce.

In 1948, a survey of Prishtina was drawn up by a local architect, Milorad Prljević; this plan served as the basis of a master plan drawn by the architect, Nikola Dobrović.[21] Dobrović, a pioneer modernist architect

FIGURE 1.4   Aerial view of Prishtina in the late 1930s. Photograph from Nikola Dobrović, *Urbanizam kroz vekove* (1950).

in Serbia, had studied in Prague and worked in Prague and Dubrovnik before the war.[22] After the war, in 1945, he was appointed director of the Urban Planning Institute of Serbia, and in 1946 he became director of Belgrade's Department of City Planning (Sekretarijat za urbanizam). In 1950, Dobrović published a textbook that set forth principles of modern urbanism and analyses of towns and cities throughout Yugoslavia.[23] He included an analysis of Prishtina, a city whose planning he would soon undertake.

Dobrović's analysis of Prishtina was illustrated with an aerial photograph from the late 1930s (Figure 1.4) and a photograph of an urban tableau, probably taken at around the same time (Figure 1.5). The aerial photograph shows the bazaar at the center of the city—an urban environment that, at the time of the book's publication, no longer existed. The urban tableau

FIGURE 1.5 Urban tableau in Prishtina from the late 1930s. Photograph from Nikola Dobrović, *Urbanizam kroz vekove* (1950).

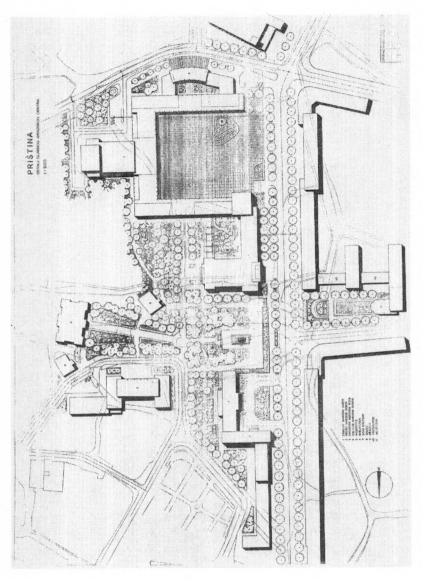

FIGURE 1.6 Nikola Dobrović (attributed), proposal for adminstrative center on site of demolished bazaar, Prishtina, 1952. Drawing from Municipal Archive of Prishtina.

shows two structures adjacent to the bazaar: the fifteenth-century Imperial Mosque and the Sahat Kula, a clock tower built at the end of the nineteenth century. The clock tower was one of hundreds built at the same time in the Ottoman empire in the frame of a modernization project undertaken by Sultan Abid al-Hamid II; the towers allowed calls to prayer from mosques to be scheduled with new accuracy and precision.

For Dobrović, however, what the aerial photograph of Prishtina revealed was "the amorphous constitution of the Turkish-Oriental city," and what the urban tableau displayed was not historical artifacts, much less artifacts involved in modernization, but rather "a composition of contrasting Euclidean forms."[24] On the one hand, then, Dobrović viewed the Ottoman city as formless, a vision that implied the need for modern planning to provide that missing form; and on the other hand, form, in the guise of an abstract Euclidean geometry, was a template for visualizing architecture. The clock tower and mosque were visible to Dobrović but the mud-brick market buildings of the bazaar were not. This was a regime of vision that defined the setting for Dobrović's urban plan for Prishtina, drawn up in the early 1950s and approved by the city in 1954.

Dobrović's modernism did not entail a neglect of heritage. Rather, heritage was crucial as a contrasting foil for Dobrović's modernist architecture. In 1951, just as he began to become involved in the planning of Prishtina, Dobrović published an essay on heritage in *Zbornik Zaštite Spomenika Kulture*, the journal of the Institute for the Preservation of Monuments of Serbia. In this essay, he pointed out how "old and new parts of the city are interconnected through an indispensable symbiosis," a relationship in which the city's "old historical parts are dispersed and put into contrast (with its new parts) so as to become beautified into eminence."[25] This "indispensable symbiosis" precisely describes the status of heritage as a supplement to modernization, crucial to its manifestation.

Yet the city's "old historical parts" manifested modernization, not only by being preserved in the guise of cultural monuments, but also by being destroyed in the guise of abject heritage. Dobrović's urban plan for Prishtina registered the latter by locating the city's new municipal and provincial government buildings on the site formerly occupied by its bazaar (Figure 1.6). This placement was a crucial dimension of Dobrović's plan; it rendered the destruction of the bazaar as the condition of possibility for the construction of the new city center. In 1952, a draft urban plan for Prishtina was publicly exhibited in the city's newly built National Theater, and an article in the state Albanian-language newspaper, *Rilindja*, thus reported on the plan's proposed modernization as including the "construction of a modern administrative center on the site occupied the city's old bazaar."[26]

The key elements of the city's new center were a building for Kosovo's provincial government, a building for Prishtina's municipal government, and a large square between the two, with the remains of Prishtina's partially demolished Ottoman-era architectural heritage on the periphery.[27] The Square of Brotherhood and Unity lay between the Provincial Assembly and Prishtina's already-constructed City Hall. Squares of Brotherhood and Unity were key urbanist figures in Yugoslav city planning of the 1950s and early 1960s, accompanying or (as in Prishtina) replacing earlier city centers and representing a central tenet of Yugoslav socialist ideology. Like many of its counterparts, Prishtina's Square of Brotherhood and Unity was centered on a Monument of Brotherhood and Unity. In Prishtina, this monument took the form of a tower with three separate concrete pylons, clustered together at the base and becoming increasingly distant from one another as they rose. According to the recommended interpretation, the pylons represented the three constituent peoples of Kosovo—Serbs, Montenegrins, and Albanians—the peoples whose brotherhood and unity was to be nurtured and maintained in socialist Kosovo.

The monument was performative; it produced a new representation of Kosovar society. In the years after World War II, Kosovo's social composition was complex and heterogeneous, with a population composed of a number of groups whose definitions were not only ethnic and whose relations were at once shifting and overlapping.[28] Not all Slavs were Christian, not all Albanians were Muslim, and not all communities were either Christian or Muslim: there were Muslim Slavs (Gorani); there were Christian Albanians; there were Jews who were neither Christian nor Muslim; there were Roma who celebrated both Christian and Muslim holidays; and there were small communities of Greeks, Croatians, Turks, and Roma, some of whom called themselves Egyptians (Egipćani). Yet, as Benedict Anderson has pointed out, the modern bureaucratic state requires simple and fixed categories to identify its population, with ethnicity often furnishing a basis for such categories.[29] The Yugoslav state's project to categorize its population according to ethnicity made anomalous minorities of the aforementioned communities and made dominant majorities of Christian Serbs and

Montenegrins and Muslim Albanians. In order to promote "brotherhood and unity" among Yugoslavia's ethnic communities, the Yugoslav state had to first produce those communities; the Monument of Brotherhood and Unity was a part of that process of production.

The Architectural Diacritics of History

The Monument of Brotherhood and Unity, however, was not the only representational element of New Prishtina's ensemble of architectural forms. As I mentioned in the beginning of this chapter, state-sponsored representations of modernizing Kosovo towns and cities persistently juxtaposed abject heritage and modernist architecture, a juxtaposition that framed this heritage not as an invisible absence but as a fragmented and ruined presence. Modernization was manifested by ascribing significance to destruction as the destruction of the premodern, the past that was overcome by modernization. Modernist destruction thus did not yield simply an elimination of its targets, but a reinscription of those targets into new contexts.

Each book on the progress of socialist modernization in Kosovo thereby comprised a perceptual apparatus, a device to structure the experience and interpretation of modernization's architectural manifestations. *Prishtina*, published in 1965, is both a visual and textual explication of the progress of modernization in the city, and thus, of the architectural diacritics of premodernity and modernity.[30] The book's narrative of modernization begins with the evocation of Prishtina's architectural transformation that forms one of the epigraphs to this chapter.[31] Modernization is staged as a product of postwar socialism, a product that is visible in the very form of the city itself.

An image of Prishtina from the early 1960s thus shows the city's newly constructed main street in the foreground, the complex of new government buildings in the upper-left corner of the background, and the remains of the "Oriental" city surrounding all of the above (Figure 1.7). The caption of the picture, almost exactly the same as the caption of the image from Gjakova discussed at the beginning of this chapter, focuses precisely on the contrast between old and new: "Modern constructions rise more and more above the low roofs of the old houses." Modernization, in other words, is a difference from and destruction of the premodern. This staging is reprised in an image of Prishtina's Square of Brotherhood and

FIGURE 1.7   "Modern constructions rise more and more above the low roofs of the old houses." Photograph from Esad Mekuli and Dragan Čukić, eds., *Prishtina* (1965).

Unity (Figure 1.8). The square is shown with the Monument of Brotherhood and Unity in the foreground and the minarets of three of Prishtina's Ottoman-era mosques in the background; architecture is cast here as an immediate manifestation of socialist history, with the new era initiated by socialism rising above and beyond its Oriental predecessor.

In the book *Yugoslav Cities*, also published in 1965, it is the remains of Prishtina's bazaar that are staged as signs of socialism's superceded prehistory.[32] In one image (Figure 1.9), nineteenth-century mud-brick buildings in a still extant section of the bazaar are juxtaposed with a new, white modern building. The caption points to the remains of the bazaar not simply as abandoned but as endowed with new significance as an outmoded and

FIGURE 1.8 Square of Brotherhood and Unity, Prishtina. Photograph from Esad Mekuli and Dragan Čukić, eds., *Prishtina* (1965).

FIGURE 1.9 "Dilapidated small houses, a relic of the past, can still be seen in some parts of the town, but they are fast disappearing. The people of Priština want large, modern blocks of flats." Photograph from Ivan Vučković, ed., *Yugoslav Cities* (1965).

rejected landscape, "fast disappearing." This was a landscape seen as if from an ever-receding distance, the distance from the past enabled by modernization. Architecture, in the guise of "a relic of the past," became both foil for and target of modernization, a manifestation of premodernity produced through modernization itself.

Politics, History, Architecture

The meanings and effects of Kosovo's modernist destruction exceeded the modernizing intentions and agencies that motivated it. Destruction drifted, necessarily, in time and across interpretive communities, and other readings of it emerged within a short time. In 1967, for example, just a few years after the Yugoslav state declared modernization's initial victory, a Kosovar architect, Zoran Petrović, reflected on this victory in the pages of the Yugoslav journal *Arhitektura Urbanizam*.[33] This journal often pictured modernism's clean and white architectural avatars jutting boldly into the future. Petrović was a frequent contributor to the journal's section on heritage—a section whose presence, in a journal devoted to modern architecture, reiterated the supplementary status of heritage in modernization. Petrović's writings usually struck a cautionary note about modernization, but, in his essay on architectural and urban heritage in contemporary Serbia and Kosovo, his note was damning. Petrović pointed out that even after the Second World War, even after the vast destruction inflicted during the war years, it was possible to see Ottoman-era bazaars and entire Ottoman-era urban districts in Kosovo. In the intervening years, though, these historic environments—"characteristic, picturesque, and historically evocative"— had been almost all destroyed, having fallen victim to "rapid economic development, the wish to replace the old and outmoded socioeconomic conditions with new and modern ones, and an ignorance of the real value of architectural and urban heritage." It was a "real wonder that so many architectural and urban values survived war's destruction and devastation," but these values did not survive the other values of modernization.[34]

Petrović thus confirmed that modernization was a war and that the target of the war was heritage, but, for him, the loss of this heritage was not a gain. Ottoman-era heritage was not an obsolete remainder of an outmoded past but a valuable reminder of that past; it should therefore be preserved as a cultural monument instead of being debased and destroyed. Yet precisely by arguing *for* the preservation of heritage, Petrović's criticism of modernization invoked and reproduced its particular architectural ideology: that history resided in architecture. Petrović's criticism of modernization thereby reprised a politics of architecture, a way of conducting politics through and about architecture, that was rehearsed in modernization itself. Modernization thus stood, for both its advocates and critics, as an inscription of political conflicts about the present and the future onto architecture and history—an inscription that remained even after modernization itself became historical, as it was becoming even in Petrović's writing.

For Petrović, the destruction of Prishtina's bazaar was at once deleterious and contingent: "Some towns, like Priština, have in a very short time done away with characteristic and picturesque parts of markets or urban districts, unnecessarily and without due consideration." The incompleteness of the destruction of such "characteristic" architecture was also, for Petrović, a contingency, but one that was fortunate. Destruction's remainders provided the only way to discern the specificity of a modernized city: "If not for a few preserved mosques and other characteristic buildings, it would now be difficult to assert that these cities had their own local color and belonged to the geographical area in which they are situated."[35]

In Kosovo's modernization, however, destruction was not "unnecessary" and its incompleteness was not an accident, whether happy or otherwise. Modernization manifested itself specifically through the destruction that Petrović posed as unnecessary; that destruction comprised a crucial aspect of modernization's appearance, the form in which modernization was represented and explained to its apparent beneficiaries. And the incompleteness of this destruction, too, was crucial; the few "characteristic buildings" that were preserved as cultural monuments also manifested the premodernity that modernization left behind. Yet I do not wish to "correct" Petrović in order to expose the "error" of his observations. His observations do not merely resolve into either truth or error; rather, I would like to resolve them into desire and thus into mimesis—a desire for history, identified in and with architecture, that was exactly the desire of modernization. This desire bequeathed architecture to history as its supplement, with the "cohabitation" of architecture and history thereby becoming "as strange as it is necessary."[36] Architecture is, therefore, precisely where to recover another past for another future—which is also my (mimetic) desire here, and in the following chapters.

PART II

EMERGENCIES

2

It Is Not Only Vandalism

They are stealing my memory,
Curtailing my history,
Robbing my centuries,
Turning my churches into mosques,
Ransacking my alphabet,
Hammering my graves,
Uprooting my ground,
Dismantling my cradle.
Yet where can I carry Dečani Monastery?
Where can I put the Peć Patriarchate?

MATIJA BEĆKOVIĆ, "Kosovo Polje" (Kosovo Field)

The enigma of what has been, is no more, and yet offers itself as a present
sign of a dead thing.

ROLAND BARTHES, "The Discourse of History"

Desecration and Sacralization

On the night of March 15, 1981, a fire burned down a guesthouse on
the grounds of the patriarchate of the Serbian Orthodox Church in Peć,
Kosovo. A church investigation committee arrived at the patriarchate the
following afternoon. One member of the committee described the scene
in the next issue of the Church's bimonthly newspaper:

It was a sad sight in the courtyard: parts of the guesthouse roof collapsed by
the walls, the chimneys rising menacingly above the site of the fire, and various

FIGURE 2.1 Ruins of guesthouse at Peć Patriarchate after fire, March 1981. Photograph from *Pravoslavlje*, 1 April 1981.

FIGURE 2.2 Ruins of guesthouse at Peć Patriarchate after fire, March 1981. Photograph from *Pravoslavlje*, 1 April 1981.

objects, burned and wet, strewn about the grass. The firemen, in full form, were pouring water on the site of the fire, where life peacefully and actively went along until this morning. Upon noticing us in the courtyard, the nuns came to meet us. Their faces showed the full tragedy of the conflagration, while their dresses and catechisms were the only property they had left.[1]

This report was accompanied by photographs of the guesthouse ruins (Figures 2.1 and 2.2)—but, despite the textual and visual documentation, nothing about the fire was at all apparent in some interpretive communities.

Did the fire destroy merely an "outbuilding," constructed at the end of the nineteenth century and of little historical value, or "the patriarchate" itself, founded in the thirteenth century and the mother church of the Serbian Orthodox Church's patriarch? Did the fire start by accident, or was it deliberately set? If an accident, was it due to a faulty electrical connection, as the Peć municipal court eventually found, or a malfunctioning chimney, as the Peć fire department originally believed? Or were both these claims political cover-ups by Albanian officials for Albanian vandals? If so, were the police, mostly Albanian, in on the cover-up, too, because they never arrested anyone for the crime? And what about the fire department, also staffed largely by Albanians: did firemen fight the fire the best they could, or did they sabotage their ostensible effort by arriving at the patriarchate with empty water cisterns? And if Albanian vandalists set the fire, were they linked to the Albanian students who demonstrated four days earlier at the University of Prishtina? Were they linked to the Albanian students, workers, and unemployed workers who demonstrated across Kosovo in the succeeding two weeks, demonstrations that also included vandalism and that "provoked" the imposition of a state of emergency in Kosovo? And what were these demonstrations, anyway? Were they aimed at political self-determination for Kosovo's majority Albanian population, as the demonstrators proclaimed, a counterrevolution against socialist Yugoslavia, or violence against Kosovo's minority Serb population? If the aim was violence, did that project include the burning of the patriarchate and the destruction of other Orthodox patrimony, which, in Kosovo, included many hundreds of Byzantine-era churches, chapels, and monasteries? Was the fire at the patriarchate, then, an act of ethnic violence?[2] An answer to this latter question was ventured just a month later on the cover of *Ilustrovana Politika*, a popular Belgrade magazine; the cover superimposed the figure of a traditionally dressed Albanian man, in the guise of the monastery's traditional Muslim caretaker, or *voyvod*, holding a submachine gun in the foreground of the ruined guesthouse (Figure 2.3).[3]

Each of these questions mediate not only the mystery of the event that provoked them, but also the way in which that event, in its very mystery, had already been defined and identified to its audiences: the way, in other words, that the mystery was, with its very appearance, iterable, its surprise contained, its singularity compromised, its relation to other

FIGURE 2.3 "The oath is not returned." Fictionalized Albanian monastic caretaker (*voyvod*) before ruins of guesthouse at Peć Patriarchate on cover of *Ilustrovana Politika*, 26 May 1981.

events, both past and future, established.[4] In the case of the fire, those other events involved Kosovar Albanians acting simply *as such*: as members of an ethnic community rather than as workers, students, citizens, or in any other nonethnic guise. For the Serbian Orthodox Church and other Serbian interpretive communities, this ethnic agency was dangerous; the fire thus furthered an ongoing investigation of Albanians as ethnic others and intensified an already extant fear of their presence.

Yet it would have been difficult to think about the fire otherwise. The fire took place in a period when, for the Serbian Orthodox Church, ethnic alterity was manifested precisely in violations of its architectural patrimony. For the Church, these violations were revelations. They immediately exposed the truth of ethnic antagonism, conflict, and violence: their authors were Albanian and their targets were Serbian—identities that were determinative of violence's intentions, meanings, and effects. Architecture thereby functioned as a medium of violent exchange; attacks against the Church's patrimony were attacks on Kosovo's Serbian community by that community's ethnic others.

The Church's identification with its patrimony in Kosovo thus comprised an interpellation by architecture, by an irresistible inheritance, at once primordial and decisive. As *memory, history, ground,* and *cradle*— words commonplace in the discourse of the Church—the patrimonial monuments were not simply *symbols* of identity, but irreplaceable *components* of it. "For how can the Serb nation exist at all," a 1988 essay on Kosovo asked, "separated from its spirituality in the spiritual centers of the Peć Patriarchate, Dečani Monastery, Gračanica Monastery, and the other shrines of Kosovo and Metohija?"[5] Architecture is here not the mimesis of a preexisting and self-sufficient ethnic or national identity, but a constituent part of that identity.

Patrimony thus filled a lack in ethnic identity, supplementing that identity and rendering it complete. This supplementation of identity, however, took place in the course of violence, whether actual or imagined. Posed as a targeting of the architectural supplements of Serb ethnic and national identity, this violence became ethnic, with both its authors and their victims cast as representatives of ethnic communities. The Church's discourse on violence was thus an architectural discourse. Its narratives were performative, endowing architecture with a patrimonial identity that was taken as eternal and sacred. The Church's access to its own inheritance thereby proceeded through an ethnic other, seemingly dead set on that inheritance's violation. Mediated through that other's violation of sacred monuments, the Church received ethnic alterity as insuperably violent; the ethnic identity of its own constituents as irrevocably threatened; and ethnicity as founded in architecture.

The 1981 fire at Peć Patriarchate comprised both a repetition within a history of architectural manifestations of ethnic alterity and an alteration of this history, the initiation of its shift from a chronicle of the recent past to a *longue durée* structure of epochal violence. This history formally commenced in 1968, when the Church's Holy Council delegated Church personnel in Kosovo with the task of reporting on violations of Church property by Albanians. The violations that were reported included toppled gravestones in Orthodox cemeteries, vandalized Orthodox churches, and trespassing, unauthorized cattle grazing and unauthorized harvesting on Orthodox monastery fields. These violations became the primary space of appearance of Albanians in the Church's collective imagination. The fire at the patriarchate in March 1981 fit within this chronicle of violations but also instigated its conversion into an epochal history of recursive violence against the Church. The reports made and collected by Church personnel on violated architecture before 1981 fit seamlessly into post-1981 narratives; what was previously cited as evidence of crime was cited as evidence of ethnic cleansing and genocide. Architecture remained a privileged medium of alterity, even as the forms of alterity underwent radical revision. An architectural representation of alterity, then, stood in for the political representation of others: a crisis of representation that the Church produced and perceived as a crisis of violence.

It was also a crisis of agency. For the Church, agency emerged in response to an interpellation by sacred architecture. This interpellation was to hold both for the Serbs who identified with sacred architecture and mourned its violation and for the Albanians who allegedly inflicted and celebrated that violation; both Serbs and Albanians were defined, that is, by their supposed relationship to architecture. But the Church's discourse on desecration was a solicitation to and for another agency, as well—a protector of threatened monuments and a defender of a beleaguered community. This discourse took form, therefore, as entreaties to authorities and audiences, at first the formal authorities of the Yugoslav state and then, after 1981, to various international and intranational institutions, communities, and publics. What has often been posed as the "appropriation" of the Church's discourse on desecration by the Milošević regime, then, was precisely inscribed in the discourse itself.

Actual Crimes

Until 1981, ethno-nationalist antagonism in Kosovo, as throughout Yugoslavia, had no place in state or state-sponsored narratives. For the state, the "brotherhood and unity" of Yugoslavia's ethnically and nationally defined peoples was public policy and expressed reality.[6] The relations between these peoples were acknowledged and reified in sanctioned displays of cultural difference, from the constitution of Yugoslavia's ethno-nationally defined republics, through festivals of ethno-national cultural traditions, to Monuments of Brotherhood and Unity like that constructed on the site of Prishtina's destroyed bazaar. Differences were only admissible, that is, as mutually supportive and reinforcing in the frame of state socialism.

Yet at the end of November 1968—two days before a national holiday in Yugoslavia (Day of the Republic) and a day before a national holiday in neighboring Albania (Day of the Flag)—Albanian students demonstrated at the University of Prishtina, marching with banners proclaiming "Dole kolonizacija na Kosovu!" ("Down with colonialism in Kosovo," in Serbian) and "Duam republika!" ("We want a republic," in Albanian).[7] When demonstrators began to overturn cars and smash windows, the police dealt with the event as a riot; in the resulting violence, one student was killed and injuries were inflicted on police and students alike. The demonstrations spread through Kosovo and beyond, to Albanian-majority areas in neighboring Macedonia; explicitly demanded were republican status for Kosovo, freedom to fly the Albanian flag, an independent university for Kosovo (in 1968 the recently established university in Prishtina was a branch of the University of Belgrade), and the removal of the Serbian name "Metohija" from Kosovo's official name (this name, Kosovo-Metohija, was formed from the Serbian names of Kosovo's two regions; in Albanian, the name for the province was Kosova).[8]

In the wake of these demonstrations, the federal government enacted a series of "liberalizations" in Kosovo. In the frame of Titoist governance, these policies and programs were designed to equalize political status and social relations between Serbs and Albanians and to placate Albanian discontent: to restore, in other words, a "brotherhood and unity" presumed to have existed before the demonstrations and to have been disturbed by them. Federal constitutional amendments passed in December 1968 devolved various legislative and judical authorities to Kosovo and Vojvodina, Serbia's other province, and these provinces were also given direct representation in Yugoslavia's federal parliament. The Serbian parliament adopted a new constitution for Kosovo in January 1969, further expanding the province's autonomy and establishing an independent University of Prishtina. In 1974, a new constitution in Yugoslavia devolved still more governmental functions to the federation's six republics, as well as to Kosovo and Vojvodina, which then became constituent elements of the federation, alongside, in many ways, the republics.

It was during this time of perceived violence against the state carried out by partisans of Albanian sovereignty and state efforts to placate Kosovo's Albanian citizenry that the Serbian Orthodox Church took on the responsibility of documenting violence against its properties and members. According to subsequent church narratives, the church began to be concerned with vandalism against its properties after the 1968 demonstrations in Kosovo because vandalism itself intensified after those riots: "From then on, attacks on churches, monasteries, graveyards, and monuments of Serbian nationality, spirituality, and culture only increased and widened."[9] This is, already, an architectural interpellation: the Church posed violence against its architecture as the origin of its concern for that architecture. In so doing, however, the Church exchanged the mystery of vandalism for the manifestation of ethnic alterity.

Enacting this exchange, the Church recalibrated its relationship to the state. Prior to 1968, the socialist state was the Church's central antagonist. The state mandated the destruction of churches, the listing of church properties as cultural heritage managed by the state, the seizure of church and monastery artifacts as heritage to be displayed in state museums, and the appropriation of monastery property for state functions, all issues protested by church leaders prior to 1968.[10] After 1968, though, the Church relied on precisely the authority that had been responsible for violence against its property in the past to respond to violence against that property in the present. The Church's relation to the state began to be mediated by the Kosovar Albanians whom the Church cited as responsible for attacks against its property and members. The Church was still protesting to the state, but now about the actions of Albanians.

In the wake of the 1968 riots, the Church's diocese in Kosovo complained to the Holy Council of Bishops (Sveti arhijerejski sinod), the Church's governing authority, that state authorities in Kosovo had not brought any perpetrator of assaults on church property or members to justice.[11] The Holy Council of Bishops then petitioned President Tito for redress from what were described as "not only outrages but also actual crimes against the Serbian Orthodox Church and its members in Kosovo."[12] In the petition, these "actual crimes" were enumerated to include, "not only damage to crops, destruction of forests, and demolition of tombstones, but also bodily assaults, even against women and nuns." The petition ends with an appeal "to address your attention to our distress so that similar unlawful acts might be prevented from happening again."[13] Tito replied by letter to the Holy Council, writing that he would pass its petition on to the Executive Council of Serbia.[14] Several months later, however, the Church newspaper, *Pravoslavlje*, reported that the government had done nothing and so seemed to be uninterested in putting a stop to the "savagery."[15]

At that time, the Holy Council instructed its ecclesiastical personnel in Kosovo to collect data "on all instances of attacks on the clergy, churches and church property committed by citizens of Albanian nationality in the Kosovo area."[16] While the Church staged its documentation of vandalism after 1968 as a "response" to the upsurge in vandalism, its documentation also involved the production of a new discursive object—a new event. Attacks against property of different sorts, in different locations across Kosovo, were aggregated together as "actual crimes" inflicted by Kosovar Albanians against the Church. Just as violated architecture was received by the police in 1968 as a sign of the transformation of "demonstrations" into "riots," it was received by the Serbian Orthodox Church as a sign that transformed a series of local incidents of vandalism, harassment, and trespass into province-wide violence against the Church and its members.

In the documents collected by the Church, violent events are reported but not interpreted; these documents were written shortly after the events they reported took place; they emplotted these events in short-term chronologies and circumscribed spatial contexts; they took the form of messages to authorities; and they were for the most part not circulated beyond the Church. All of these features subsume the content of these documents under the category of "actual crimes" as defined by the state. One group of these documents takes the form of first-person testimonies that report vandalism and violence directly witnessed or experienced by their authors. The following, for example, is a report cited in the Holy Council's petition to President Tito, made by Prioress Paraskeva of the Dević Monastery to the Eparchy of Raško-Prizren, the Church's diocese in Kosovo:

On May 28, 1968, we introduced a notification and request to the Municipal Committee and the National Police in Srbica against the sons of Osman and Azem Deljević from Rezala, who attacked the chief of Dević Monastery, Prioress Paraskeva, hitting her on the head with canes inside the monastery. On June 13 one of the same sons found me; he grabbed my arm and twisted it so that it almost fractured. On June 14, around 9 A.M., someone came to Dević and told me that I shouldn't go down from the monastery because they are waiting to kill me. . . . Their cattle are grazing freely in our cornfields, our gardens, and our meadows. What can we do when they come and stay for several hours, destroying all our silence?[17]

A second group of documents take the form of reports that summarize testimonies made by or information collected by others. The following, for example, is a report by Bishop Pavle of Prizren to the High Commission of the Autonomous Province of Kosovo:

In the cemetery of the village Sipolje near Kosovska Mitrovica during the summer of 1972 some youths of Albanian nationality, singing insulting songs against Serbs, demolished fifteen gravestones. Similarly, not long ago in the village of Srbovec near Kosovska Mitrovica, eight gravestones were destroyed. In this way in the cemetery at Orahovac, where not only wooden crosses were broken but also seven gravestones from marble, two from cement, and fourteen from stone. In the village of Opteruši near Orahovac, three stone crosses were broken and all wooden crosses except three. In the village of Retimlju near Orahovac the wooden crosses were broken so that, concerning the graves, there is quite a large emergency.[18]

The "existents," or thematic objects, of these narratives are people, places, and things classified as either Serbian or Albanian. The events reported by the narratives are violations: people being harmed, places being trespassed, things being damaged or destroyed. The function performed by architecture in these narratives is thus to be violated. In all cases, Albanians are the source of violation and Serbs are the victims of violation; from trespass to desecration, the violation of Serbian Orthodox architecture mediates the antagonism of individuals or groups of Albanians against Serbian Orthodox people, places, and things.

These documents exemplify the two predominant forms in which the Serbian Orthodox Church narrated violence against its members and property before 1981. The first document comprises a narrative about different forms of violence occurring in the same place; the second document comprises a narrative about the same form of violence occurring in different places. In both cases, time, space, and violence are precisely coordinated. "Dević Monastery" names a site where a number of acts of bodily violence, threats, and trespassing took place over the course of two weeks; the rural villages around the towns of Kosovska Mitrovica/Mitrovicë and Orahovac/Rahovec name sites where a number of graves and gravestones were vandalized over the course of one summer. In each document, the narrated period of time is also close to the time in which the narrative itself was produced; each document was submitted to the eparchy only weeks or months after the events it narrated took place. Even reports covering a year of criminal activity in the Kosovo diocese carefully demarcate temporal and spatial boundaries, describing how, for example, "the attacks will usually stop for some time, only to begin in another place."[19]

Articulated by violence, space and time are organized by the formulation of the crime scene, the site of the "actual crimes" reported by the Holy Council to President Tito. The explicit genre of each document is a crime report. The first document is a report on a crime made to the municipality or police, and the second, a report made to provincial authorities. In each document, a crime or crimes are reported to an authority endowed with power to investigate that crime and bring its perpetrators to justice. The temporal and spatial descriptions of each narrative are comprehensible within the crime report's expectation of precise presentation of evidence: places are named, dates and sometimes even times are given, and, when possible, protagonists are identified by name.

The status of these documents as crime reports places these documents *in* history, as opposed to *on or about* history. The narratives for the most part stage themselves as indicative: merely describing, reporting, or stating events. This indicative function can be distinguished from an interpretive function: to explain, to make meaningful, to understand. As reports, the documents work to extricate themselves from historical discourse. As Roland Barthes puts it, "for history not to signify, discourse must be confined to a pure, unstructured series of notations"; the spatial and temporal circumscription of the reports above attempt such a series.[20]

But the indicative status of discourse cannot be "pure."[21] Barthes' description of indicative discourse presumes and reproduces its own indicative status, its own purity, its own separation from ideological interpretation—the ideology, that is, of a structuralism whose descriptions perfectly subsume their objects. Yet the presumed neutrality and objectivity of this structuralism, as well as of the descriptions, reportages, and statements it attempts to subsume, are a function of protocols of interpretation outside structuralism and its objects of analysis. Thus, that Prioress Paraskeva named her antagonists as "the sons of Osman and Azem Deljević" (whose first names are marked as Albanian), and that Bishop Pavle reported on "some youths of Albanian nationality," cannot be confirmed as either indicative or interpretive on the basis of the texts those phrases are included within. The relevance of ethnicity in these reports, that is, is undecidable. What can be ascertained, by contrast, is that ethnicity is included within these reports, along with other presumably indicative descriptions, *as if* it, too, is a neutral and objective description: a performance of indication that works to de-ideologize ethnic reference.

On one level, this performance refracts a disinclination or impossibility to contradict the concept of "brotherhood and unity," a sociality in which ethnic antagonism had no place. For the most part, these narratives were not publicly circulated; their addressees were usually limited to state authorities or else the eparchy. Only in a few cases did the Serbian Orthodox Church publish a report of violated monuments in one of its newspapers.[22] If these "actual crimes" were the subject of interpretation, these interpretations left little or no public traces. On another level, however, this performance is a solicitation of agency. The addressees of these narratives were posed as agents who not only could interpret the narratives but also respond to them. As messages sent to authorities, the narratives fit within an implied division of labor by means of which the narratives *report* crimes while other author(itie)s, who are endowed with agency, *interpret* these crimes and then provide redress.

It Is Not Only Vandalism

In the spring of 1981, the state injunction against public references to ethnic or national antagonism broke down. In response to a number of events that took place in Kosovo from the middle of March to early

April 1981, the state shifted from hiding antagonism to mobilizing it as an explanation for disorder, whose manifestations were subsequently categorized as demonstrations, protests, riots, uprising, counterrevolution, or the commencement of open and total war between Albanians and Serbs in Kosovo. Besides the fire at the patriarchate, these manifestations of disorder included a series of public assemblies and street marches by Kosovar Albanians in Prishtina and then throughout Kosovo; forbidden speech acts, vandalism, and violence deployed by or attributed to the protestors; violent measures of crowd control on the part of security police trying to suppress the protests; and finally the declaration of a state of emergency and the mobilization of the Yugoslav National Army to restore that particular state of affairs known as "order."

Over the course of their duration, the meanings of the above events were mediated by a diverse and shifting array of texts.[23] Some of these texts were verbal or written: proclamations, shouted slogans, graffiti, signs, and banners, indexing political positions from Yugoslav socialism to Albanian nationalism. But verbal signs, written signs, and violence were enmeshed in a complex communicative network of apprehensions, responses, and counterresponses, so that the longer the events lasted, the more repressive were the means to control them, and the more the means were violent, the more radical were the political programs that demonstrators called for. The events were shaped, that is, by the names given to them and the texts in which they were narrated, by demonstrators and authorities alike, in an ongoing process of definition—a process that escaped the rationalities and agencies of all protagonists involved.

The state originally attempted to conceal the violence of the demonstrations, just as it handled other events that appeared to contradict brotherhood and unity. The Yugoslav press was subsidized by the state; it was expected to follow official policy and doctrine and was subject to banning and confiscation if it transgressed these.[24] The disorder of spring 1981, however, became a crisis for state media control; it was the first time that the Yugoslav state could not sustain its control over the appearance of events. Slavoljub Djukić, the editor of one of the leading daily newspapers in Belgrade, *Politika*, described the media as "adhering to the rule that what is not published in newspapers had not happened," but added that exchanges of information over the telephone between Prishtina and the rest of Yugoslavia rendered that rule obsolete.[25] Communication technology had developed to the point that, for the first time, it became impossible to make a mass public event disappear; "now the dam burst: Yugoslav newspapers openly competed to give the most complete and probing coverage to Kosovo, and this new spirit quickly spread to other topics."[26]

While the state could not make the demonstrations disappear, however, it could semantically colonize them. Programmatically avoiding reflection on its own role in the violence, the state introduced a concealed enemy that, it claimed, lay behind the events' status as "counterrevolutionary." The presence of this concealed enemy—named Albanian nationalism and irredentism—rendered the state's reaction as a necessary counterviolence. The discord between the explicit demands of the demonstrators (for Kosovo to become a republic in the Yugoslav federation) and the nationalist and irredentist program of this enemy was explained by recourse to the latter's necessary concealment. As one newspaper article put it shortly after the demonstrations:

The basic platform of counterrevolution in Kosovo is nationalism and irredentism, with rather skillfully interwoven pseudo-Marxist slogans by which part of the youth in the province was deceived. Even the most confirmed nationalists and chauvinists are aware that they cannot appear in public without a mask. With slogans about equality, the right to self-determination, exploitation, low standard of living, and similar things, it was possible, although only temporarily, to conceal the real nationalist and irredentist nature of counterrevolution.[27]

Yet the counterrevolution was revealed, according to the state's interpretation, in architectural media, or "vandalism." Thus, as the League of Communists official report on the events claimed, "the vandalism displayed by participants in the demonstrations assumed such proportions that our system of socialist self-managing democracy exhausted all political means and was compelled to resort to appropriate measures to counter this violence."[28] Nationalism and irredentism were concealed by the demonstrators' explicit demands for republican status for Kosovo, encomiums to Marx and Tito, and so forth, but were revealed by the demonstrators' recourse to "vandalist" violence.

Just as it did for the Church, that is, vandalism supplemented an otherwise absent contextual agent; violated architecture allowed that agent's presence to be discerned—and thus annihilated. Reports about vandalism against Church properties that previously circulated only among Church and state authorities then began to appear in daily newspapers and magazines. This, too, was an interpellation by architecture, but it was now received by the state, suggesting that the state was the target of violence whose formation was exterior to it. Here, for example, is a report about the desecration of a Serbian cemetery published a month after the end of the demonstrations, from the Prishtina daily newspaper *Rilindja*:

During the night between April 29 and 30, an unknown person or persons in the village of Bresje, in the municipality of Prishtina, damaged nineteen graves and dug up seventeen others. This type of vandalism is unprecedented in this village, entirely inhabited by Serbs. There have never been complaints regarding cohabitation with Albanians and members of other ethnic groups who live in nearby villages, and even today they do not doubt that this act is the work of someone else, allied with the hostile elements that reject this cohabitation.[29]

Vandalism was thus rendered comprehensible by linking it to the origin point of the demonstrations, with the agency behind the vandalism then becoming the same "hostile elements" as those behind the demonstrations themselves. Another report of cemetery desecrations in Kosovo, from the Belgrade daily newspaper *Borba*, reads:

During the night between November 28 and 29, an unknown person or persons desecrated a number of Orthodox and Catholic gravestones in Prizren Cemetery. The official report of the Prizren Secretariat of Internal Affairs says that one marble Orthodox gravestone was knocked down and decorative stones at two other Orthodox graves were damaged. In the same fashion, five Catholic gravestones were desecrated and nine wooden crosses were pulled out of the ground, one of which was broken and the rest tossed around. A session of the Committee for All Peoples Defense and Social Self-Protection was immediately held, in which this most barbaric vandalistic act was sharply condemned as aimed against the brotherhood and unity of our nations and nationalities.[30]

It is vandalism, but, as the headline of another report on vandalism in *Politika* pointed out, "it is not only vandalism."[31] Vandalism exceeded itself as a supplement of nationalist ideology and agency. This supplementation was not only semiotic—yielding a sign that could be read—but instrumental—yielding a threatening form of violence. The threat of this violence lay precisely in its supplementary dimension; each act of vandalism was read as targeting the state's most fundamental principles. As one characteristic account put it, reporting the vandalism of twenty-nine gravestones in an Orthodox cemetery in the Serbian village of Dvorane: vandalism was "an enemy act that represent[ed] a brutal attack on intranational and interpersonal relationships, brotherhood and unity, and the oneness of Yugoslavia's peoples."[32]

The state, concerned with nationalisms of whatever sort, did not segregate reports of vandalism against Serb targets from those against Albanian or Yugoslav targets. Indeed, the cemetery desecration in Prizren included both Serb (Orthodox) and Albanian (Catholic) targets and newspapers after 1981 also reported vandalism not only in Orthodox cemeteries but also against Albanian-owned shops and Yugoslav government buildings. Reclaiming its capacity to conceal and reveal, the state cast vandalism as a sign of nationalisms of any sort, forces that were deemed responsible for social insecurity and disorder and that necessitated the use of state violence as a means to restore order.

An Atmosphere Created by Vandalist Methods

Before the spring of 1981, the Serbian Orthodox Church posed vandalism as a crime against state law, posed state authorities as the addressees of its narratives, and framed those narratives by the state ideology of brotherhood and unity. After that spring, the Church's narration of vandalism bypassed the state both materially and ideologically. Appealing to witnessing publics both international and intranational, this narration posed vandalism as a manifestation of "genocide" and "ethnic cleansing," the former a crime against humanity and the latter a crime against the Serbian people. The Church's post-1981 narration of vandalism reflected and performed a dissolution of state authority—an authority that was, after the spring of 1981, approached as weak and conflicted, its ideology fragile if not fictional, its law inadequate to the nationalist forces that, it was claimed, threatened it.[33] Indeed, by 1987, Patriarch German, the head of the Serbian Orthodox Church, was claiming that state authorities "knew" the Albanians who set fire to the patriarchate in 1981 but concealed the fact in a (failed) attempt to maintain the appearance of brotherhood of unity.[34]

The Church's post-1981 narration of vandalism also comprised a shift from presuming to write *in* history to presuming to write *on* history—to produce the discourse of history. This history was one of epochal and recursive Serb suffering, so that contemporary vandalism became a historical reenactment, a mimetic repetition of the infliction of damage on church property by a series of violent others. While, to the post-1981 state, vandalism was a manifestation of antistate nationalism, to the Church it manifested the recursive history of Serb victimization. Church narratives of vandalism thus explored its historical position, posing it in relation to sequences of past acts of violence. As Patriarch German's claim above indicates, the fire at the patriarchate was soon transformed from a *mysterious* event to a *historical* one, "the first public rendering," according to one account, "of the crimes of Albanian [*arbanaske*] separatist aggression against all things Serb in Kosovo and Metohija."[35]

After the patriarchate fire, Patriarch German met with Sergej Kraigher, the chairman of Yugoslavia's post-Tito collective presidency, to discuss the threat to Orthodox heritage in Kosovo.[36] Most post-1981 narratives, however, replaced the addressees of pre-1981 narratives—Serb and Yugoslav state authorities, from President Tito on—by international and intranational audiences. The former was consolidated both by Serb publications published by émigrés in England, Canada, and the United States and by international relations pursued by Church officers through official visits to Europe and North America. In February 1982, several priests sent an open letter to Patriarch German, asking that he take action to prevent the "extinction" of Serbs in Kosovo; this letter was then published in a Serb émigré monthly published in England.[37] Three months later, a second open letter written by twenty-one priests, monks, and nuns was published in *Pravoslavlje* and then in émigré publications in England and the United States.[38] Reporting on endangered Serbs and Serb heritage in Kosovo, the authors of the "Appeal" were, they wrote, "compelled by our conscience to raise up our voice in defense of the spiritual and biological existence of the Serbian people in Kosovo and Metohija."[39]

As in pre-1981 Church reports, the "Appeal" emplotted smashed tombstones and vandalized churches as manifestations of ethnic alterity and, as in those reports, an authority was solicited to prevent the further occurrence of such violence. Yet the "Appeal" aggregated the acts of violence it narrated into a single narrative block, named "genocide" and "ethnic purification":

Our grievous sufferings, the frequent migrations of Serbs from Kosovo, and the destruction of our national shrines were all comprehensible from the Battle of Kosovo (in 1389) until the most recent times. . . . There is no example from the suffering of the past which has not reoccurred for the Serbs in Kosovo over the past twenty years, from the threatening of life and property to the burning of the Patriarchate at Peć, the desecration of sacred graves, criminal offences committed against students and monastics, and even the blinding of livestock just because they belong to Serbs. . . . One can say that a planned, premeditated genocide is gradually being carried out against the Serbian people in Kosovo! Because, if it is not so, what does the theme of an "ethnically pure" Kosovo mean—a theme which, disregarding everything, is actively being carried out by continuous and incessant expulsions. . . . Especially since 1969, the expulsion of Serbs has continued up to the present, and has moreover intensified over the last year! It is being intensified through an atmosphere created by vandalist methods, on the basis of a long-term program that is being carried out with planning and organization, secretly and openly, before the eyes of the whole world.[40]

The counterpart to what Barthes described as indicative discourse *in* history was interpretive discourse *on* history. The latter, historical discourse, according to Barthes, is marked by two linguistic features. The first, which Barthes terms a "shifter of listening . . . designates all mention of sources, of testimony, all reference to a listening of the historian, collecting an *elsewhere* of his discourse and speaking it."[41] In the "Appeal," this elsewhere is comprised of time since the 1389 Battle of Kosovo, a moment marking the inaugural violence of Serbia's loss of Kosovo. The second feature of historical discourse, writes Barthes, is the "shifter of organization," which establishes the relation between "two time spans: the time of the speech-act and the time of the material stated."[42] Here, that relation is one of recursivity: acts of violence take place as repetitions or "recurrences" of prior violence, stretching back to the arch-violence of Serbia's loss of Kosovo in 1389. What Barthes calls the "lesson" of this history is thus "continuity": history extends into the moment of historicization itself, so that the very form of this historicization is that of an appeal for protection against a violence that originates in the past and persists "up to the present."

Yet this continuity is at least partly comprised on the basis of events "since 1969"—events that the Church had documented in the form of seemingly indicative crime reports. In the "Appeal," these reports, aggregated together, are spliced into an epochal temporal sequence along with prior instances of "suffering," "migrations," and "destruction." The citation of multiple *indications* thereby yields an *interpretation*, a historical claim, a rendering of a recursive history of violence. In this history, architecture maintained its position as a manifestation, a rendering of the actuality of the past, which was, recursively, also a rendering of the future: "With its

700-year duration, Kosovo is really present in our present and future, with the Patriarchate at Peć, with the monasteries at Dečani and Gračanica, the martyrs of Kosovo and the Serbian decision and testament of Kosovo; Kosovo is our memory, our hearth, the focal point of our existence."[43]

The persistence of architecture as patrimony here confirms the repetition of time as recursive history. Yet this representation of patrimony emerged in an appeal for its protection. The claim to an architectural inheritance was made in the moment when this inheritance was perceived to be under threat. The sacralization of architecture, in short, was conjoined to that architecture's desecration, with the historicity of sacralization always already suppressed by its status as an inheritance.

By scripting vandalism as a component of "genocide" and "ethnic purification," the Church participated in the introduction of ethnic antagonism, of both the past and of the present, into Yugoslav public discourse. In Yugoslavia, the terms *genocide* and *ethnic cleansing* emerged in the context of the Second World War and its aftermath.[44] The socialist narrative of the Second World War excluded these terms, and the politics associated with them, by de-ethnicizing the war and presenting it as a conflict between communist partisans and bourgeois of all nationalities. All nationalities, the socialist narrative posed, contributed to the fascist bourgeois enemy and to that enemy's victims, so that neither *genocide* nor *ethnic cleansing* were appropriate names for the violence inflicted on those victims.[45] In the early 1980s, the victimization of Serbs in wartime Croatia was broached by Serbian writers, who reintroduced the term *genocide* and the concept of Serb victimization into public discourse about the Second World War.[46] Simultaneously, the Church mobilized this new term, as well as *ethnic purification* and *ethnic cleansing*, to narrate current events in Kosovo.[47]

At the same time, as the "Appeal" already indicates, Church discourse emplotted genocide and ethnic cleansing in an epochal temporality. The "Appeal" cited both 1389 and 1968–69 as origin points for a continuum of violence in Kosovo. Other Church accounts that pose 1968–69 as an origin point explicitly consolidated the reports of crime collected after 1968, framing them as components of a single, long-running violent event. In July 1982, for example, the Serbian Orthodox newspaper *Glasnik Srpske Pravoslavne Crkve*, published a chronology beginning in 1968 recounting vandalism against churches, trespassing on church property, and injury to church personnel and other Serbs in Kosovo since 1968.[48] Each act of vandalism in the present evoked and extended Kosovo's post-1968 history, a history that became one of repeated or continuous ethnic violence against Serbs.

After 1981, journals and newspapers represented this history not only textually but also visually, publishing photographs of such images as vandalized graves (Figure 2.4), vandalized cemeteries (Figure 2.5), and, in one instance, an armed nun guarding a monastery (Figure 2.6), the latter after an Albanian policeman's reported rape attempt on Abbess Tatjana of Gračanica Monastery.[49] As in the texts they accompanied, these photographs, too, conjured the presence of ethnic others; the signs of violence inflicted on Serb monuments were, here, traces of that other's presence. Photography staged a corroboration between the materiality of those traces and their semantic function; violence against or at historical sites was, it was asserted, a historical violence, a violence that repeated itself through history.

The framing of contemporary violence in Kosovo as "genocide" also suggested a repetition of the genocide inflicted on Serbs in Yugoslavia during the Second World War.[50] This repeated or continuous genocide was narrated through figurations of or parallels between Kosovar Albanian

FIGURE 2.4 Vandalized Serbian Orthodox graves in Srbica, 1985. Photograph from *Književna Reč*, 10 January 1987.

FIGURE 2.5 Vandalized Serbian Orthodox graves in Begov Lukavac, 8 October 1985. Photograph from *Književna Reč*, 10 January 1987.

FIGURE 2.6 "Mušutište: Prioress Ilirija guarding the sanctuary with a rifle in her hand." Photograph from *Duga*, 17–30 September 1988.

"irredentists" and "Albanian Nazis" (*Albanske Naciste*) or Ustaša, the fascist organization that governed Croatia during the Second World War. Posed as such, contemporary Albanian vandalism comprised yet another iteration of an attempted "extermination [*istrebljenje*] of the Serbian people in Kosovo and Metohija."[51] Many Church narratives that mobilized the term *genocide* were authored by Atanasije Jevtić, bishop of Zahum-Herzegovina and a Serb nationalist activist. In a series of articles entitled "Od Kosova do Jadovna" (From Kosovo to Jadovno), published in *Pravoslavlje* during 1983 and 1984, Jevtić compared the violence against Serbs in fascist Croatia during the Second World War (Jadovno was a Croatian concentration and death camp) to ongoing violence against Serbs in Kosovo.[52] Both violences were "genocides," Jevtić claimed, with Jadovno itself a "continuation" and a "culmination" of the loss of Kosovo in the 1389 battle.[53] Moreover, according to Jevtić, both the Second World War genocide at Jadovno and the contemporary genocide in Kosovo were suppressed by the Yugoslav state in the interest of maintaining brotherhood and unity, so that Albanian violence and state apathy themselves became recursive.

In 1990 Jevtić published another book, *Stradanja Srba na Kosovu i Metohiji od 1941 do 1990* (The Sufferings of Serbs in Kosovo and Metohija from 1941 to 1990), which posed the relationship between the Second World War and contemporary Kosovo as not only recursive but continuous. The book narrates an unbroken campaign of violence waged by Albanians against Serbs from the war on: "The chronicle of contemporary suffering of Kosovar-Metohijan Serbs begins in the difficult war years of 1941 to 1945, with the basic characteristics of this suffering comprising violence against people and families, robbery of property, defilement and destruction of Serb sacred heritage, persecution against believers, forced emigration, in short, a biological and cultural *genocide against Serbs*."[54] The book included reports from the 1960s, 1970s, and 1980s collected from the Church archive, as well as newspaper reports on vandalism and expulsion that began to be published in Kosovo and Serbia after 1981, citing all of these as evidence of genocide.

Jevtić also emplotted contemporary violence in Kosovo in an epochal temporality that began in 1389, when the medieval Serbian kingdom was thought to have lost Kosovo to the invading Ottoman army. This emplottment was made, for example, in the book edited by Jevtić, *Zadužbine Kosova: Spomenici i znamenja srpskog naroda* (Endowments of Kosovo:

Monuments and Symbols of the Serb Nation). This book opens with a map that displays "important churches and monasteries" in Kosovo. These churches and monasteries are classified in two ways, in terms of time and in terms of architectural condition: those built before and after 1459 (when the Ottoman conquest of the medieval Serbian kingdom was completed) and those intact or ruined. The map shows these churches and monasteries densely filling Kosovo's territory. This spatial occupation is then narratively reprised in the book itself, which opens with histories of the major churches and monasteries and ends with testimonies about violence inflicted on these buildings and their clergy and congregations from the fifteenth century to the present.

The Sufferings of Serbs in Kosovo and Metohija from 1941 to 1990 ends with "Kosovo Polje" (Kosovo Field), a poem by a leading figure in the Serb nationalist opposition, Matija Bećković.[55] The poem, whose beginning forms an epigraph to this chapter, explicitly conjoins architectural violence with architecture's status as a repository of Serb ethnic and national memory, history, and identity. The poem, and the discourse in which it resonates, suggests that it was this status that provoked the violence against architecture, that Albanians targeted Orthodox churches, monasteries, and graves precisely because they were symbolically significant to Serbs. As a 1995 novel about Kosovo by Danko Popović, another writer in the Serb nationalist opposition, was to put it: "The Albanians knew what graves meant to the Serbs; that's why they were destroying them."[56] But it was the experience of spatial violation, whether actual, anticipated, or remembered, that intensified if not produced the symbolic significance attributed to its target. "Kosovo Field," written in 1987 amid the growing attention in Serbian public culture to the plight of Kosovar Serbs, testifies to the refraction of perceived violence against space into spatial symbolism.[57] The protagonists of the poem are left unnamed because, in the discourse of desecration, they name themselves through the violence they inflict. Their alterity manifested in and through violence. The title of a 1988 article on the plight of Kosovar Serbs from the Belgrade biweekly *Duga*, functions similarly: "They burn, rape, beat, stone, destroy, break, and desecrate."[58] Here, Kosovar Albanians are named simply via the alleged violence by means of which their presence is made manifest to their Serb ethnic others. In so doing, *Albanian* becomes not only an incarnation of historical alterity, but also a compendium of varieties of violent otherness.

Desecration as a Political Text

In the beginning of the 1980s, while Serbian, federal Yugoslav, and Communist Party institutions were attempting to maintain the relevance and authority of socialism, the discourse on desecrated Kosovo was oppositional. Church officials were often criticized or censured by the state, and sometimes arrested, for the overly nationalist dimensions of their statements and events. The 1983 rededication of the Peć Patriarchate's newly rebuilt guesthouse occasioned one such criticism.[59] State media denounced the "nationalistic and chauvinistic demonstrations" expressing "greater-Serbian hostility" that took place during the rededication, along with the presence of "oppositional elements"—who included Matija Bećković, the author of "Kosovo Field," along with other Serb nationalist activists.[60] At the same time, the Communist Party in Kosovo was denouncing the "extremist part of the clergy" of all denominations; the views of this extremist clergy were "based on nationalist hatred and backed by an alien ideology seeking to create compact religiously and ethnically pure entities."[61]

In the course of the second half of the 1980s, however, the Church's discourse of desecration gradually shifted from oppositional to hegemonic as it circulated through the language of politically organized Kosovar Serbs, the Serb nationalist opposition, and then the Milošević regime.[62] This circulation is typically termed "appropriation," but it was also a response to the Church's own solicitation for an external agency to protect, defend, and secure itself, the patrimony that it identified with, and the community that it claimed to represent. The discourse of desecration, that is, fabricated a space for the "savior of the Serb nation"—the space that the Milošević regime would claim to occupy.

Architecture was not simply "politicized" as it passed from a subject in Church discourse to a subject in the discourse of Kosovar Serbs, nationalist opposition, and the Milošević regime; architecture's agency was, rather, reinscribed in other contexts. These other contexts were explicitly centered around human rights, civil liberties, the rule of law, and the brotherhood and unity of Yugoslavia's national peoples. A distinctive situation ensued: the defense of ethnically neutral legal and juridical principles summoned Kosovo's status as desecrated space, at once violated by Albanians and sacred to Serbs. Human rights abuses and civil rights violations became *desecrations*.

When Kosovar Serbs began to organize to protect their rights and liberties in the early 1980s, then, the violence that jeopardized them was situated in an epochal history of violence inflicted on and resisted by the ancestors of the protestors.[63] In the first of several petitions that protesting Kosovar Serbs sent to Yugoslav, Serbian, and Communist Party institutions, the "human rights" of the Kosovar Serbs were posed as threatened by a "fascist genocide" taking place "in the cradle of our own fatherland."[64] This genocide was inflicted by "Albanian [*šiptarski*] chauvinists against us and our families, farms, cemeteries, and places of worship." While maintaining its position as a privileged manifestation of ethnic alterity, violated architecture has here become a human rights abuse, as well.

This petition requested the guarantee of human rights for Serbs in Kosovo, but also rewards for the Serbs' "sacrifices" to the nation, which were to comprise various measures limiting the rights of Kosovar Albanians (expulsion from Kosovo of immigrants who had come from Albania after 1941, prohibition on the display of the Albanian flag, and so on). The petition was condemned as "nationalist" by the Serbian presidency and the Central Committee of the Communist Party of Serbia, which then prompted the Serb nationalist opposition to mobilize in support of the Kosovar Serbs.[65] A number of Belgrade intellectuals then sent a second petition to the Yugoslav and Serbian assemblies and Serbian media outlets through the Committee for the Defense of Freedom of Thought and Expression (Odbor za odbranu slobode misli i izražavanja).[66] This Committee was founded in 1984 in order to defend an ethnically neutral subject—the "citizen of Yugoslavia"—on the basis of the Yugoslav constitution and the Universal Declaration of Human Rights.[67] The explicit content of the committee's petition was "a demand for democratic reforms that would establish strong legal order and ensure legal rights." Yet the committee's petition situated the source of disorder and rights violation in Kosovo in a recursive history of violence:

Histories and memories still alive tell us that the exodus of Serbs from Kosovo and Metohija has been going on for three centuries. Only the mentors of those who are pushing Serbs out have changed: instead of the Ottoman Empire, Austria-Hungary, Fascist Italy and Nazi Germany, this role is now filled by the state of Albania and by the ruling institutions of Kosovo itself. . . . The only new feature is the blend of tribal hatred and genocide hidden beneath the Marxist veil.[68]

The "violation of legal rights" in this petition is identical to the violence narrated by the Church: it is epochal, generated by a generic violent other, a fixed feature of a space of desecration. Indeed, the committee's petition explicitly stresses that "the methods [of violence] have not changed either. . . . Old women and nuns are raped, youngsters beaten up, cattle blinded, stables built from gravestones, churches and shrines desecrated, economic sabotages are tolerated, and people forced to sell their farms and land for next to nothing."[69]

The 1986 "Memorandum" of the Serbian Academy of Arts and Sciences, often posed by historians as a key text in the emergence of Serb nationalism in late Yugoslavia, displays the same scripting of rights discriminations against Kosovar Serbs as a violation of sacred space.[70] The "Memorandum" discusses these discriminations in economic, social, and cultural terms but situates them in the space of epochal desecration:

The Serbs in Kosovo and Metohija not only have their past, embodied in cultural and historical monuments of priceless value, but also their own spiritual, cultural and moral values now in the present, for they are living in the cradle of the Serbs' historical existence. The acts of violence which down through the centuries have decimated the Serbian population of Kosovo and Metohija are here and now, in our own era, reaching their highest pitch.[71]

The narrative movement from *monuments of priceless value* to *acts of violence* shuttles between the two reference points of the discourse of desecration: as violence endows architecture with sacred—here "priceless"— value, monuments endow violence with the status of desecration. Serbian nationalism becomes a defense of rights, liberties, and the rule of law, and Albanian nationalism a perpetuation of centuries of decimating violence: an ideological rendering of these nationalisms—but, also, an architectural rendering, with Serbs posed as the inheritors of monuments and Albanians as their destroyers.

In the three years following the "Memorandum," Slobodan Milošević rose through the hierarchy of the Serbian Communist Party, becoming president of Serbia in 1989. This rise is usually understood to mark, correspond to, or itself instantiate a shift in Serbian politics and political culture from a socialist to a nationalist orientation. Historians often pose the Milošević regime as "appropriating" or "mobilizing" the victimization of Kosovo Serbs as a means to consolidate power in Serbia.[72] Milošević's speeches in the years leading up to his presidency often referred to Kosovo as the "cradle" or "hearth" of the Serbian nation.[73] Slogans during the 1988 "antibureaucratic revolution" fomented by Milošević often referred to desecrated Kosovo.[74] State-controlled media outlets followed suit with proliferating reportage on

Kosovo's history and meaning.[75] The regime's representation of Kosovo as a desecrated space thus appears as an "instrumentalization" of Church discourse, with the desecration of sacred monuments becoming a political resource to legitimize violent measures to protect Serb sovereignty in Kosovo, as well as analogously endangered Serb spaces in Bosnia and Croatia.[76] But this "instrumentalization" of desecration also renames an interpellation by architecture. That is, the endowment of monuments with political (profane) presence as legitimizing instruments in the Milošević regime simply iterates the Church's endowment of them with a patrimonial (sacred) one. Consideration of this interpellation suggests that Serbian sacred and origin spaces in Kosovo were not simply usable geographies discursively deployed in the context of contemporary political exigencies—instruments at hand to history's agents—but were always already spaces in which agency was historically determined by architecture in the guise of "sacred monuments."

Assuming a position as a defender of the beleaguered Kosovar Serbs—a respondent to the appeals, petitions and memoranda both from them and on their behalf—in 1989 Milošević mobilized Serb support for the revocation of the autonomy of Serbia's autonomous provinces, Kosovo and Vojvodina, and asserted Serbia's authority in both places. The revocation of Kosovo's autonomy, however, was instantiated and maintained by state violence. The revocation was protested by a general strike and large-scale demonstrations of Kosovar Albanians.[77] These demonstrations, termed "war" by the Milošević regime and popular Serbian media, were subdued by police violence and the installation of a state of emergency in Kosovo—the second after 1981.[78] Following the emergency's official termination, it was practically prolonged through the enactment of special laws for "extraordinary circumstances" (*posebne okolnosti*), as well as a thorough extralegal repression of Kosovar Albanians in public and private life.[79] Yet this state violence, too, was enmeshed in the recursive history of desecrated Kosovo. In that history, it was endowed with value, significance, and sanctity; it had been paid for by centuries of desecrations and it comprised a legitimate counterviolence against an unremittingly violent ethnic other. State violence, the terminal phase of which is the subject of the following chapter, thus completed the summoning of ethnic alterity that the discourse of desecration had initiated; it finally conjured alterity into existence, in the very process of managing and destroying it.

History legitimized this conjuring and architecture confirmed this history. For Barthes, critic of "the discourse of history," this history was the product of a semiotic operation. In historical discourse, he writes, "it is the signified itself which is repulsed, merged in the referent; the referent enters into direct relation with the signifier, and the discourse, meant only to express the real, believes it elides the fundamental terms of imaginary structures, which is the signified." Historical discourse thereby performs a collapse of the past into mere signifiers: "The 'real' is never anything but an unformulated signified, sheltered behind the apparent omnipotence of the referent."[80] At the same time, however, Barthes also attests to the cultural "prestige" of these otherwise "mere signifiers" of history—their privileged capacity "to signify that the event represented has *really* taken place."[81] The staging of this capacity as mere semiosis is not, however, a simple unveiling that substitutes the latter for the former; semiosis and reality-effects are conjoined in historical discourse, and this conjunction conveys the status of this discourse as a supplement of the past, at once additive and indispensable. This was the supplementation that was enacted, as tragedy, by the Church, in its narration of ethnic alterity, a narration that set history "into direct relation" with its architectural signifiers.

Barthes ended his essay "The Discourse on History" with an observation on precisely those signifiers. "The profanation of relics," he writes, "is in fact a destruction of reality itself, starting from the intuition that the real is never anything but a meaning, revocable when history requires it."[82] In a footnote, Barthes refers this observation to an attack on a temple at Confucius's birthplace, in 1967, during China's Cultural Revolution and in the year Barthes' essay was published—his own interpellation by architecture. Barthes imputes the "intuition" about history that he describes to the Red Guards who authored the violation of the temple. Yet I want to claim this intuition, also, for those who felt themselves victims of such violations. The Church's narration of desecration—"a destruction of reality itself"—becomes, then, not only an ideological historicization of alterity but, implicitly, the recognition of an other's presence. The Church's historicization hollowed out the agency of this other, fabricating a violent other's eternal return, translating the other's mystery into history—but, at the same time, this historicization also allows for a retranslation, a restoration not of reality—at least, not for me—but of the mystery that throws what passes for reality into question.

Warchitecture

This is war, unfortunately.

COLONEL SLOBODAN STOJANOVIĆ, Yugoslav Army spokesman,
on the burning of the village of Krush e Madhe / Velika Kruša, Kosovo

Violence, Performance, Ethnicity

"I would like to go to the village of Racaj. There you see buildings in flames—that is what happens when the Serb forces come to town."[1] The speaker was NATO spokesman, Jamie Shea; the date was May 14, 1999, the fifty-second day of the NATO bombing campaign against Serbia; the occasion was NATO's daily press briefing during that campaign; and the subject was the violence that Serb military and paramilitary forces were wreaking in Kosovo. Shea termed his survey of this subject "Milošević's battle damage assessment." This description, it quickly emerged, was ironic. While Serbia claimed its forces were fighting a war against a violent insurgency, Shea's survey did not depict Serb forces in military battle but in violence against civilians. More specifically, his survey depicted *architecture*: not violence against civilians in their homes, villages, and towns, but violence against those homes, villages, and towns themselves.

Shea's words about the village of Racaj/Rracaj glossed the first of a series of images that depicted damaged and destroyed buildings (Figure 3.1). Sometimes these buildings comprised the homes of expelled Kosovar Albanians—"nice smart suburban-style villas," according to Shea, in the case

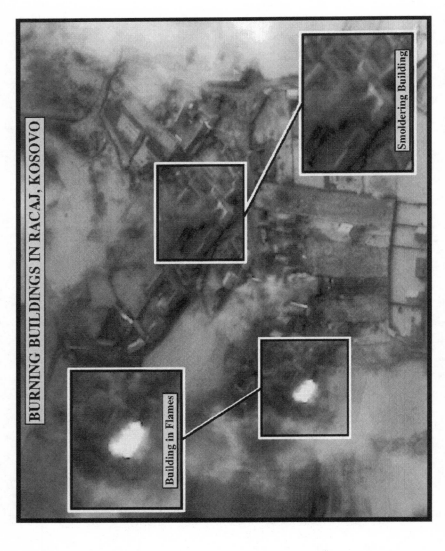

FIGURE 3.1 Satellite image of burning buildings in the village of Racaj, Kosovo, shown in Operation Allied Force press briefing on the Serb counterinsurgency campaign, 14 May 1999. Image courtesy of NATO.

of Podujevo/Podujevë (Figure 3.2). Sometimes they comprised mosques in emptied-out villages (Figure 3.3). Some images showed the same scene before and after Serb forces "visited," to use Shea's once-again ironic term: "the buildings intact and then the buildings obliterated," as Shea described the juxtaposed images (Figure 3.4).

Shea's ironic distance from his subject matter reflected, inadvertently, the ambivalent immediacy of his presentation. On one level, this ambivalence was technical: Shea took his global audience to the small village of Racaj, and to other sites of violence, via annotated images produced by U.S. Defense Department satellites circling far above the earth. The subjects of these images, pictured in a bitmapped haze of pixels, had to be enmeshed in a complex apparatus of written, graphic, and verbal signs in order to become legible. The image of a building in flames, or damaged or even destroyed, was incomprehensible without an accompanying text signifying flames, damage, or destruction. The rhetorical distance of irony in Shea's presentation thus mapped onto the spectatorial distance of his satellite imagery. Was it possible to get up close and personal to a satellite image in 1999? Was it possible to lead spectators from a network of pixels to a vale of tears?

On another level, though, the ambivalent immediacy of Shea's presentation was structural. His blurry images of distant violence were not extraordinary in their dependence on mediation: no matter the media, no matter the precision of rendering, burning buildings do not speak, either for themselves or for those who set them alight. Immediacy is always ambivalent, always constructed: a flimsy discursive facade that conceals the machinery of mediation, machinery that has to be ignored, avoided, or forgotten for there to be a "direct" experience of the content that mediation delivers. *Violence* (the word) is a mediation, just as is violence (the phenomenon), not despite but through the very materiality of the injury and damage that violence produces. Flames put architecture in jeopardy, but flames have to be endowed with meanings for that jeopardy to be revealed as violence.

The key mediation in Shea's presentation was that of "ethnic cleansing"; pixels labeled "fire" and pixels labeled "ruin" were portrayed as signs of the ethnic violence Serb forces were wreaking on Kosovo Albanians. "Remember when we see these pictures and hear these stories," Shea concluded, "these are just ordinary decent people—farmers, doctors, teachers, mechanics—whose lives were destroyed for one reason and one reason

FIGURE 3.2 Satellite image of damaged houses on the outskirts of Podujevo, Kosovo, shown in Operation Allied Force press briefing on the Serb counterinsurgency campaign, 14 May 1999. Image courtesy of NATO.

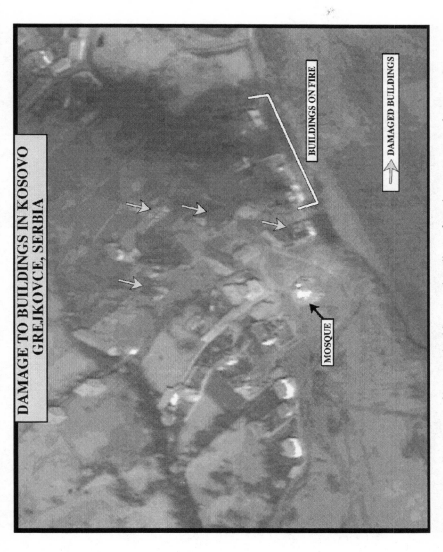

FIGURE 3.3   Satellite image of burning buildings in the village of Grejkovce, Kosovo, shown in Operation Allied Force press briefing on the Serb counterinsurgency campaign, 14 May 1999. Image courtesy of NATO.

FIGURE 3.4   Before and after satellite images of damaged buildings on the outskirts of Mitrovica, Kosovo, from Operation Allied Force press briefing on the Serb counterinsurgency campaign, 14 May 1999. Image courtesy of NATO.

only: their ethnicity."[2] With this substitution of (barely) present buildings for absolutely absent people, Shea staged a discovery: the disclosure
of Milošević's "battle damage" as "ethnic violence." But this disclosure was
more a confirmation than a revelation: in mass media, political rhetoric,
human rights reports, and an emerging historical discourse alike, political violence—in Kosovo as throughout the former Yugoslavia—was and
continues to be regarded as incontrovertibly "ethnic." *Ethnic violence* thus
serves as a cover term under which are sited multifarious forms of domina-
tion, repression, and injury.

But what does it mean to call this violence "ethnic"? In most discursive contexts, the predominant meaning of *ethnic violence* is violence oriented in some way around ethnic difference.[3] Sometimes ethnic violence
is posed as the result of a top-down manipulation of ethnic communities
by states or elites; sometimes it is posed as the result of a bottom-up appropriation of ethnic ideologies in local conflicts; occasionally it is posed as
the result of primordial antagonism between ethnic communities.[4] Com-
pressed within many of these formulations, however, is the assumption
that ethnic identity historically preexists and theoretically stands apart
from the violence that supposedly mediates that identity. Ethnic identity
is posed as prior to and separate from its material representations, violent
or otherwise, in a realm of self-constituting and freestanding ideology or
imagination. Discourse on "ethnic violence," then, often posits a (usually
but not always) socially constructed ethnic identity that is manifested in
violence: it is precisely this manifestation of identity that makes and marks
this violence as "ethnic."

Thus, the destruction of architecture was recruited in Shea's presentation as a representation of ethnic violence, as if, in the very act of burning buildings, Serb forces revealed or manifested the truth of their identity
as Serbs, of their victims as Albanians, and of architecture as an index of
the identity of its inhabitants or its territory, or indeed of culture or history
more generally. But architecture, as a supplement of identity, leads only
to other supplements. Identity is never *not* supplemented; it emerges precisely in the guise of its supplements. "Through this sequence of supplements," Derrida writes, "a necessity is announced: that of an infinite chain,
ineluctably multiplying the supplementary mediations that produce the
sense of very thing they defer: the mirage of the thing itself, of immediate
presence, of originary perception."[5] The materials that Shea represented as

evidence of ethnic violence, that is, can be nothing other than representations. This is not to minimize the violence of this representation; it is, rather, to insist on violence as a *form of representation*, a novel and unprecedented rendering, irreducible to its supposed reference, as well as a *represented object*. It is to pose buildings in flames as an architecture of violence, a scene prepared for spectatorship and cognition—by its victims, by distant witnesses, and even by its authors. It is, then, to understand identity as the subject of a performance rather than a historical subject in its own right, so that the "ethnic identity" that Shea and almost every other witness of the 1998–99 Kosovo conflict has discovered at the origin of its violence becomes not a critical description exterior to that violence, but an ideological representation scripted in and by it. And the insistence on violence as representation also maintains the status of architecture as representational, even—or especially—amid its destruction. Instead of an objective, all-but-natural ethnic "sign" or "symbol," then, architecture becomes a prop in the performance of ethnicity: a "representation *in the abyss* of presence."[6]

The representation of the Serb military campaign as "ethnic violence" was set against its representation, authored by officials of the Serbian state and its armed forces, as "war"; ethnic violence was illegitimate and unjustifiable violence, inflicted against civilians, over and against the legitimate and justified violence of war, inflicted against military targets. But both representations share in a parallel reification of architecture. Each reduces architecture to a mere manifestation, a representation of a presence "whose plentitude would be older than it, absent from it, and rightfully capable of doing without it."[7] This presence—whether named "war" or "ethnic violence"—suffuses architecture to the point where it is transmuted into a target, in the case of war, or into an ethnic sign or symbol, in the case of ethnic violence. The destruction of either becomes an acting-out, a distribution of a force—both semantic and material—held elsewhere in reserve. In the exchange between *war* and *ethnic violence* as adequate names for the Serb counterinsurgency, then, the adequacy of architecture as a manifestation of one or the other is both presumed and reproduced.

I appropriate the term *warchitecture* to foreground this recruitment of architecture as manifestation of presence. The term was coined by Sarajevo's Association of Architects during its city's siege in the 1990s.[8] It was coined in an attempt to come to terms with that siege as a war in, and against, a city: a strange war because it was a war against architecture. The Association of Architects thus applied architecture's particular techniques of spatialization and visualization to its city's destruction: architects mapped damage in terms of its architectural space of infliction (roof, facade, direct hit on building); they diagrammed its architectural effect (roof damage, partial burning of building, complete burning of building, total destruction); and they inserted the targets of damage into a new architectural history of Sarajevo, a history that was composed in terms of the received historical categories but whose architectural exemplars were all in varying states of war-induced ruin.

For Sarajevo's architects, the semantic force of warchitecture lay in its representation of a war *on* architecture, which, for them, was a war on history, memory, and culture—another recruitment of architecture, that is, as a manifestation of presence. For me, the force of the term lies in its additional potential to represent a war *by* architecture—to pose architecture as a supplement to a violence that requires architectural completion. Warchitecture suggests that architecture—the very medium of war—is made, or remade, both semantically and materially, in the very course of destroying it. I posit what follows, then, neither as a reassessment of "battle damage" nor as a rediscovery of "ethnic violence"—each of which are terms of reification—but as an account of another form of warchitecture. This, too, of course, is a reification, but it is one that can defamiliarize the seemingly objective availability of architecture—whether construed as target; as sign or symbol; as repository of history, memory, or culture; or as an instrument in its own right—to destruction.

The Mise-en-Scène of Counterinsurgency

The Serbian military campaign presented by Jamie Shea formally commenced in February 1998. It was undertaken in response to an insurgency movement to liberate Kosovo from Serbia, led by what became known as the Kosovo Liberation Army (Ushtria çlirimtare e Kosovës; KLA). This liberation was necessitated, according to the KLA, by Serbia's thorough repression of Kosovo's majority Albanian population and its denial of that population's political sovereignty. The KLA's initial targets were posed as representatives of Serb state authority in Kosovo, primarily police but also Serbs and Albanians deemed to be loyal to the Serbian state—a violence that was itself representational, with its objects posed as delegates of an institution absent in space (the state of Serbia) and its authors posed as delegates of an institution absent in time (the projected state of Kosovo).

After an increase in KLA attacks against Serb police forces at the beginning of 1998, these forces began an active counterinsurgency; first they attacked villages in the Drenica region of Kosovo, where the KLA was thought to be based, and then their counterinsurgency spread, carried out by military and paramilitary forces in response to actual or suspected KLA activity throughout the rest of Kosovo. As a guerilla army, the KLA was difficult to find and engage. The Serbian counterinsurgency, then, focused on destroying the "infrastructure" (*infrastruktura*) of the KLA. The positing of such an infrastructure was a performative speech-act in the form of a constative one: its putative presence allowed for the rendering of all Kosovar Albanians living in areas where the KLA was understood to be a threat as elements of this infrastructure. Thus they became the objects of what has normatively been described as "ethnic violence" or "ethnic cleansing."[9]

The counterinsurgency proceeded according to what may be regarded as a precise dramaturgy, or system of performance, whose protocols have emerged in testimony by Serb military personnel and their victims alike. Interviews with members of Serb forces conducted by the journalist Miroslav Filipović have suggested that this dramaturgy was structured by, among other principles, a temporal ordering of violent acts.[10] In one interview, a member of a tank unit in the Yugoslav Army reported that:

We wouldn't sit and plan how to hit, with what and from where, and discuss the number of terrorists, and their firing power. . . . Once the order was given, we would sit in our vehicles and attack. . . . Everything came to this: we would stop in front of a village and from a distance fire a few times, after which they (the police) would go in, clean it, rob it, burn the houses. . . . Only then would we go in.[11]

Firing, cleaning, robbing, and *burning* name types of violence and organize violence into a signifying structure. The key signification, attested to repeatedly in Filipović's interviews, was that of propriety: violence had proper and improper forms, and interviewees were invested in distinguishing the difference between these forms. One dimension of propriety lay in agency: proper violence was executed in response to orders, as a volunteer in the Yugoslav Army suggested:

We had an order to get them (KLA members) from the hills, and that's what we did. After that, there were groups of people that wanted to go into cleaning actions of their own accord. That's not cleaning. That's theft, robbery. . . . A few villages were done until a General saw one of the unauthorized actions. He ordered the soldiers to stop. . . . When volunteers are accepted, sometimes even thieves turn up. You can't control everything.

Yet, in the very invocation of "cleaning" as model violence, another, even more fundamental dimension of propriety is adumbrated—one that was left unnamed by Filipović's interviewees but that emerged in narratives by victims of the violence they inflicted.

One such victim was Halil Morina, the third prosecution witness called to testify in the trial of Slobodan Milošević.[12] Morina was a retired farmer, sixty-five years old when he testified in February 2002. He lived in a village called Landovica/Landovicë—"a large village," he said, of about 120 houses. Morina was called as a witness because after Serb forces attacked his village he did not immediately flee, but hid instead; thus he was an eyewitness to the village's destruction.[13] In his testimony, Morina told of the arrival of four Yugoslav Army soldiers in Landovica at around nine o'clock on the morning of March 26, 1999; of a clash resulting in the death of three soldiers and a villager; and of the arrival an hour later of more soldiers in armored personnel carriers and tanks. These vehicles, said Morina, parked at the hill on the edge of the village and began to shell it.

Morina testified that, when the shelling started, "there was alarm in the population," which then fled the village with "only the clothes they had on their bodies." Morina, his brother, and his sister-in-law, however, hid in the cellar of his house. From the cellar, Morina said, he heard the shelling stop and then, at around three o'clock in the afternoon, he saw the arrival of infantry troops and police from the Serbian Ministry of the Interior, who began to set fire to the village. "I saw them," he said, "while they were burning the village. They killed a Gypsy. And when they came down, they killed Avdi Gashi, an Albanian. And a paralyzed woman, they set fire to her in her own home." At around five o'clock, Morina described, he and his family members fled the cellar and took refuge in the outlying house of a neighbor, about five or six hundred meters away from the village.

He returned to his village the following day. His own house, he said, was "razed to the ground," so he went to his brother's house, where he spent the night. Early the next morning, Morina described his walk through the empty village, where he found thirteen dead bodies lying on the floor of the house next door and three-quarters of the village's houses burned.[14] After unsuccessfully looking for members of his family, Morina returned to his brother's home. From that home he saw the following: "A group of soldiers came and examined the corpses [of villagers killed during the shell-ing] and three of them went to the mosque. They entered the mosque. . . . In ten minutes I heard the explosion, a blast, and the minaret fell. . . . Then they [the soldiers] came back and borrowed a private Zastava [a kind of au-tomobile], on which they loaded the bodies of the dead people."

Morina's story, visualized not from the distant aerial perspective of a surveillance satellite but from proximate perspectives, terrestrial and sub-terrestrial, differs in important ways from generic descriptions of destruc-tion—differences that were, nevertheless, left unregistered in the Milošević trial. Morina's testimony suggests that the violence carried out by Serb forces was highly dramaturgical, with different forces carrying out differ-ent types of violence, with some acts of violence concealed and others re-vealed, with some acts making their objects disappear and others rendering their objects in novel guises. In his testimony, that is, violence is not simply an object of representation, but is itself representational, already prepared for and soliciting further representations that, as in the Milošević trial, are usually framed as exterior and critical.

In Landovica, the dramaturgy of destruction played a crucial and complicated role in violence's mise-en-scène. The shelling and burning of Landovica's houses yielded a village that was uninhabited and almost un-inhabitable. The primary audience of this destruction was its victims, in whom it produced, as Morina said, "alarm," and who then fled their soon-to-be-destroyed homes. But the toppling of the minaret of Landovica's mosque occurred in an empty village in conjunction with the removal of corpses killed during the assault on the village. The audiences of these acts were not the victims of violence; these acts yielded representations whose audiences were both their authors and imagined interpretive communities of these authors' actions.

The removal of the bodies of villagers killed during the assault on Landovica allowed that assault to be interpretable as a population displace-ment, an act, albeit violent, that was credible in the context of a hard-fought counterinsurgency campaign. NATO's bombing campaign against Serbia, which began two days before the assault on Landovica, was an ex-plicit response to a claim that forty Albanian civilians were killed in the vil-lage of Račak/Reçak after it was assaulted by Serb forces.[15] This claim, first made by the Kosovo Verification Mission, a team of observers in Kosovo sent by the Organization for Security and Cooperation in Europe (OSCE), interpreted these killings as a war crime. The key condition of possibility for this interpretation was the presence of the corpses themselves, which Serb forces did not remove from Račak until eight days after their assault on the village. In Landovica, by contrast, the removal of corpses was part of the final act of the assault on the village; this removal prevented interpretive communities critical of violence from finding what they would regard as evidence of war crimes.

Morina's testimony, however, described how the removal of corpses in Landovica occurred with what should be regarded as another component of this final act of scene-setting—the toppling of the minaret of the mosque in the village. The *disappearance* of evidence of mass killing occurred alongside the *appearance* of other evidence. This evidence, a damaged mosque, was produced by a specific act of violence, and one inflicted at both a temporal and spatial remove from the ethnic others of its authors.

Architecture and the Ethnicization of Violence

The attack on Landovica's mosque was reprised throughout Kosovo during the eighteen months of the Serb counterinsurgency campaign. Approximately 225 of Kosovo's 600 mosques were vandalized, damaged, or destroyed during that campaign. In some urban neighborhoods and villages, mosques and other Islamic buildings were the only targets of architectural violence; in other settings, all mosques and Islamic buildings were targeted.[16] In the trial of Slobodan Milošević, and in an emerging historical discourse, as well, the above serves as key evidence of the "ethnic" dimension of the violence inflicted against Kosovar Albanians, with mosques posed as objective ethno-religious signs or symbols. But this destruction provides, more fundamentally, evidence of the performative dimension of "ethnic violence"—of the way in which violence "does not essentially limit itself to transporting an already constituted semantic content guarded by its own aiming at truth."[17]

In Landovica, Serb forces toppled the minaret of the village mosque following their attack on the village and the flight of its inhabitants. This was typical of attacks on mosques and other buildings identified as examples of Islamic heritage. Though widespread, most violence against mosques and Islamic architecture occurred *after* the populations who used those buildings had been expelled from their villages, towns, and cities. In the most comprehensive survey of Kosovar refugees, for example, less than half of respondents reported seeing mosques or other places of worship attacked.[18] Reports by human rights organizations on the actions of Serb forces during the counterinsurgency also corroborate the limited visibility of violence against religious sites to their intended victims.[19] The initial audience of violence against putative ethnic "signs" or "symbols," that is, was composed of the authors of that violence.

Considered instrumentally, violence against architecture is understood to intend the eradication of its targets.[20] The function of this eradication is understood to be self-evident: "The aim is immediate (expelling/preventing return of communities) and the political intention obvious."[21] Yet in only a handful of cases were targeted building or complexes of buildings destroyed. Typically, rather, they were transformed through particular sorts of damage and vandalism: mosques were vandalized; minarets were toppled or their tops were shot off; walls were riddled with bullets; and facades were graffitied with texts and images (Figures 3.5–3.8).[22] The subsumption of these transformations under a putative aim or intention is, then, both empirically inaccurate, as this violence against ethnic "signs" or "symbols" did not erase its targets as much as *intensify* their visibility, and theoretically imprecise, as this violence ramified on the identities of its targets, authors, and victims alike.

As graffiti, some of the representations comprised by violence were linguistic texts. Frequent graffiti on mosques were "Srbija" (Serbia), "Kosovo je Srbija" (Kosovo is Serbia), and "Mi smo Srbi" (We are Serbs) (Figures 3.6–3.8). In these graffiti, that is, Serbs represented that they were Serbs and that Kosovo was Serbian: the very presumptions of Serb collective agency in Kosovo. The most common graffiti was a cross with the Cyrillic *C* in each corner (Figures 3.6 and 3.8). This cross, a Serbian national symbol, was used by Serbs in Kosovo during the 1998–99 war to identify their homes and apartments to Serb military and paramilitary forces; identified as such, these properties were marked as Serb-occupied so that military and paramilitary forces passed over them as they moved through towns and cities to expel Kosovar Albanians.[23] Yet these forces often graffitied this same symbol on mosques, appropriating a representation of ethnic identity and ethnic space and inscribing it on a representation of ethnic alterity.

In this context, other forms of violation, from vandalism to destruction, emerge as nonlinguistic representations of similar identities or similar representations of alterity. The violation of architecture becomes a means of representation and self-representation. These violations have been posed as

FIGURE 3.5   Mosque in Reti e Poshtme, dynamited in March 1999. Photograph by author.

FIGURE 3.6   Mosque in Novosellë, burned and graffitied with Serbian national cross, 1999. Photograph by author.

FIGURE 3.7 Mosque in Cernicë, burned and graffitied with "Srbija" (Serbia), 1999. Photograph by author.

FIGURE 3.8 Mosque in Gjyfatyn, vandalized and graffitied with "Mi smo Srbi" (We are Serbs), "Srbija" (Serbia), and Serbian national cross, 1999. Photograph from Sabri Bajgora, ed., *Barbaria Serbe ndaj Monumenteve Islame në Kosovë* (2000).

arch-sites of "ethnic violence," the sites where violence was finally revealed to be "ethnic," but consider the curious performances that took place at these sites: Serbs declaring to themselves that they are Serbs by means of violations of architecture identified with violated ethnic others. The two apparent redundancies here are crucial. Each comprises a seemingly "symbolic" reiteration of a seemingly "actual" social fact: Serbs symbolically declaring their Serbian identity and symbolically violating the architecture of violated Albanian communities. It is the very redundancy of these acts, however, that suggests their supplementary status. Neither ethnic identity nor ethnic alterity, that is, is self-sufficient as a construct: they have to be performed. These performances, then, are not manifestations of preexisting and self-sufficient identities as much as solicitations of those identities, conjurings of them, compensations for their otherwise fugitive presence.

These performances did not end the supplementation of ethnic identity during the counterinsurgency; their redundancy was multiplied in other scenes, other media, other representations, temporally taking place both prior to and after their architectural counterparts. But architecture was not only a counterpart to these supplements; it was the supplement that was left behind and made available, by its authors, to other audiences and so to discourse and history. The traces of other supplements remain with their authors—participants in the Serb counterinsurgency—or their victims. The reconstruction of these traces, however, only adds to the enigma of identity.

Warchitectural Photography

The photography carried out by Serb forces during the counterinsurgency comprises one such trace. Testimony at both the International Criminal Tribunal for the Former Yugoslavia and in war crimes trials in Serbia has at times referred to photography, carried out by both Serb military and paramilitary forces in the midst of violence these forces were carrying out.[24] In one case, the trial of the Škorpioni (Scorpions) paramilitary group in Belgrade in 2006, a video of a massacre of Bosnian Muslim men at Srebrenica also became a primary piece of evidence. Yet precisely because it comprises evidence incriminating its authors in often severe crimes, this photography circulates in highly circumscribed networks of viewers. In the summer of 1999, however, in the weeks after the departure of Serb forces from Kosovo, the human rights organization Human Rights Watch obtained several sets of photographs taken by paramilitaries in Kosovo.[25] One set was given to the organization's researchers in Kosovo in July 1999; this set was provided by KLA officials, who said the photographs came from the homes of Serbs who had lived around the city of Peć/Peja and then fled after the arrival of NATO troops. A second set came from a roll of undeveloped film found in the summer of 1999 by a German journalist in a field near Orahovac/Rahovec.

Each set of photographs collected in Kosovo in 1999 depict Serb paramilitaries before, during, and after counterinsurgency operations; some photographs comprise "live action" shots, while others show their subjects posing in various settings (Figures 3.9 and 3.10). These images fit within a particular photographic genre, a hybrid of the photojournalism of war and tourist photography. While the explicit content of the photographs is violence, their thirty-five-millimeter format and casual formal structure suggest their relation to tourist photography. Thus, as is typical for this genre, photographs are organized around the relationship of people to places, usually with people posing in the foreground and resonant signifiers of place in the background. Here, these people are members of paramilitary groups and the signifiers of place are often burning buildings before which these members are grouped and posed.

These poses comprise still further performances of ethnic identity. In Figure 3.9, paramilitaries have placed themselves before the concrete walls of what appears to be a compound of residential buildings, with the flames of a burning building reaching over the walls. The three standing paramilitaries each make the three-finger salute (*tri prsta*), a gesture that emerged in Serbian nationalist political parties in the 1990s and one that became a prominent form of Serb self-identification in violence in Bosnia and Croatia. In Figure 3.10, paramilitaries pose before a free-standing building, possibly a mosque or school, amid rolling green hills; they display as a trophy an ostensibly captured Albanian flag.

These photographs also reproduce violence's architecturalization. The violence that is represented is arson, the burning of buildings presumably owned or occupied by Albanians. Violence appears, then, as violence against architecture; violence against bodies—the bodies that built, occupied, and identified with that architecture—reciprocally disappears. Just as soldiers choreographed the scene of violence in Landovica by hiding corpses and toppling a minaret, these photographs depict a scene of violence inflicted on buildings rather than bodies. This architectural representation of violence is also creative: it creates an image of disembodied violence, violence that does not kill but only destroys.

FIGURE 3.9   Serb paramilitaries posing in front of burning building, Kosovo, 1999. Photograph from Fred Abrahams, ed., *A Village Destroyed: May 14, 1999* (2002).

FIGURE 3.10   Serb paramilitaries posing with burning building in background, Kosovo, 1999. Photograph from Fred Abrahams, ed., *A Village Destroyed: May 14, 1999* (2002).

Embodied Ethnicization

Yet the violence of the Serb counterinsurgency was profoundly embodied: it included myriad forms of abuse against bodies, from the expulsion of people from their homes to the infliction of a range of physical injuries, some lethal in effect. Architectural violence was at least partly intended to displace embodied violence as a representation of the Serb counterinsurgency. But architectural violence also precisely mimicked the embodied violence it was intended to displace, as both forms of violence recruited objects to display texts of ethnic identity. That is, even at the very moment when "Serb" bodies encountered "Albanian" bodies, ethnic identity was the subject of performance; encounters with ethnic alterity became occasions to produce or reproduce the meanings and values of that alterity, the identity that stood over and outside of it, and the violence that mediated the former and the latter.

Albanians detained or imprisoned by Serb forces during the counterinsurgency have testified that, among the abuses inflicted on them, they were at times forced to perform as Serbs—occasionally in exactly the same ways as Serb paramilitaries performed as Serbs before the cameras they aimed at themselves. Sometimes Albanian detainees were forced to sing Serbian nationalist songs; sometimes they were forced to shout Serbian nationalist slogans; and sometimes they were forced to make the three-fingered Serbian nationalist salute.[26] These performances accompanied often brutal interrogations, physical abuse, and, at times, murder.

With these performances, the Serb performance of ethnicity was extended to abject Albanian others, who were compelled to participate in and mirror the performances of ethnicity carried out by their Serb captors. In so doing, even the alterity that made Albanians targets of violence was evacuated. As Serb police compelled Albanian detainees and prisoners to parody Serbian identity, Albanian identity was symbolically voided—but the symbolic dimension of this voiding was crucial to its actual efficacy. If Albanian detainees were only momentarily, symbolically, and parodically Serbian, their status as Albanian was, by contrast, fixed, actual, and tragic.

These performances rendered ethnicization reciprocal. Dominant Serb community and abject Albanian alterity were simultaneously materialized and displayed. The one became the seemingly necessary counterpart of the other. The Albanian body was fabricated in just same way as the architecture deemed by Serb forces to represent that body; both body and architecture not only were targets of violence but also media on which to inscribe, display, and circulate representations of ethnic identity. Attention to this dynamic ramifies on the fixity and stability of ethnic identity on the part of authors of this presumably ethnic violence. This was not, simply, violence against the bodies, objects, and places of the ethnic other; it was also the fabrication of those bodies, objects, and places as ethnic. Identity was thus rendered fungible, the topic of a performance, rather than a property possessed by legal, ethical, or biological bodies.

This extended to the identity of "Kosovo" itself. The parodic-tragic performances of embodied Serbian identity that Albanian detainees were forced to carry out reiterated the statements of geography that members of Serbian forces made to Albanians in the course of their expulsion from Kosovo. As reported in refugee interviews and testimonies to the International Criminal Tribunal of the Former Yugoslavia, when Serb military, paramilitary, and police forces evicted Kosovar Albanians from their homes during 1998 and 1999, they often declared to their victims, "This is Serbia," "This is Serbian land," "This is not your land," "Albania is your country," or "Go to your country."[27] Kosovo was, according to the rule of state sovereignty, a province of Serbia. But these declarations were performative; at the same time as they invoked "Serbia" as a territorial frame, they produced the meaning of this frame as a territory devoid of Albanians.

We Are Paid by Serbia for Everything We Do and You Must Do What I Say

The repeated, though not redundant, performances of ethnic identity undertaken by Serb forces were also performances of violence. This violence included the mass expulsion of Albanian civilians from Kosovo and the infliction of a wide spectrum of abuses, from robbery and extortion to rape and killing, before and during these expulsions. Yet, carried out by self-declared "Serbs" against a target declared as ethnically other, this violence—physical, sexual, and economic—was reduced to and represented as ethnic. The legitimacy of this representation did not have to be accorded truth value for it to produce effects: enmeshed with the authority of the Milošević regime, "ethnic violence" functioned as a mode of authorization, engendering legitimacy by inscribing itself in a history of national victimization by violent ethnic others—a history that, as the previous chapter posed, was also supplemented by architecture.

"Ethnic violence" is not, then, a critical formulation of this violence; it is, rather, a representation scripted by that violence's very authors, an ethnicization of violence that possesses other forms with far more obscure modes of legitimization. Indeed, though tropes of revelation are fundamental to much critical discourse on ethnic violence, the ethnicity of the violence inflicted in the Serb counterinsurgency was not hidden by its authors; on the contrary, it was foregrounded. For these authors, the ethnicity of the violence they inflicted was its desired meaning, its intended message, its cultural value, its redemption. What, then, did warchitecture and other representations of ethnic violence conceal? What violence disappears in the course and discourse of ethnic violence?

In response to these questions, I refer to the following testimony, given in the trial of Slobodan Milošević by a witness only identified as K15.[28] K15 was described as a twenty-five-year-old Albanian woman from Kosovo; not only was the violence inflicted against her hidden, but the public revelation of this violence compelled her identity itself to be hidden. I begin to cite her testimony after she has described the burning of her village, how she had walked in a group of displaced people for four days to the Albanian border, had been turned back from the border by Serb border guards, and then returned on foot to the border in another convoy. Her testimony here emerges in response to questions by the prosecuting attorney, Geoffrey Nice.

Q. What happened while you were walking in this convoy?
A. After a few hours walking, the Serbian army and police came, and they stopped the convoy, and they came in cars and started mistreating people. And then they came up to my mother and asked my mother where her husband was, and my mother said her husband has died, and they said, "No, your husband is a soldier." And my mother said, "No, I don't have a husband." And they went up to my brother and he had a red handkerchief on his head, and they asked why. And they said, "He's a boy." And then they came up to me and they started to mistreat me and asked me for money, and they said, "Come to us in our car."
Q. I will stop you, Witness. Can you describe the person who came and talked to you and your mother? Was he—how was he dressed? Was he wearing any uniform?
A. Yes. And he had a handkerchief around his head.
Q. And what color was the uniform?
A. Green.

Q. If I show you a photo, you will be able to recognize?

(Ms. Romano: Can I have the witness be shown Exhibit 18 again, please?)

Q. Again, looking at the series of photos you have in front of you, can you see in any of the photos a uniform similar to the uniform that man was wearing at the time?

A. Similar to number 8. He had bandanas, but the colors are the same. Something like that.

Q. Thank you. So, Witness, you said that you—you asked him—sorry. He said to you that he wanted to take you away from the convoy. How did it happen?

A. Yes. He came up to me and said, "Come in a car with me." I thought he was making a mistake, and I waited for him to say something else. But he grabbed hold of me and said, "Come, because you are a whore." And then he hit me and slapped me and said, "Come in the car with me," and he pushed me into the car.

Q. Were you the only person that was taken away from the convoy?

A. There was another girl in the car . . .

Q. And in the car, did they—did they tell you anything? Did they talk to you?

A. When they pushed us into the car, I asked this girl where they were taking us, and she said, "Don't say anything." And they took us in an unknown direction, and they took us out of the car, and one took me and another took the other girl. And the one who took me told me to take off my clothes, but I refused. . . . He said, "You will become a woman. You will become a whore." And his mistreatment started. . . . He took my clothes off and started to rape me . . .

Q. You said that he raped you. I'm sorry, but I have to ask some specifics the Court will need to know. What did he do to you?

A. It's the truth. Besides the rape, he started other kinds of mistreatment. I remember very well how he grabbed me by the hair and forced his penis in my mouth and began a lot of mistreatment. After that, he started to rape me, so at every moment I was—it was very difficult for me to cope with this mistreatment of his, and he began to rape me. And I know that I was a virgin, and I had a lot of pain. He wouldn't leave me go—he didn't leave me go until I had become a woman.

Q. When you say "become a woman," what do you refer with that?

A. I mean until I had lost my virginity.

Q. So he penetrated you?

A. Yes.

Q. During all the time that he was mistreating you, Witness, did he threaten you with any weapon? Did he show you any weapon?

A. He—he took out of his car all his equipment he had for a massacre, and he said, "You have to do what I say. Look at these things." And he started to say that, "We are paid by Serbia for everything we do and you must do what I say."

You must do what I say: this command is a paradigmatic performative utterance, a speech act that does not refer to a preexisting reality so much as transform reality and render it anew. This horrific performative, however, was preceded and sustained by a whole series of performances of identity. Some of these performances involved the ascription of identity to violence's victims: the witness's mother as a soldier's wife rather than a widow; the witness's brother as a boy rather than a girl, the witness herself as a whore rather than a virgin. Other performances involved the assumption of identity on the part of violence's perpetrator: the rapist as part of a collective "we" and that collective as an ethnically defined contractor of the state. This assumed collective identity is the one the rapist represented to his victim and, reciprocally, to himself. Whether or not the rapist's statement was empirically true, his statement had the effect of rendering what was experienced as sexual violence by his victim as state-sponsored ethnic violence.

For the prosecution in the Milošević trial, however, *violent performance* was taken as *violence as such*, so that the prosecutor sought evidence of precisely the sort of violence that its perpetrator explicitly performed. Seeking evidence of ethnic violence, the prosecutor glossed over the sexual violence of rape warfare. After hearing K15 describe her rape, the prosecutor's exclusion as a "weapon" the rapist's penis is here symptomatic; understanding violence as ethnic rather than ethnicized, the prosecutor failed to acknowledge the representational work that was done on rape, by its very perpetrator, to render it ethnic.[29] Indeed, the prosecutor precisely followed the perpetrator in inscribing sexual violence in a discourse of ethnicity.

Warchitecture comprises the public(ized) form of this inscription. It enlists architecture as a manifestation of ethnic violence, a just and legitimate violence inflicted by representatives of a victimized ethnic community on representatives of that community's victimizers, and a representational and representative violence that renders other forms of violence—sexual, physical, and economic—covert and exceptional. To pay attention to warchitecture, then, should be to receive it, like architecture itself, as a mise-en-scène, a representation of violence designed to be viewed and to interpellate its victims, authors, and audiences—including those who condemn it.

4

The Right Place:
A Supplement on the Architecture
of Humanitarian War

At some stage during this operation, we may have one weapon or two weapons
that fall in the wrong place. . . . What I can assure you is that we do everything
that is humanly possible to make sure that our weapons are targeted on the right
place, that we have done our homework to make sure that we are not targeting
civilians, we're not targeting people, and we're not targeting civilian infrastructure.

AIR COMMANDER DAVID WILBY, Operation Allied Force spokesman,
on NATO's bombing campaign against Serbia

Humanitarianism, Violence, Architecture

From March 24 to June 11, 1999, a coalition of armed forces from
the NATO nations, led and dominated by forces from the United States,
dropped bombs onto and flew missiles into a series of buildings, structures, vehicles, equipment, and human beings located in Kosovo and Serbia. The preceding were, according to NATO, components of Serbia's "war
machine," "command-and-control system," "military network," or "infrastructure." Each of the preceding were at least a nominal equivalent to the
"infrastructure" of the Kosovo Liberation Army that Serb forces were themselves targeting in Kosovo—an amorphous semantic field on which violence's various targets could be renamed and displayed. NATO undertook

its bombing campaign in order to compel Serbian forces to end their violence against Albanian civilians in Kosovo. NATO's campaign—often termed the "Kosovo War"—has subsequently been framed as the first "humanitarian war," a war waged wholly in the interests of victims of human rights abuses; as the first manifestation of "humane warfare" in which moral concerns shaped military actions; as the first project of a "military humanism" that enforces human rights claims by military power; and as the simultaneous anticipation and promotion of a transnational "cosmopolitan state" that would protect human rights across the globe by any means necessary.[1] When it emerged in the early twentieth century, aerial bombing was sometimes regarded, from positions both within and beyond the military, as a breach of fundamental ethical principles as well as the laws of war.[2] The perceived military utility of aerial bombing made opposition to it untenable. The Kosovo War marked a moment of historical reversal, when aerial bombing became not only a military necessity but also an instrument to advance precisely the ethics it was once thought to contradict.

The representation of mass violence as a specifically ethical necessity is time-honored, if not honored by all vectors of ethical imagination. In the Kosovo War, writes Paul Virilio, "the *missionary* element of the colonial massacre or the *messianic* dimension of the world wars with their mass slaughter are supplanted by the *humanitarian* impulse."[3] But the Kosovo War also involved an innovation in the relationship of violence and ethics; not only was the end of violence defined in ethical terms, but so too were its means—NATO officials and spokespeople posed its precision-guided weaponry and seemingly strict rules of engagement as instruments of a moral, even "humane" violence. The Kosovo War, Virilio writes, was supposed to be "a *clean war*, which went beyond the principle of the *just war* of the old free-world fighters."[4] From the perspective of military humanitarianism, the means and ends of the Kosovo War were therefore continuous. In Kosovo, so advocates of this humanitarianism argued, the practice of war was brought into line with war's ethical objectives. In the words of one postwar assessment prepared for the United States Army: "Since the alliance's primary goal was to compel Yugoslav forces to end violence against the Kosovar Albanians, it could not afford to be seen as acting inhumanely, as applied to both Kosovar Albanians and Serb civilians. The rules of engagement were therefore highly restrictive, reflecting NATO's goals and moral values."[5]

As the invocation of "civilians" in the quotation above indicates, "humanitarian war" is almost always understood as having something to do with the forging of new relationships to human beings in the context of warfare. Humanitarian war is a war in which human exposure to violence—for the authors of war, for innocent bystanders, and sometimes even for adversaries—is supposed to be minimized. Yet with this minimization comes a corresponding, reciprocal, and often overlooked maximization: humanitarian war is also a war in which artifacts—material representations of the adversary under attack—come to be exposed to violence to an unprecedented degree. Thus, humanitarian war also has something to do with the forging of new relationships to things that come to represent and undergo destruction in place of the human. These things are, often, architecture. If humanitarian war places the individual in the center of *moral* imagination, whether as victims who must be protected by military means, civilian bystanders who must be protected from military means, or the military forces who must be protected during their infliction of these means, then this form of war also places architecture in the center of *military* imagination to an unprecedented degree. Precision-guided weaponry allows individual buildings or even parts of buildings to be targeted for destruction, while injunctions against "collateral damage" render such focused targeting normative rather than ideal. Humanitarian war, then, may be redescribed as a war on architecture: another form of warchitecture, another architecture by other means. This was the war that NATO representatives described in their almost daily exclusions of "civilians" and "civilian infrastructure" from NATO's targeting categories, exclusions that left architecture as an unstated object of inclusion, an appropriate(d) target of violence, a supplement of humanitarian war—the "right place" for humane destruction.

The performance of humanitarian violence in the Kosovo War ostensibly materialized what previously had been an ideological representation of war focused on damage to buildings instead of injury to bodies. This representational displacement was based upon the perceived intolerability of encounters with images of war's awful effects on the human body, even the bodies of dehumanized enemies, and the reciprocal visualization of other effects of war perceived to be tolerable, desirable, or even sublime. War's legitimization, that is, was partly informed by an aesthetics, a system structuring sensory experience.[6] Before the advent of precision-guided weaponry, the transfer of wartime violence from bodies to buildings occurred on the level of postviolence representation. In World War II, the U.S. and British firebombing of German cities, the U.S. firebombing of Japanese cities, and, most of all, the U.S. atomic bombing of Hiroshima and Nagasaki—many acts explicitly aimed at both architectural and human targets, the latter often narrated as "workers in war industries"—produced deformations of the human body whose descriptions and visualizations were and have remained highly circumscribed.[7] This circumscription was partly instituted and maintained by the substitution of damaged and destroyed architecture and cityscapes for damaged and destroyed bodies. There is a precise relationship, that is, between the well-known images of the ravaged cityscapes of Dresden, Tokyo, and Hiroshima and the almost unknown images of human bodies destroyed in those ravages.

The emergence, in the late 1980s and 1990s, of real-time news coverage, alternative platforms of new media, and the twenty-four-hour broadcast cable-news cycle have each given the visual representation of war a new public prominence.[8] The postulation of a "CNN effect" at this time registered the new status of mediated images in political consciousness and the correspondingly new salience of these images in political conduct.[9] The development of "humanitarian war," then, may be seen as a response not only to a new ethical framing of war but also to war's increased visibility and accessibility to witnessing publics. In "humanitarian war," the displacement of bodies by buildings ostensibly does not occur on the level of postviolence representation, which is now produced by a proliferating array of authors and circulated on a proliferating array of media platforms, but rather on the level of violence itself. As precision-guided weapons hit the "right places" for humanitarian destruction, the gap between the horribly violent actuality of war and the ideologically cleansed representation of war seemingly collapses. The war specified by humanitarianism is thus supposed to be a war that can be watched, a war that can be known, a war that we can not only tolerate but also appreciate and even desire. It is a war not only made *for* imaging but also, partly, *by* imaging: a war in which visual representation is not an exterior addition but a constitutive supplement.

The politics and aesthetics of destruction in the Kosovo War placed architecture in the field of public vision in a new way. If architecture's reception is consummated by a public in a state of distraction, as Walter Benjamin famously described, then the precision-guided aerial bombing of the Kosovo War made this claim only tenable for those places and times outside a state of emergency.[10] The Kosovo War marked a key moment in the transformation of architecture into a privileged mediation of violence, and thus into an object of scrutiny for a public guided by military image capture and aesthetics. In the Kosovo War, architecture was rendered *attractive*, not only for violence but also for gazes that tracked that violence, both critically and uncritically. During and since that war, then, a militarized public attention has at times been fixed on architecture, on buildings whose destruction is threatened, imminent, in process, complete, or even feared. These buildings comprise decoys, lures, or ruses, substituting for or repressing other sites or sights of violence; but, precisely as such, they are also traces of that other violence and thus of the visual economy of war's representation.

The Mise-en-Scène of Humanitarian War

Beginning in 1998, when human rights organizations and international observers implicated Serbian forces in a wide series of human rights abuses in Kosovo, the "Contact Group" of nations began a series of diplomatic attempts to force Serbia to withdraw those forces or curtail their activities in Kosovo.[11] In 1999, after the Contact Group diplomats perceived negotiations with Serbia to be ineffective, the leaders of the group authorized NATO to bomb Serbia to force a withdrawal of Serbian forces from Kosovo. NATO officials and spokespeople thus proclaimed the bombing campaign as a means "to put a stop to the atrocities, the violence, the human suffering in Kosovo."[12] The targets of the bombing campaign were explicitly posed as the Serbian forces responsible for these atrocities, this violence, this suffering. In the words of General Wesley Clark, the commander of the NATO Operation Allied Force:

The military mission is to attack Yugoslav military and security forces and associated facilities with sufficient effect to degrade its capacity to continue repression of the civilian population and to deter its further military action against his [*sic*] own people. We aim to put its military and security forces at risk. We are going to systematically and progressively attack, disrupt, degrade, devastate and ultimately destroy these forces and their facilities and support, unless President Milošević complies with the demands of the international community.[13]

The distinction between "military and security forces" and "associated facilities" that General Clark invoked was formalized in NATO's two target categories, one termed "tactical" and the other "strategic." This categorization of targets was drawn from the military theorization of aerial bombardment; "tactical bombing" targets military forces on or near battlefields while "strategic bombing" targets those forces' ostensible sources of power. In the words of the United States Air Force manual of military doctrine, those sources are defined, using Clausewitz's famous term, as the enemy's "centers of gravity," which are then specified as "command elements, war production assets, and supporting infrastructure (for example, energy, transportation, and communication assets)."[14] The abstract figurations of the preceding definition ("centers of gravity," "elements," "assets," "infrastructure") are characteristic of the prose of strategic bombing. The conceit of strategic bombing, which leads directly to the tragedy of this bombing, is that such abstract figurations have precise material and spatial correlates—correlates that can be, as General Clark put it, attacked, disrupted, degraded, devastated, and destroyed. Architecture thus emerges in strategic bombing as a privileged site of translation, something that is at once visible through the cross-hairs of a bomb sight but also conceivable according to the categories of strategic targeting: a node in a "network," a piece of an "infrastructure," a component of a "system."

At the inception of the Kosovo War, General Clark elaborated how NATO would pursue "a tactical line of operation against the Serb forces deployed in Kosovo and in southern Serbia" and "a strategic line operating against Serb air defenses, command and control, VJ [Vojska Jugoslavije, or Yugoslav Army] and MUP [Ministarstvo unutrašnjih poslova, or Ministry of Interior] forces, their sustaining infrastructure, supply routes, and resources."[15] Attacks on these targets were to be phased, so that they would begin with the establishment of NATO "air superiority" and then follow with the exploitation of this superiority through the destruction of an expanding array of tactical and strategic targets. This phasing was to allow Serbia the opportunity to agree to NATO's demands before it suffered vast destruction; phasing was thus conceivable as a dimension of NATO's humanitarian violence, as well as a product of the alliance members' quite distinct concepts of acceptable destruction.[16]

The agents directly responsible for committing the violence that the bombing campaign was instituted to stop—Serb military and paramilitary in Kosovo—fit under the category of "tactical targets." Yet these targets proved difficult for NATO forces to locate and destroy. As factors contributing to this difficulty, military analysts have pointed to the absence of a threat of a NATO ground invasion, which would have required Serb forces to construct defenses easily visible from air; to the high altitude at which NATO bombers flew, to guarantee that Serb antiaircraft weaponry could not reach them; to Kosovo's almost constant cloud cover during the spring and summer of 1999, which prevented many visual surveillance technologies from functioning; and to the length of time required by NATO pilots to learn how to see and find Serbian forces in an environment with which pilots were unfamiliar.[17]

Substituting for attacks on the forces responsible for violence in Kosovo, NATO then pursued attacks on what it termed "strategic targets." In the first weeks of the beginning of the bombing campaign, these targets comprised air-defense systems, military "command and control" facilities such as headquarters and administrative buildings, and ground-force installations such as the barracks accommodating military forces. Each of these targets had determinate relations to Serbian military and security forces—the ultimate target of NATO's violence. But as these strategic targets were destroyed and the bombing campaign continued and expanded through the delivery of additional equipment, other strategic targets had to be provided for NATO to attack.

A month after the bombing campaign began, then, NATO representatives decided to inflate the strategic target set to include "military-industrial infrastructure, news media and other targets of a strategic nature."[18] Architecture provided a key resource to effect this inflation. NATO targeting discourse figured strategic infrastructure in the form of individual buildings and structures, and precision-guided weapons provided the technical means to destroy these targets, even in dense urban environments where "collateral damage" often included the killing of a building's occupants and bystanders. Among the buildings and structures thus figured and destroyed were the headquarters and studios of Serbian state television and radio in Belgrade; the Socialist Party headquarters in Belgrade; electrical power plants across Serbia; and rail and road bridges across Serbia and Kosovo.

The role played by architecture in the discourse and practice of strategic bombing is exemplified in the case of the bombing of the building that housed the headquarters and studios of Serbian state television and radio (Radio televizija Srbije, or RTS) in downtown Belgrade on April 23, 1999. The bombing was explained by NATO's Colonel Konrad Freytag as part of the alliance's mission to "disrupt the national command network and to degrade the Federal Republic of Yugoslavia's propaganda apparatus."[19] Implicit in such characterizations was the status of the RTS building *itself* as a key component of the cited "network" and "apparatus"; the building, that is, furnished an ostensible materialization of otherwise abstract or at least highly mediated forms.

This materialization was imprecise. First, it was based on two separate readings of the building, one as a vital part of the "national (military) command network" and the other as a vital part of the Milošević regime's "propaganda apparatus." Second, the relationships of these two parts were posed in contrasting, even contradictory ways. NATO linked the building's "propaganda function" to the control network, as when a NATO spokesman claimed that "strikes against TV transmitters and broadcast facilities are part of our campaign to dismantle the Federal Republic of Yugoslavia's propaganda machinery which is a vital part of President Milošević's control mechanism."[20] But it was also claimed that the military control network appropriated an otherwise civil communications network, rendering that network of "dual use" to civilians and military; NATO officials thus stressed that the destruction of the building struck at the regime's capacity to "transmit their instruction to the troops in the field."[21] Third, and most important, the civil communications "network" in Serbia was a diffuse and highly reticulated open system, so that the broadcasting of Serbian state television broadcasting could be quickly diverted to local networks as a result of the RTS building attack, which only served to interrupt this broadcasting for a little more than three hours.[22]

The above ambiguities sponsored wide debate on the legitimacy of the targeting of the RTS building, both before the attack, by NATO's military staff, and afterward, by human rights organizations responding to the deaths inflicted by the attack. According to Amnesty International and Human Rights Watch, the targeting comprised a violation of international humanitarian law, and human rights sources also testify to British and French objections to the targeting, recommended by U.S. officials, on the basis of this law.[23] And yet, at the same time, the destruction of the RTS building was extraordinarily precise. This destruction was inflicted by satellite-guided long-range Tomahawk cruise missiles launched by a U.S. Navy vessel.[24] These missiles were apparently targeted on the front entrance of the building, a targeting that determined where and how the building was destroyed and that ostensibly limited collateral damage (Figure 4.1).

The *imprecision* of the RTS building's status as a military target and the *precision* with which this target was destroyed must be considered together. Conjoined, they testify to the military knowledge of architecture, a knowledge focused on the destruction of a material artifact rather than on that artifact's social, cultural, political, and even technological functions. For NATO, the metric of architectural interpretation was that of function,

FIGURE 4.1   Radio Television Serbia Building, Belgrade, after NATO attack, 23 April 1999. Photograph from Federal Ministry of Foreign Affairs, *NATO Crimes in Yugoslavia: Documentary Evidence, 24 March–24 April 1999*, vol. 1 (1999).

but interpretation reduced to classifying functions onto a truncated set of civilian categories and an expanded set of military ones. Further, the concept of "dual use" buildings allowed the supposition of *any* military function to trump *every* civilian function and thereby render a building a legitimate target. Thus, for NATO, architecture furnished an almost inexhaustible resource for the production of destruction—but not a repository of information about the various "infrastructures," "networks," or "systems" that this destruction was meant to destroy.

NATO officials and spokespeople insisted that, through the use of precision-guided weapons and "strict rules of engagement," so-called "collateral damage" to civilians would be limited to an unprecedented degree in the course of destroying tactical and strategic targets in Kosovo and Serbia.[25] As General Clark put it, in words repeated constantly through the bombing campaign, "We are taking all possible measures to minimize collateral damage or damage to innocent civilians or nearby property that is not associated with the target."[26] Yet NATO's production of destruction militated against its humanitarian framing. In the case of the RTS building, while the use of precision-guided weaponry resulted in the killing of "only" 16 of the 120 people working in the building and the injuring of 16 others, these deaths and injuries were inflicted in order to interrupt state television broadcasting one morning from 2:20 A.M. to 6 A.M.[27] More generally, because NATO's violence was focused on so-called strategic targets, it did little to curtail the violence inflicted by Serb forces in Kosovo. During the course of the NATO bombing campaign, the violence that NATO termed "ethnic cleansing" not only continued but intensified, with around six hundred thousand to seven hundred thousand Kosovar Albanians expelled from Kosovo during the NATO bombing and an estimated ten thousand killed.[28] Finally, because "strategic targets" were often buildings used, inhabited, or surrounded by civilian populations, NATO's violence, though precise, is estimated to have killed as many civilians as it did members of Serbian forces carrying out ethnic cleansing.

For NATO, however, destruction *for* humanity was posed as identical to destruction *without* humanity, to the destruction of buildings and structures that could be narrated as legitimate military targets and destroyed as such by precision-guided weaponry. Though unnamed, the concept of "destruction without humanity" underscored almost all NATO reactions to reports of "collateral damage." NATO's fully architectural interpretation of buildings and structures as strategic military targets was assumed to be universal, the only legitimate interpretation, so that alternative architectural interpretations become not only excluded but even potentially fatal. For NATO, then, it was the Serb government that was responsible for the presence of civilians in the buildings and structures that NATO bombed, as the latter comprised nothing other than targets for destruction. In the case of the RTS building, for example, Prime Minister Tony Blair of the United Kingdom blamed Serb government officials for not evacuating the building: "They could have moved those people out of the building. They knew it was a target and they didn't."[29] NATO officials made similar arguments after people were killed while traveling across bridges that were being bombed.[30] In the words of Colonel Freytag during a NATO press briefing, "We target bridges and I am sure that the Serb authorities know that these bridges are of extreme value to their lines of communication and when they allow public traffic over these bridges, then they risk a lot of lives of their own citizens."[31]

Many critics of the NATO bombing campaign have pointed out and criticized the focus of the campaign on dubiously strategic targets. "In the end," writes William Arkin, "attacking Serb forces in Kosovo meant bombing fixed facilities, such as garrisons and headquarters buildings, most of them probably empty."[32] Less acknowledged is the architectural ideology that such a bombing campaign was based on and legitimated by. This ideology posited the status of architecture as objective, as capable of articulation via a schematic set of functionalist concepts. The interpretation of a building as a machine to be destroyed thus displaced any other status with which a building or structure could possibly be endowed. NATO's knowledge of architecture, that is, was an entirely modernist one. It accurately refracted a modernist presumption of architecture as a social and technological machine, a device for regulating individual bodies and social spaces. NATO's targeting process was an epistemic ideology of architecture—a presumptive International Style for destruction.

The Aesthetics of Humanitarian Destruction

As the destruction of buildings and structures, in the guise of "strategic targets," substituted for the destruction of Serb military forces during the NATO bombing campaign, NATO represented that campaign with images and data documenting the supposedly precise destruction of those

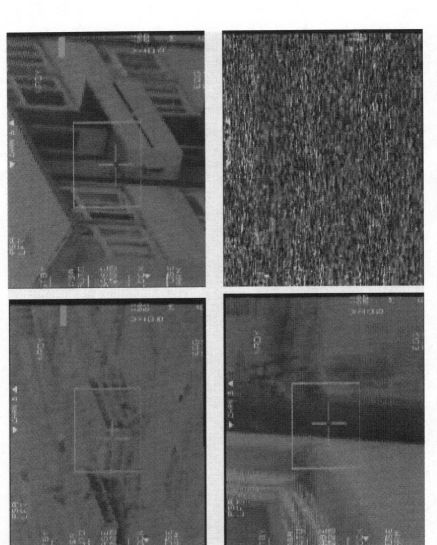

FIGURE 4.2 Destruction of Ministry of Interior Affairs headquarters, Rahovac, Kosovo, 3 April 1999, from video shot by bomb-mounted camera. Video courtesy of Federation of American Scientists.

buildings and structures (Figure 4.2). Videos shot by cameras mounted on precision-guided weaponry zoomed unerringly in on a targeted building or bridge and then abruptly ended, ostensibly at impact, with a screen of gray fuzz; video images of attacks filmed with cameras on surveillance aircraft circled around a targeted building until that building disappeared in a flash of flame or cloud of smoke; and surveillance photographs showed an airport runway or petroleum refinery before and after it was attacked, demonstrating the precision of the attack with accompanying arrows or legends. Further, all of the preceding were calculated daily in pie charts, bar graphs, and tables of numbers and statistics.

Each of these image-texts mediated the architectural aesthetics of humanitarian destruction. The bombing campaign, that is, involved the production and circulation of architectural *representations* as well as architectural *destruction*. These representations supported the classification of other destruction—that of human bodies—as ancillary or what in military discourse is termed "collateral." Thus, not only did architecture provide a resource for the manufacture of destruction, but images and data of this destruction provided resources to displace images and data of injury inflicted on human bodies, especially on those of "civilian bystanders." In so utilizing the documentation of destruction, NATO attempted to evacuate "collateral damage" of visual and statistical description and thereby render it politically neutral. NATO's destruction was maintained as humanitarian, then, partly through a system of representation that deployed destroyed buildings in place of injured or killed human bodies. Here, architecture's status as an object of humanitarian violence becomes contradictory: at once a military target substituting for human bodies, it was also a site of spectacular violence drawing public attention away from violated bodies. Human bodies were often violated in the course of violating buildings; in these cases, the videos shot by precision-guided weaponry and surveillance aircraft were snuff films screened as architectural studies.

"Let me now show you some imagery of some of our recent attacks" began a typical commentary accompanying such videos during a NATO press briefing. "The film clips that you are about to see are of a recent attack on the large MUP headquarters complex in Priština. It is a large complex. The whole image you are about to see represents just one part of this extensive complex. Each clip depicts aircraft targeting different impact points on the facility. You will also notice secondary explosions resulting from the attack" (Figure 4.3).[33] While the depiction of these "impact points" seemingly confirmed the precision of the bombing, the implicit subject of such imagery was the status of architecture as the target of NATO violence and thus of the war gaze—whether the military's own gaze or that of the military's civilian spectators.

The videos produced by precision-guided weapons effected, in the words of Judith Butler, "a phantasmic distinction between the hit and its consequences."[34] This distinction, Butler continued, "systematically derealized" these consequences and, in particular, the manifold forms of human injury that such hits inflict. But this was a "derealization" only of the missing human body—the site of the only consequences that Butler acknowledged, her own tacit implication in the military's disappearance of the same—as it accompanied, and was accomplished by, a corresponding hyperrealization of architectural destruction. In the seventy-eight days of

FIGURE 4.3 Attack on Ministry of Interior Affairs headquarters at three "impact points," Prishtina, 31 March 1999, from video shot by camera on surveillance aircraft. Video courtesy of Federation of American Scientists.

the NATO bombing campaign, architectural and other nonhuman targets were the only referents of NATO's visual representation of that campaign. While human beings were often injured and killed in the course of damaging or destroying buildings or structures, and represented as such by Serb media, no damaged or destroyed bodies were ever visualized in NATO's documentation.

This visual occlusion of such bodies accompanied their discursive repression and political nullification. Consider, for example, the following exchanges, which took place during a U.S. Department of Defense press conference on June 2, 1999. First, a journalist asks Department of Defense spokesman Major General Chuck Wald to verify his claim that "of all the bombs we've dropped, 99.6 percent have actually hit the target out of the 20,000 bombs."

Q. What percentage?
A. 99.6 percent.
Q. Out of how many thousand?
A. Nearly 20,000 . . .

Less than two minutes later, another journalist attempts to shift the focus to the question of human casualties in such a precisely targeted bombing campaign:

Q. The British defense minister briefer was asked about an estimate of Serb casualties of up to 2,000. He said he felt that was quite low and it was more like 10,000. Do you have a figure?
A. I have no idea whether 2,000 or 10,000 is the number. I don't know the number. I haven't even read what the number is. I suspect there are some casualties on the ground. When they're around certain targets, you would expect that, but we don't know what the number is. We're not there.[35]

NATO's claim of precision, that is, is an architectural claim—a claim about destroyed buildings and structures, which were not only rigorously visualized by NATO during the course of the bombing campaign but also counted, classified, verified, and distinguished from the destroyed human bodies that, in Major General Wald's words, may have happened to be "around certain targets"—another figuration of those targets purely as places without bodies. Thus, the effect of precision bombing on human bodies was rendered not just imprecise but invisible, at least on image platforms outside of Serbia.

The dynamic by means of which destroyed architecture appeared as a displacement of destroyed human bodies—in contrast to its appearance as a substitute for the destruction of those bodies—continued through the bombing campaign and determined the content of the so-called final assessment of the campaign, completed in October 1999. At the press conference introducing this assessment, a U.S. Department of Defense spokesman announced that "we're going to see multiple on-site pictures of actual digitized photos where you'll be able to graphically see the level of destruction was catastrophic." Yet, despite the seeming precision of this display, when this spokesman was later asked to assess the number of Serb troops killed in the course of inflicting this catastrophic destruction, he was unable to answer, except to say, "I can give you no estimate of that whatsoever. We have no way of knowing."[36]

"Because they do not think the other, they do not have time."[37] Thus, the U.S. Department of Defense counted the number of "strike sorties" it launched during the Kosovo War (10,484); it counted the number of bombs and missiles it launched (23,614), breaking down this number by type of weapon and delivery platform; it counted the number of "target aimpoints" against which these weapons were directed, breaking down these aimpoints between "fixed" and "mobile" targets; it counted the number of each type of "fixed" and "mobile" target it damaged or destroyed, including airfields (10), railroad bridges (11), command posts (14), highway bridges (29), tanks (93), armored personnel carriers (153), other military vehicles (339) and artillery and mortar guns (389); it estimated the percentage of Serbian military and infrastructure assets it degraded; and yet it was (or claimed to be) unable to estimate the violence it inflicted on human bodies, either those of the enemy, termed "Serb forces," or those of civilian bystanders, termed "collateral damage."

Estimates of violence against bodies inflicted by NATO forces were readily produced both by the Serb government and human rights organizations: somewhere between 132 and 462 Serb military, paramilitary, and police members were killed by NATO bombing, according to the Serb government, and somewhere between 488 and 572 civilians were killed by this bombing, according to Human Rights Watch.[38] The Department of Defense's claim to have "no way of knowing" this violence is, then, a claim about the value of this knowledge: unimportant enough to be performatively disregarded and important enough to recruit architectural destruction as its replacement. Left unacknowledged by NATO, then, was the fact that its bombing campaign destroyed more bodies of civilians through "collateral damage" than bodies of Serb military or paramilitary—the agents of the violence that the bombing campaign was intended to bring to an end.

The Identification of Architecture

The registration of those unacknowledged bodies makes possible other representations of the Kosovo War; so, too, does the registration of other dimensions of the architecture that was used to suppress the registration of those bodies. NATO interpreted its architectural targets according to the functions that these targets ostensibly fulfilled. In NATO's military gaze, architecture was a site where certain sorts of programmed activities took place, activities that were classified, analyzed, and destroyed according to their putative relation to the Serb military's "centers of gravity." Yet the functionalism of NATO's modernist architectural discourse provides only a partial purchase on architecture. As architectural critics of modernism stressed, architecture is not only a site of programmed activities but is also a product of individual and collective labor; a location of licit and illicit social practices; an article of affective and cultural investments; a historical artifact; an object of memory; and an array of other dimensions whose limit can only be conditional. "Devastation is never solely material; it has multiple aspects, multiple meanings": Dubravka Ugrešić's observation, made with reference to the shelling of the National and University Library during the siege of Sarajevo, points to the correspondence between architecture's multiple modes of existence and the multiple modes of violence therefore capable of being inflicted against it.[39]

Just as the Kosovo War's human victims, left unrepresented by NATO, were reclaimed in other discursive contexts, so too have authors or audiences narrated strong affective, historical, or cultural relationships to some of the war's architectural targets. These projects of reclamation comprise countermemories of destruction opposed to the militarized memory of war. Excerpts from three such projects follow, each focused on a work of architecture that was destroyed by NATO as a strategic target. These narratives each posited the meaning and value of their object—a tower, a bridge, an office building—as stable and continuous, as "remembered" rather than produced. Here, as elsewhere, loss worked alchemically, transforming the banal into the beautiful, the everyday into the indispensable, the interesting into the indescribable. Performative acts of mnemonic recall thereby approached or even took the form of constantive acts of description. Yet these performances recovered NATO's architectural targets *as* architecture and therefore complicated the seemingly secure boundary between "civilian" and "military" functions that underscored wartime destruction.

The Avala Tower (Avalski toranj), on the outskirts of Belgrade, was bombed and destroyed on April 29, 1999, as a component of the Serb military's communication infrastructure. The 202-meter-tall tower supported a television transmitter owned by RTS and comprised one of twenty-five such transmitters and relays that NATO destroyed. In 2001, the Avala Tower Fans Association (Udruženje ljubitelja Avalskog tornja) was formed in Belgrade in order to sponsor the tower's rebuilding. On the association's Web site, the tower is remembered as a tour de force of modernist architecture—"the only tower in the world that had an equilateral triangle as its cross-section" and "one of the most beautiful TV transmitters in Europe and the whole world"—that was constructed along with New Belgrade itself (Figure 4.4).[40] This tour de force was carried out by "hundreds of construction workers working in all kinds of weather," becoming a site of collective urban memory. Under the transmitter, the tower supported a glass-enclosed bar and restaurant which gave onto panoramic views of Belgrade. As it is recalled on the association's Web site, "People used to say 'see you at the tower' and now the asphalt road that leads to the tower is all covered with grass. People used to queue so that the elevator could take them to see the sight. It was a matter of prestige to have a drink at the top of the tower, to have dinner and watch the city glittering at night."

The Petrovaradin Bridge (Petrovaradinski most), in the Serbian city of Novi Sad, was bombed and destroyed on April 1, 1999; it was the first of the eight bridges over the Danube River that NATO attacked, each targeted as a piece of the Serb military's transportation infrastructure (Figure 4.5). The Petrovaradin Bridge was located where the distance over the Danube near Novi Sad was shortest and thus at the site of the river's earliest bridging; it connected downtown Novi Sad, the capital city of the province of Vojvodina, with the seventeenth-century Petrovaradin Fortress. German POWs built the bridge as a temporary structure in the winter of 1945 out of the remains of a former bridge mined by the Germany army in 1944. The destruction of this permanent temporary bridge was mourned by citizens

FIGURE 4.4 Avala Tower, Belgrade, 1965–99. From Web site of Avala Tower Fans Association (www.avalskitoranj.com, accessed 11 January 2008).

FIGURE 4.5 Memorial image of Petrovaradin Bridge, Novi Sad, Serbia. From the Web site of Vojvodina Province (www.vojvodina.com, accessed 12 January 2008).

of Novi Sad in many newspaper and magazine articles and Internet postings. One such posting, circulated on nettime.org, by the theater director Dragan Klaic, was a reminiscence:

> I remember the uneasiness I felt every time crossing the bridge, even in the daytime: the wooden planks of the side board got lose [*sic*] and rotten and one could see the water underneath. I feared I'll step into the void and even sink into the Danube, little as I was. . . . In the years before I had a driver's license I was crossing it often on foot in the sunset, going to the fortress for a stroll or to some of the inns on the Petrovaradin side with wild Gypsy music, only to return in the small hours, admiring the dawn above the city. Ugly as it was, this bridge was part of my childhood and adolescence.[41]

The Yugoslav Army headquarters, in the heart of Belgrade, was bombed on April 29, 1999, as a key landmark of the Serb military's command and control network (Figure 4.6). In an essay by the architect Srdjan Jovanović Weiss, the building was posed as a key work of the Serb modernist architect Nikola Dobrović—the architect who authored the plan for Prishtina discussed in Chapter 1.[42] For Weiss, the headquarters was particularly significant as an object designed on the basis of what Dobrović called "Bergsonian diagrams." These diagrams appropriated Henri Bergson's concepts of vision and motion to depict relationships between the building's masses and voids, the most important of the latter being the street around which the two parts of the building were located. According to Weiss, Dobrović's choreography of form and void was designed "to be experienced by a contemporary citizen always on the move," or what Dobrović termed *homo spatiosus*. As such, the building suggested that "the identity of the nation was to be found in the void, in nonmatter, and in the action of the individual moving through the void"[43]—a suggestion of particular and novel appropriateness, for Weiss, given the radical transitions that took place in post–Second World War Yugoslavia.

A view of a city glittering at night, a site of childhood memories, a choreographed experience of urban space: these countermemories emerged as critical responses to an objectifying, imperial, and destructive mode of architectural interpretation. Yet they, too, could be objectified. Indeed, in Serbia, countermemories furnished ample resources to the state-sponsored hegemonic memory of the NATO bombing campaign. No matter their poignancy—or, perhaps, precisely because of that poignancy—countermemories were often appropriated in nationalist narratives of Serb victimization and sacrifice, of lost glory, of noble causes lost and found, narratives in which Kosovo stood as prime example and arch-metaphor. Countermemories thus become enmeshed in precisely the functionalist aesthetics they emerged to oppose. Nowhere was this clearer than in those narratives that claimed NATO destroyed certain buildings or sites because it knew "what they meant to the Serbs."[44] Such narratives mirrored those of NATO itself in assigning to architecture fixed and universal identities, constant over time and across interpretive communities. Thus, just as NATO blamed the government of Serbia for not acknowledging that

FIGURE 4.6 Yugoslav Army headquarters, Belgrade, after NATO attack on 29 April 1999. Photograph by Vladimir Kulić, from Srdjan Jovanović Weiss, "NATO as Architectural Critic," *Cabinet* 1 (2000–2001).

certain buildings were, "objectively," military targets, so too did the government of Serbia criticize NATO for destroying what were, "objectively," cultural monuments or social landmarks. Each identification bracketed the violence that comprised its horizon—prospectively for that of NATO, retrospectively for that of the Serbian state—as if it was produced in a timeless present, as if the identity of architecture could be recovered for all time. But, emerging as a legitimization or a criticism of violence, the identity with which architecture was endowed bore the trace of the violence that this endowment explicitly refused to acknowledge.

To recover that trace for history, as I am attempting, is of course to provide yet another identification of architecture, to necessarily participate in the economy of identities that is my object of historiographic study. I posit this economy as one of supplements, compensating for and adding to architecture's irreducible discursivity. This is not to deny identity but to locate it within the minimal form of supplementarity. Identification becomes, then, potentially strategic, rather than "objective," as for NATO, or "subjective," as for the authors of countermemories. It thus offers a possibility of maintaining a gap between itself and its object—precisely the gap that is denied when architecture contributes to human rights by being destroyed *in the name of humanity.*

PART III

AFTERWAR

Reconstruction/Redestruction

The Serbian aggressors, by destroying all that was built through centuries, caused irreparable damage to the cultural heritage of Kosova. . . . [They] did not even spare objects of great architectural value of the Islamic heritage.

REXHEP BOYA, "The Serbian Genocide, Culturocide, and Urbicide in Kosova"

It is clear that we are facing the organized and deliberate destruction of monuments and religious objects, aiming to erase any trace of the Christian civilization and the Serbian cultural heritage in this territory under the interim administration of the UN Mission, belonging to Serbia and Europe.

DRAGAN KOJADINOVIĆ, "The Fate of Cultural Heritage in Kosovo and Metohija"

Alternation constitutes a *relationship.*

RENÉ GIRARD, *Violence and the Sacred*

Violence and Mimesis

June 1999: the war was over. NATO ended its bombing campaign against Serbia, Serb forces departed from Kosovo, NATO forces arrived to replace them, and Kosovar Albanians quickly returned to their homes, traveling from refugee camps in Albania and Macedonia and makeshift havens from violence in the Kosovo countryside. The generals from NATO declared "mission accomplished" and the politicians from the NATO nations

declared "peace." President Slobodan Milošević declared, somewhat ob-
scurely, "victory," and Kosovar Albanian politicians declared, somewhat
prematurely, "independence." General Wesley Clark visited Kosovo and
got a parade. President Bill Clinton spent Thanksgiving in Kosovo and got
a street named after him in Prishtina. NATO initiated "peacekeeping" and
the United Nations initiated "reconstruction"—yet the violence in Kosovo
continued, some of its forms hardly different than those of war. Families
were expelled from their homes; bodies were beaten, abducted, murdered,
and disposed of; buildings were vandalized, burned, and blown up. Only
the identification of victims and victimizers had changed; after the war,
representatives of Kosovar Serbs became the object of violence and representatives of Kosovar Albanians, primarily the Kosovo Liberation Army
and its successor organizations, became violent subjects. "Thanks to you,"
President Clinton told the American troops in Kosovo, "we have reversed
ethnic cleansing."[1] But in fact it was ethnicizing violence itself that had reversed, its targets and apparent beneficiaries exchanging places. This was
the afterwar, a time when the violence of war did not so much end as shift
its direction, becoming a resource for new constituencies, a terror for new
victims, a thematic for new narratives.

"In tragedy everything alternates."[2] Yet the *tragedy* of alternation was
hardly acknowledged by the authors of violence, whose spokespeople issued
justifications, condemnations, and disavowals of that violence, and the *alternation* of tragedy was hardly acknowledged by its victims, whose spokespeople complained of permanent historical oppression. The alternation of
violence was, if anything, even more occulted in and by the NATO nations.
Their declaration of victory in Kosovo—a victory over the Serb forces committing ethnic cleansing against Kosovar Albanians, figured as a victory for
"freedom," for "human dignity," for "human rights"—could only be sustained by ignoring the subsequent violence inflicted by (representatives of)
Kosovar Albanians on (representatives of) Kosovar Serbs. And so it was
largely ignored, which is to say, tolerated, if not abetted, by the UN officials
administering Kosovo and the NATO forces charged with the keeping of
what passed for Kosovo's peace.

At moments, however, tragic postwar narratives did emerge. One
signal instance was an editorial by Veton Surroi published in August 1999,
two months after the arrival of the United Nations and NATO in Kosovo,
in the Albanian newspaper, *Koha Ditore*. Surroi, the newspaper's publisher,

precisely articulated the transformation of identities that had taken place in Kosovo after the war: "We are dealing with a most vicious, organized system of violence against Serbs. And we are also dealing with a conviction that lurks behind such violence, that every Serb should be condemned for what happened in Kosova. This system, based on such a conviction, is called fascism. It is exactly the same conviction-based system that the people of Kosova stood up against in their ten-year struggle with Slobodan Milošević."[3]

Kosovar Serbs were now victims of the violence that had been inflicted on Albanians; "I know how these Serbs feel," Surroi wrote, "because I, along with nearly two million other Albanians, was in the same situation." At once empathizing with Serb victims of postwar violence and criticizing Albanian perpetrators of that violence, Surroi acknowledged how violence prompts imitative counterviolence and thereby renders antagonists doubles of one another. Surroi described a situation in which Serbs and Albanians effectively reversed positions, the former becoming collective victims of violence and the latter perpetrators of that violence; "fascism" became an ideology that passed from one ethnic community to another and thereby evacuated them of distinguishing features.

The reaction to Surroi's editorial only substantiated his points. A press release issued a month later by Kosovapress, the press agency founded by the Kosovo Liberation Army, called Surroi and the editor-in-chief of *Koha Ditore*, Baton Haxhiu, "paid spies of the Milošević regime," who "should not be left unpunished for their criminal acts, since their idiosyncracies deliver water to arch-criminal Milošević's mill."[4] The response to Surroi's narration of reciprocal violence, that is, was the claim that Surroi and Haxhiu were acting like and for Serbs, so that reprisal attacks against them "would be perfectly understandable." To be a Serb or even "pro-Serb" was to be a legitimate target of violence: this was a performative confirmation of Surroi's original assertion and, perhaps as such, the press release was then published, along with Surroi's response, in the pages of *Koha Ditore* itself.[5]

The dynamic that Surroi saw developing in postwar Kosovo was theorized by René Girard as mimetic violence. For Girard, violence is contagious; it invites mimesis, or imitation, an invitation that is expressed in common figurations of violence as "revenge," "vengeance," or even "reaction" or "response" to prior violence: "Only violence can put an end to violence, and that is why violence is self-propagating. Everyone wants to strike the last blow, and reprisal can thus follow reprisal without any true conclusion ever being reached. . . . Vengeance, then, is an interminable, infinitely repetitive process."[6]

For Girard, violent reciprocity destroys distinctions between antagonists, rendering them doubles of one another. But these are "monstrous doubles," doubles sharing both an identity and an investment in one another's annihilation: by setting out to destroy one other, antagonists become increasingly similar to each other. Surroi's concern—that "our moral code, according to which women, children, and the elderly should be left unharmed, has been violated"—testifies to what Girard describes as the destabilization of a community's social order by the chronic or extreme violence it both suffers and inflicts. Mimetic violence, that is, also reproduces itself *within* a community, eroding the "regulated system of distinctions in which the differences among individuals are used to establish their 'identity' and their mutual relationships"[7] Hence, established structures for regulating violence become obsolete or irrelevant and violence emerges in the forms that Surroi describes as "monstrous acts." Pointing out this monstrosity, Kosovapress responded, was the act of a "pro-Serb vampire"—but both "monster" and "vampire" are terms that suggest the same fear and anxiety, a fear of and anxiety over the nullification of political, cultural, and ethical differences between Serb and Albanian identity. "The representation of nondifference ultimately becomes the exemplar of difference, a classic monstrosity."[8]

Against Surroi's insistence on the mimetic dimension of postwar violence inflicted against Kosovo's Serbs was the insistence, on the part of former KLA officials but also a wide range of other Albanian public figures, that this violence was punitive: not an *imitation* of violence but a *retribution* for violence. For defenders of retribution, the distinction between imitation and retribution refracted on a range of other distinctions: between illegitimate and legitimate violence, between disordering and ordering violence, between the incessant exchange of violent acts and the termination of those acts through the achievement of a final equivalence. For Girard, by contrast, retribution was only an ideological framing of imitation and could not secure passage from illegitimate to legitimate violence. That passage, rather, was one from de-differentiating mimetic violence to the singular differentiation of sacrificial violence, a violence inflicted on an object that symbolically condenses the other into a single form. The destruction of this object—what Girard terms "sacrifice"—stops the uncontrolled de-differentiation sponsored by imitation-retribution and thereby reorders society.

While Surroi represented mimetic postwar violence by attacks on Serb "women, children, and the elderly," the narrators of retribution represented it not by attacks on people but by the justified, even necessary destruction of architecture: Serbian Orthodox churches and monasteries posited as sites, symbols, and institutions of violence. The destruction of the preceding was framed as a violence that both responded to and could put an end to violence. Yet what retribution responded to was itself the object of a proliferating array of definitions: initially confirmed as a reaction to the Milošević regime, as postwar retribution continued the violence that was cited as its origin both reached back to a mytho-history of autochthonous Albanian religious sites violated by premedieval Serb Orthodox churches and reached forward to encompass current political conflicts between Serbs and Albanians. Destruction, that is, not only re-presented prior acts of unavenged violence but also invoked such acts. Its mimesis was performative, with violence defined as retributive creating a space that could be filled by violence defined as unavenged. Destruction thereby comprised a supplementary mediation of retribution's putative origin—a mediation that both filled a lack by avenging that violent origin but also added an excess by conjuring that origin in the very process of responding to it. Contra Girard, what was "original" in this mimetic violence was not an empirical act of violence but rather the supplementation of the other's presence simultaneously through and as violence. The agency that Girard attributes to violence and that renders violence "self-propagating" is, in this sense, the artifact of an agency present to itself as violated by an other.

Redestruction

June 1999: the war was over. Yet as Albanian refugees were returning to their homes in Kosovo, Kosovar Serbs were becoming refugees themselves. Some Serbs left Kosovo immediately after the war, traveling to Serbia along with Serb forces. Others, remaining in Kosovo, faced threats and violence in the villages, towns, and cities where they were a minority or a marginalized population. Homeowners were threatened with death if they stayed in their homes; homes were vandalized, robbed, and burned; men were at times abducted, beaten, and killed; women were at times abducted and raped.[9] Serb refugees reported being threatened in precisely reciprocal terms to the threats made by Serb forces against Kosovar Albanians ("This is not your home," "Go to Serbia"), and the many of the forms of violence that Serb forces inflicted on Kosovar Albanians were, in turn, inflicted after the war on Kosovar Serbs.

Serb refugees and survivors of violence often testified that they were threatened and harmed by men wearing the uniform of the Kosovo Liberation Army or claiming to be KLA soldiers.[10] At this time, the KLA had assumed the role of the provisional government of Kosovo, taking over former Serb government offices, setting up ministries, municipal administrations, and police departments, and appointing its members to official positions, from prime minister on down. Each of the preceding, along with violence inflicted on Kosovar Serbs, comprised an act of mimesis, of opposition to the Serbian state and imitation of that state assuming one and the same form. But this mimesis of governance placed the KLA in conflict with the three other organizations that claimed to be governing Kosovo: not only the government of Serbia, within which Kosovo was still a province, but more saliently the Democratic League of Kosovo, the Kosovar Albanian political party that led Kosovo's decade of nonviolent resistance to Serbia in the 1990s, and the United Nations, which was in the process of setting up Kosovo's interim government as stipulated by the UN resolution defining Kosovo's postwar administration. These conflicts, separate but enmeshed, comprised a political culture in which retributive violence was a crucial resource, producing social effects that were endowed with instrumental rationality and that ramified on the identities and agencies of all participants in the conflict.

Attacks on Serbian Orthodox churches and monasteries comprised a key form of retributive violence. Along with Kosovar Serb bodies and homes, Serbian Orthodox architecture was the object of widespread violence immediately after June 1999. In rural areas or villages whose Serb population had left or been forced out, Serbian Orthodox churches and monasteries were vandalized, burned, or destroyed by explosives. Cathedrals in the center of Prishtina, Gjakova, and Rahovec were also attacked, with either dynamite or fire. These acts of representation were themselves often represented, through photography, by the Serbian Orthodox Church (Figures 5.1 and 5.2). These photographs, along with accompanying texts,

FIGURE 5.1 Ruins of Church of Holy Trinity, Petrić, August 1999. Photograph courtesy of Serbian Orthodox Eparchy of Raško-Prizren.

FIGURE 5.2 Ruins of Church of Apostles Peter and Paul, Suva Reka, July 1999. Photograph courtesy of Serbian Orthodox Eparchy of Raško-Prizren.

were circulated in pamphlets and books and on the Church's Web site, in each of which the Church presented postwar destruction as the latest phase in its long-standing victimization by a violent ethnic other.

In many cases, vandalized or burned buildings were graffitied with the initials of the KLA (Figure 5.3). Graffiti literalized the recruitment of these buildings as political media, mimicking the recruitment of mosques as such by Serb forces in the previous two years. Graffiti was both a form of violence and a claim to violence; inscribed with the initials of the KLA ("UÇK" in Albanian), churches and monasteries were represented as objects of and responses to the violence that Serb forces had previously inflicted on mosques. Indeed, the signature UÇK signified the *reciprocity* of violence over and beyond the *authorship* of violence; while the particular authors of these signatures were covert or unknown, the signatures themselves projected the KLA, one of the protagonists of war, into the afterwar. The violence of the afterwar was thereby sutured to that of the supposedly concluded war. Reciprocity was performed, if not actualized; the war, in effect, was continued.

FIGURE 5.3   Fresco with graffiti of Kosovo Liberation Army (Ushtria Çlirimtare e Kosovës [UÇK]) inside Church of St. Paraskeva, Drsnik, September 1999. Photograph by author.

By the end of 1999, approximately one hundred Serbian Orthodox churches and monasteries had been damaged or destroyed in Kosovo.[11] While KLA officials in some cases disavowed responsibility for specific and highly visible attacks on architecture, and while officials from the Serbian Orthodox Church and the Republic of Serbia attempted to direct international attention to these attacks, legitimizations of destruction were prolifically narrated by Kosovapress and circulated in postwar Albanian media. These narrations initially posed the destruction of Serbian Orthodox architecture as a moral retribution for the violence inflicted by the Milošević regime. As one Kosovapress press release, from the end of July 1999, detailed,

The Serbian Orthodox Church has for many years, but especially with the fall of Yugoslavia, completely served Serb policy, including ethnic cleansing. The Milošević era has been marked by a policy of building churches in places where Serbs never lived. Such a construction policy caused Albanians to feel threatened and to view the Serbian Orthodox religion as a tool of nationalism. In those churches, Serb nationalist propaganda was openly distributed. Among other things, these pamphlets called for the deportation of Albanians. Today, nobody should be surprised, therefore, that these churches, built as symbols of Serb fascism and in contradiction to any religious norms, are being attacked and destroyed by Albanians. It would be correct for such churches built in the last ten years to be destroyed by KFOR (NATO forces in Kosovo, termed Kosovo Force or KFOR) and the international community. These churches are being destroyed by Albanians who lost children, wives, brothers, and husbands to an ideology of hatred.[12]

Milošević-era churches are here described as *institutions* serving the Milošević regime, as *instruments* of Serb nationalism, and as *symbols* of Serb fascism; as such, churches were portrayed as legitimate targets of retribution. The danger of conceiving this violence as merely mimetic is the tacit motivation of this press release; the various determinations of the Church (institutional, instrumental, symbolic) therefore rationalized imitative violence by suturing it to prior violence and finalizing it as justice. This was an attempt to pose the church as a legitimate target of retribution—an attempt that faltered at the press release's conclusion, when an appeal was made not to the guilt of the object of revenge but to the victimization of the avenging agency—the agency of mimetic violence.

This shift, from the ascription of guilt to the victims of retributive violence, to the ascription of victimization to that violence's perpetrators, also played out in the proliferation of objects that could fill the category of retribution's targets. The collective accountability of the Serbian Orthodox Church for ethnic violence marked one aspect of this proliferation. This accountability, scripted in the preceding press release, was widely addressed and amplified in postwar Albanian media. "Milošević is only the peak of the pyramid of crime," began one typical editorial, published one month after the war. "A wide specter of organizations were involved in the preparation of genocide. . . . The Serbian parliament and government, Serbian Socialist Party, Serbian United Left Party, Serbian Radical Party, Serbian Orthodox Church, Serbian Academy of Sciences and Arts, Serbian Writers Association, and so on."[13] This is a list of supposedly legitimate targets of retribution. Yet the institutional location of each target, except for the Serbian Orthodox Church, was in Serbia proper; the Church, in any and all of its representations in Kosovo, thus became singularly exposed to violence.

This exposure was concretized, framed, and publicized through frequent reports in the Albanian media on such topics as Serb paramilitaries hosted in monasteries, Serb war criminals escaping Kosovo via assistance by monastery personnel, and monks' practice with heavy weaponry.[14] At the same time, unavenged violence inflicted by Serbs against Albanians was projected into history and onto Orthodox architecture in other narratives. One prominent narrative posited Orthodox churches and monasteries as sited on, and therefore destructions of, proto-Albanian holy places. In a typical article, by Naser Ferri, a professor of history and ethnology at the University of Prishtina, the violence of Serb tribes against Dardanians, the putative ancestors of contemporary Albanians, in premedieval Kosovo mimetically produces justifications for contemporary violence against a series of Orthodox churches and monasteries:

Their history and their acts have shown that Serbs once were and still are one of the most destructive people in the world, who, during their migration from the Carpathians and occupation [of the Balkans], destroyed everything where they stepped. One of the few things they accepted without destroying was Orthodox Christianity. After they accepted it, a long period began in which they embezzled sacred Dardanian objects and adopted them for the needs of the Serb Church. Even today, the traces of this assimilation are evident in ancient churches throughout Kosovo. . . . There is information that even the Patriarchy of Peja [Peć], the Decan [Dečani] Monastery, Graçanicë (Gračanica), Kabas (Sveti Marko) Monastery, Church of Korish in Lipjan, and many other "famous" Serbian churches were constructed precisely on the foundations of earlier autochthonous churches.[15]

Violence against any of these buildings, then, would be retribution, a compensatory response to the primordial violence that enabled their being built in the first place. This is, in other words, a deep history of mimetic destruction, and one which extends from Milošević-era churches, built in the 1990s, to the oldest and most culturally significant Orthodox churches and monasteries. "We know exactly what churches were destroyed, what history they have, when they were built, how they served the politics of genocide, and even in which church this or that many Albanians were slaughtered or where Četniks and other criminals hid while planning the extinction of our nation."[16] The truth of a claim such as this, from an editorial published in 2003 in *Koha Ditore*, is at once recuperative and tautological: retribution against *any* church could not fail to hit its mark when *every* church could be subsumed as a representation of unavenged violence. At the same time, however, retribution could never approach completion. Its infliction retroactively provoked its origin; there was no reservoir of unavenged violence outside of retribution's own economy of violence.

The United Nations Interim Administration Mission in Kosovo (UNMIK), the hegemonic authority in Kosovo's postwar political culture, quickly displaced the KLA provisional government and set up its own administrative structures in the months after June 1999. Basing itself in the former headquarters of the Yugoslav Army in Prishtina, UNMIK, too, engaged in its own mimesis of governance. Thus, in concert with KFOR, UNMIK attempted to monopolize postwar violence. One means of carrying out the latter was to encourage KLA officials to disavow the widespread postwar violence against Serbs and other minorities. Such disavowals became one of the primary products of postwar political culture in Kosovo; along with exhortations, affirmations, promises, and other performative speech acts, they comprised essential forms of action by all political protagonists, allowing UNMIK to perform authority, representatives of Kosovar Albanians to perform tolerance, and representatives of Kosovar Serbs to perform suffering. This is not to say that there was not "actual" authority, tolerance, and suffering among these polities, but rather that actuality only came forth here in the guise of substitutive significations. The distinction is a crucial one; its elision allowed disavowals of violence to function, as they did for UNMIK, as direct interventions into actuality.

UNMIK's first action would prove to be typical, even down to its scripting as an "extraordinary and emergency meeting." The meeting was called on July 3, 1999, by Sérgio Vieria de Mello, the first head of UNMIK; at this meeting, representatives of the KLA provisional government, the Serbian Orthodox Church, and the main Kosovar Serb political party signed a statement of reconciliation. "We urge all Kosovo inhabitants," the signatories stated, "whether of civilian or military status, to refrain and to actively discourage others from any acts of violence against their neighbors."[17] In order to reduce the violence, Vieria de Mello said, the statement would be aired on Albanian radio and television "repeatedly." In his contribution to the press conference following the signing, Hashim Thaçi, the prime minister in the KLA provisional government, moved from exhortation to prediction—a change in speech act, if nothing else: "Albanians and Serbs have always lived together in Kosova. They know how to live together and they will know how to live again."[18]

Similar statements against collective violence continued to be made as Kosovar Serbs suffered threats, intimidation, and violence and churches and monasteries were damaged and destroyed. They were as reflective of reality as comparable statements made by Serb officials throughout the 1990s. Within one month after the war, the Serb population of Prishtina dropped from around forty thousand to less than five thousand; in Prizren, it dropped from eight thousand to less than three hundred; in Gjakova, it dropped from eighteen hundred to thirty-six; in Podujevë, it dropped from fourteen hundred to five.[19] Overall, at least 150,000 of Kosovo's minorities, mostly Serbs and Roma, would leave Kosovo for Serbia and Montenegro by the end of 1999, more than half of Kosovo's non-Albanian population.[20] Yet the "international community" proved to be a receptive audience for condemnations of violence. Indeed, taking performative words for actual deeds allowed UNMIK officials to narrate violence as beyond the control or responsibility of formal political actors and organizations, a matter of "individuals" harming other "individuals."

The connection between performative speech acts and the decollectivization of violence was made explicit in a text from November 1999 by Bernard Kouchner, who succeeded Vieria de Mello as head of UNMIK. In this text, the foreword to a report on human rights in Kosovo, Kouchner wrote: "All the parties in Kosovo-Kosova, all leaders, Serbs and Albanians, have stated their positions in favor of a multiethnic society and coexistence among all communities. The crimes we see are the acts of individuals. No political party has claimed responsibility for them. Their representatives in the Kosovo Transitional Council have condemned these abuses every time, and they themselves have expressed their concern over these acts of intolerance."[21]

Kouchner suggests that "the crimes we see" be framed by *statements, claims, condemnations* and *expressions,* that is, by disavowals of those crimes by representatives of officially recognized political organizations. Thus, he argued, the authors of those crimes must be "individuals." KFOR narrations of postwar violence similarly de-collectivized the targets of violence, rendering such targets ethnically undifferentiated individuals. The response of one KFOR spokesman to a journalist's question about KFOR's ability to provide security to Kosovo's beleaguered Serbs was typical: "I am sure you appreciate that we cannot provide protection, armed protection, for every citizen of Kosovo."[22]

This world—a world of individual subjects or "citizens" and formal political organizations with no social structures between them—was the world of neoliberalism. Established in Kosovo by UNMIK under the sign of "reconstruction," neoliberal policies provide states with means to disavow responsibility for the social welfare of its citizens. In UN-administered Kosovo, neoliberalism functioned accordingly, allowing UNMIK to disavow responsibility for the social suffering it was unable to manage, as well as allowing the KLA and its successor organizations to disavow responsibility for the violence that was inflicted by their members or in their name.

It Should Be Gently Dismantled

"Yesterday was a relatively quiet day which was unfortunately punctuated with violent outbursts involving shootings, intimidation and arson."[23] A month after the arrival of KFOR forces to Kosovo, Major Jan Joost began, typically and symptomatically, KFOR's daily press briefing. KFOR, that is, rhetorically marginalized the violence that it was unable to manage—or rhetorical marginalization itself was a technique of violence management, a means to render postwar collective violence against Kosovar Serbs as merely "outbursts" that "punctuated" the otherwise "quiet days." The reciprocal violence of redestruction slipped seamlessly into this script, with each vandalized, burned, or dynamited church comprising one more outburst punctuating the peace and quiet. The authorities of the Serbian Orthodox Church repeatedly criticized this scripting, but these criticisms, too, could be easily accommodated in the story of peacekeeping's challenges, providing still further opportunities for KFOR to renarrate the events presented as catastrophes by the Church. Thus, while Kosovar Albanian public culture affirmed the reciprocity of postwar destruction, staging it as justifiable revenge for prior violence, whether that of the war or that of mytho-history, KFOR denied this reciprocity by insistently minimizing the significance of postwar destruction. Yet these twin discourses of affirmation and denial intersected in their architectural logic, a logic in which architecture's value, meaning, and significance were posited as "objective" and thus as displacements of the "subjective" positings by those who identified with that architecture.

The 1999 UN resolution on the administration of Kosovo stipulated that after the withdrawal of Serb forces from Kosovo, "an agreed number of Yugoslav and Serbian personnel will be permitted to return" to perform a list of functions; one of these functions was "maintaining a presence at Serb patrimonial sites."[24] Serb officials repeatedly solicited this permission in the years after the war, sometimes with reference to the UN resolution and sometimes with reference to the vandalism and destruction of Orthodox churches and monasteries, but UNMIK and KFOR never granted it. Rather, in the weeks and months after the war, after some eighty-five churches and monasteries had been attacked, KFOR troops were deployed at Serbian Orthodox sites, deployments eventually made at 151 churches, monasteries, and other patrimonial sites.[25] In some cases, these troops protected churches whose congregations had fled and which therefore remained empty; in a few cases, they protected the rubble of already destroyed churches. Many churches and monasteries were protected by "fixed positions," that is, by troops positioned round-the-clock at guard posts on church or monastery grounds; other sites were periodically checked by daily or weekly foot patrols (Figure 5.4).

If a church or monastery had been damaged or abandoned after the war, then it was usually not guarded from a fixed position; thus, many buildings that were vandalized or burned in the months after the war were subsequently demolished by explosives. After explosive charges destroyed the already vandalized Church of St. Nicholas in the village of Srbinje in May 2000, Colonel Arto Raty, head of KFOR operations in the town of

FIGURE 5.4   KFOR troops guarding Serbian Orthodox Church, Podujevo, 2001. Photograph by author.

Sllovi/Slovinje, laid out the workings of this protection strategy to a journalist from Reuters: "If a church has value as a historical place, then clearly it should be guarded. But if it has no historical value and there is no chance of the Serbs returning anytime soon to the area, then it should be gently dismantled."[26]

Colonel Raty accurately represented KFOR policy, a policy based on eliminating violence against Serbian Orthodox architecture not by enhancing the protection of this architecture but by allowing "valueless" and "useless" examples of this architecture to be eliminated. KFOR assessed "historical value" by the seemingly objective and thus profoundly ideological standard of age. Thus, for KFOR, the Church of St. Nicholas was built in 1996 on the site of a sixteenth-century church, had no historical value, and so did not warrant protection. For the Serbian Orthodox Church, by contrast, the Church of St. Nicholas dated from the sixteenth century; the contemporary building comprised a "renewal" (*obnovljena*) of the original one.[27] The staging of age as an autonomous value, that is, displaced history, both as a discourse composed of often competing narratives and as a context in which the age of a building was the outcome of any number of forces and events, including any prior violence against a building that necessitated its rebuilding. Similarly, "usefulness" was assessed by architecture's functional utility; since the "users" of Serbian Orthodox churches and monasteries were Serbs, almost all of whom had left or fled the Kosovar countryside for protected enclaves or for Serbia itself, postwar violence against Serbs rendered many churches and monasteries "useless." Yet KFOR's fully modernist architectural ideology could not negotiate differences of architectural interpretation across different interpretive communities or across time. KFOR's readings of architecture transmuted the contingent conditions of a violent present into timeless facts. Because these readings determined the deployment of military forces, KFOR's knowledge of architecture was also a power over architecture and architecture's exposure to violence.

Colonel Raty's words uncannily echoed those circulating in contemporaneous Kosovar Albanian media. What were posed as sites of "Serb nationalism" by Kosovar Albanian apologists of destruction were posed as sites of valueless and useless architecture by KFOR. KFOR's marginalization of the violence it could not manage thus facilitated the exercise of reciprocal destruction. In the end, the difference between destruction inflicted by fire or explosives and the "gentle dismantling" called for by Colonel Raty was, for architecture, null; in each case, destruction was either legitimized or minimized by architectural readings of its target as devoid of value or positive historical significance.

In 2001, KFOR began to shift responsibility for guarding Serbian Orthodox sites to UNMIK's international police force and the local, mostly Albanian-staffed Kosovo Police Service. It also began to "unfix" its guard positions at many churches, substituting daily or weekly patrols as protection mechanisms. At the end of 2002, after a period in which violence against Serbian Orthodox sites had reduced to a level it assessed as tolerable, KFOR announced a decision to remove fixed positions at all churches and monasteries except those in "active use" or of "historical or artistic value."[28] In several cases, churches were attacked after their guard posts were taken down. One such case occurred at the Church of St. Basil of Ostrog, built in 1939 in the village of Ljubovo/Lupove.[29] The Serb population of the village left in June 1999; the church was vandalized thereafter;

and then KFOR established a fixed guard post at the church. This post was dismantled in September 2002 and the church was placed on a KFOR patrol route. UNMIK police periodically reported to KFOR that there were "minor attacks" (broken windows, damage to a cross) to the church in the months after the guard post was dismantled, but no change was made to security arrangements. Finally, at around eleven o'clock on a Saturday night in November 2002, the church was dynamited, along with another "abandoned" church in a nearby village. The Church of St. Basil was reduced to rubble, only a piece of its front facade still standing (Figure 5.5). The next day, Michael Steiner, the head of UNMIK, helicoptered to the site of each destroyed church, along with Bajram Rexhepi, prime minister of the Kosovo provisional government. Steiner told the press that "we're all united in condemning these acts of religious vandalism," but even his use of *vandalism* to describe the dynamiting of buildings comprised a minimization of violence and a denial of the reciprocity of destruction.[30]

FIGURE 5.5 Remains of Church of St. Basil of Ostrog, Ljubovo, November 2002. Photograph courtesy of Serbian Orthodox Eparchy of Raško-Prizren.

Bishop Artemije of the Serbian Orthodox Church protested the separation of "God's churches" in Kosovo into the categories of the "valuable and not valuable," and the latter's vulnerability to "the architects of an ethnically pure Albanian society."[31] In response, KFOR suspended the unfixing of guard positions at churches and monasteries in January 2003, but then resumed it in the spring; by the summer of 2003, KFOR had unfixed guard positions at all but twenty-six Orthodox sites.[32] Meanwhile, through 2003, churches and graveyards continued to be vandalized or damaged, at the rate of one or two a month, and KFOR and UNMIK continued to simultaneously condemn and minimize this violence: a tolerable rate of redestruction was implicitly established, with this definition serving to normalize redestruction and therefore render it politically invisible.

This, of course, was not the case for the Serbian Orthodox Church, which documented and publicized each case of violence against its property in Kosovo.[33] It was also not the case for UNESCO (United Nations Educational, Scientific and Cultural Organization), which in October 2003 issued a report that criticized UNMIK's protection of cultural heritage in Kosovo. The report stated: "Architectural monuments that make up the built cultural heritage in Kosovo have been found to be in a precarious and most vulnerable situation. . . . Three different factors account for the present sad state of cultural heritage sites: intentional destruction by dynamite, shelling and fire; vandalism and looting; the process of normal ageing and decaying of all monuments, aggravated by environmental pollution and significant neglect of protection and preservation."[34]

The response of UNMIK's Ministry of Culture, Youth, and Sports to UNESCO mentioned work on the development of a policy on the protection and preservation of built heritage; on the inventorization of built heritage; on an educational campaign to raise public awareness of heritage protection and preservation; on the capacity-building of heritage management personnel; and a suggestion on holding a donor's conference.[35] The ongoing protection of built heritage from violence was ignored. And when this protection was not ignored, its quality was reflexively proclaimed. Here is a typical proclamation, from an UNMIK press conference in December 2003: "UNMIK police together with KFOR make joint patrols to secure every historical place in Kosovo, every monument, which is of importance to the Kosovars, and we will keep on doing this way [*sic*], and we consider it our duty to protect these sites."[36]

The qualification "of importance to the Kosovars" makes the statement above less than what is might seem. Whose voices were registered in the interpretive community of "Kosovars"? How to register this community's valuation of historical places (if it existed at all)? How to negotiate between competing or contradictory valuations? The police, of course, were not concerned with such questions—and precisely because they were not, the protection of heritage, as well as its very definition, remained a matter for the police and military to negotiate.

The Situation Is Calm, While the Church Is Burning

In the context of mimetic violence, Girard argues, the function of the sacrifice is to symbolically concentrate the adversary into a single object of violence whose destruction can terminate violent reciprocity. If a symbolic object of violence does not emerge, however, reciprocal violence ends with the destruction of the adversary itself: "Only an act of collective expulsion can bring . . . oscillation to a halt and cast violence outside the community."[37] After 1999, officials of the Serbian Orthodox Church articulated and circulated their fears of just such an expulsion; each act of destruction added yet another item to the Church's list of damaged and destroyed shrines in Kosovo, bringing the Church's annihilation that much closer. UNMIK and KFOR officials, on the other hand, kept graphs instead of lists. Plotting acts of violence over time, these officials focused on what they claimed to be the growing infrequency of violence against Church property and so they rested calm, or even self-satisfied: it was as if the most receptive audience of the performative assertions of postwar reconstruction in Kosovo made by UNMIK and KFOR officials were those officials themselves. Based upon continuing statements of improvement—in development, in democratization, in security, in ethnic relations—and, correspondingly, upon continuing marginalizations of violence, KFOR decreased its troop levels in Kosovo; continued to replace fixed guard positions with "area security" patrols; and handed over security across Kosovo to UNMIK police and the Kosovo Police Service.

The destruction of Serbian Orthodox sites in anti-Serb violence that spread through Kosovo in March 2004 was facilitated by the insistence on and performance of social order by UNMIK and KFOR, a performance that led those sites to be underprotected or unprotected. But this destruction was impelled by its status as a legitimate form of violence in Kosovar Albanian public culture, a form that was legible as retribution and that could retroactively posit the violence that it avenged. The violence of March 2004 was concentrated in two days, March 17 and 18, during which crowds of Kosovar Albanian demonstrators assaulted the few remaining Serb inhabitants of villages, towns, and cities across Kosovo, along with their homes and thirty-six Orthodox churches, monasteries, and graveyards. While the Serb population of Kosovo had been halved in the years after 1999, in two days its tiny urban remnants—less than a hundred people in Prishtina, thirty-six in Prizren, five in Gjakova—were targeted, along with the Serb population of many villages and towns. This was the collective expulsion described by Girard. Its objects included people and architecture; the "expulsion" of the latter left ruins that remained as social texts—narrating, justifying, and memorializing the violence that produced them. Indeed, for all protagonists in the violence of March 2004, discursive spaces already existed for every ruin; on one level, destruction provided more evidence for each of the competing narratives on Kosovo's afterwar, evidence that could be integrated into each system of knowledge production and cultural representation.

The violence of March 2004 presumed the general availability of Serbian Orthodox architecture to collective violence—a presumption by Kosovar Albanian political leaders and demonstrators that was confirmed by KFOR troops, most contingents of which understood their mandate as "the protection of lives, not property."[38] In Prizren, after crowds in the city center threw stones at the city's well-protected UNMIK building, they then crossed a river and burned the unprotected houses of the city's remaining Serbs, the Orthodox seminary, and then the city's other Orthodox churches and monastery, all of which KFOR troops left unguarded. Some demonstrators also walked a few kilometers out of town, to the Monastery of Holy Archangels. A contingent of KFOR troops guarded the monastery; according to one news report, the demonstrators sent a delegation to the troops to assert that "we only want to burn down the monastery," the troops evacuated the monks, and the monastery was then set on fire.[39] In Podujevë, after members of a KLA veterans group dissuaded a crowd from marching to Kosovo's border crossing with Serbia, six kilometers away, the crowd went instead to the Church of St. Elias; after KFOR troops departed, the crowd vandalized the church, burned it, then knocked over headstones in the adjoining graveyard. In Ferizaj/Uroševac, a commander from the Kosovo Protection Corps, an organization composed largely of demilitarized KLA veterans, told a crowd gathered at the Church of St. Uroš to leave the town center; the crowd dispersed, first vandalizing the town's Orthodox cemetery and then burning three churches in the outlying villages of Varosh/Varoš, Softe/Softović, and Talinovc/Talinovac. In Veterinik, outside Prishtina, a crowd gathered in front of KFOR troops guarding the Serb village of Čaglavica; after Albanian politicians told the crowd to return home, some drifted back to Prishtina, gathered at the Church of St. Nicholas, the city's only active Orthodox church, and burned the church after KFOR evacuated its priest from the adjacent parish house.

Analysts have posited that this violence emerged from a network of causes, some proximate (erroneous media reports of two Albanian children chased by Serbs into a river, where they drowned; the blockade of a highway by Serbs in reaction to a drive-by shooting of a Serb teenager; the arrest of former KLA officers for war crimes), and some structural (Kosovo's stagnant postwar development and high levels of unemployment, as well as international unwillingness to deal with Kosovo's future political status). Accounts of the violence have attempted to sort through these "causes" in order to determine which were most "actionable"; the destruction of Serbian Orthodox architecture as an expression of revenge or protest has been taken, by contrast, as hardly worthy of analysis. As a supplementary mediation of a posited "cause," however, this destruction comprises not only such an expression, but also an act that conjures up the origin of revenge and protest in retrospect. From this perspective, the interpretive problem is not to distinguish the intentions behind and preceding action, but rather to acknowledge intentions as themselves products of action.

Indeed, in Kosovar Albanian political and media discourse, narrations of the March 2004 violence functioned precisely as a reflexive generation of legitimizing intentions. In its initial statement, the Kosovo Assembly posed the violence as a counterviolence against UNMIK "bias" and Serb "criminals": "The Kosovo Assembly voices its disagreement with the lack of commitment by UNMIK to provide security for all Kosovar citizens. The tolerance for Serb parallel structures and criminal gangs that murder Kosovar citizens is a wrong policy that will destabilize Kosovo."[40] Here it is the status quo that is disordered and violent (against Albanians)

and it is violence (by Albanians) that is ordering and civilizing, at once reciprocal and legitimate.

In many contexts, the destruction of Serbian Orthodox architecture
in the March violence remained as such. Albanian media thus reported
this destruction as an act of justifiable retribution for any number of acts
of ethnic violence inflicted by Serbs on Albanians. As one correspondent
from KTV (Kosova Television) described the burning of the Orthodox Cathedral in Gjakova: "The criminal acts of the Serb population in the north
[the supposed drowning of the two Albanian children] have been condemned by the population of Gjakova during peaceful demonstrations.
They demand an end to these terrorist attacks against the Albanian population. In an expression of solidarity, the protesters marched toward the
Serb street [and] the Serb church was set on fire. The situation is calm,
while the church is burning."[41]

Unlike earlier attacks on churches, photographic representations of
the destruction of Serbian Orthodox architecture on March 17 and 18 was,
at least initially, circulated on Albanian-language platforms on the Internet. The destruction of Orthodox buildings in Prizren was documented,
for example, in a photo gallery on the Web site www.besimi.com, at the
time owned and managed by a Kosovar photographer.[42] These photographs
depicted the burning of these buildings as a carnival, with crowds gather-
ing in adjacent streets to witness the fires, wave banners and flags, and
celebrate (Figures 5.6 and 5.7). After UNMIK officials forced a public dele-
gitimization of the March violence, Web sites like besimi.com were taken
down, yet legitimizing narratives of destruction continued to circulate in
the mass media. These narratives cited and extended those that appeared
in earlier years to legitimize the destruction of other Serbian Orthodox
sites. One article thus quotes Enver Bahtiu, director of the Institute for the
Protection of Monuments in Prizren, as saying that, "a great part of our
cultural heritage was destroyed (on March 17 and 18), such as the Monastery of Saint Friday and the Monastery of Holy Archangels, which are of
explicit importance to Albanian culture."[43] This article then rehearsed the
narrative of Serbs "appropriating Albanian cult sites from earlier periods"
and ended with Bahtiu's appeal to citizens "to restrain themselves and preserve the elements of their cultural heritage." This appeal, of course, was
not to Albanians to protect the heritage of ethnic others, but rather to protect their own heritage in its current fugitive—Serbian Orthodox—form.

FIGURE 5.6 Burning of Orthodox Cathedral, Prizren, 17 March 2004 (from www.besimi.com). Photograph courtesy of Serbian Orthodox Eparchy of Raško-Prizren.

FIGURE 5.7 Burning of Orthodox Cathedral and churches, Prizren, 17 March 2004 (from www.besimi.com). Photograph courtesy of Serbian Orthodox Eparchy of Raško-Prizren.

Moreover, when the illegitimacy of destruction was acknowledged in public, it was often then disavowed by attributing it to agents of Serbia or to Serbs themselves, thereby extracting illegitimate violence from Albanian responsibility. "Every Albanian knows," one post–March 2004 article stated, "that Serb churches were not burned by protestors but by individuals paid by some neighboring country."[44] This discourse relied upon a conspiracy theory of postwar violence that denied reciprocity by attributing illegitimate violence to exterior actors; as another article claimed, "many of the events of recent years (in Kosovo) have been attributed to the secret services of Belgrade, while UNMIK and KFOR have done nothing to clarify these cases."[45]

Event, Revolt, Pogrom

UNMIK and KFOR were invested, meanwhile, in their own conspiracy. This was the conspiracy of progress, expertly overseen and directed by their own good offices. For them, the violence of March 2004 comprised a series of "events" scripted by "a small group of extremists." This group could be captured and isolated from society, thereby allowing that society to "get back on track" and resume its "development." In Lipjan/Lipljan, the head of UNMIK, Harri Holkeri, visited burned Serb homes and the Church of St. Bogorodica, the facade of which was stippled by stones and bullets. Outside the church, addressing the press, Holkeri backpedaled from his statement of the previous day, in which he redescribed the "March events" as an instance of "ethnic cleansing"; at a time like this, he said, "labels are not important."[46] He then continued, apparently detailing what *was* important: "Every life lost is one too many. Every destroyed home is one too many. Every destroyed holy site is one too many." Holkerri attempted to contrast labels—the names of violence—with the pure, present, undeniable remains of violence. That these remains were, already, subsumed under the sign of the "event" is but one aporia he did not acknowledge. This subsumption occurred within a symbolic ordering of postwar reconstruction as inexorable progress, a progress that rendered lives lost, destroyed homes and destroyed holy sites, whether marked as Serb or Albanian, as empty events, mere contingencies, each one "one too many" to present itself to thought. Precisely what Holkerri upheld as more important than language was thereby made to disappear by language.

In Kosovar Albanian public culture, the violence of March 2004 comprised a popular "revolt." This was an intensification of retribution for *prior* violence that, fully performatively, transmuted its object into *current* violence—a veritable exhumation of a presumably dead enemy by wreaking revenge on it. This exhumation took the form of new representations of UNMIK and KFOR as substitutes for Serbia or the Milošević regime. Five years previously, Kosovar Albanian public culture posited UNMIK and KFOR as saviors of Kosovo from Milošević; during and after March 2004, they were seen as a regime "as bad as Milošević" which "did the Serbs' bidding." The "revolt" of March 2004, then, was in some versions enacted against Serbia, in some against UNIMIK and KFOR, and in some against both as a violent amalgam. These readings were secured by a symbolic ordering of Albanian ethnic identity as an identity of victimization. All violence inflicted in the name of this identity was always already counterviolence. The effects of this counterviolence—lives lost, homes and holy sites destroyed—once marked as Serb, were at the most historical necessities and at the least unfortunate inevitabilities. Resistance to violence reduced to legitimization for violence, with invocations of violence past and present furnishing ever renewable justifications for violence present and future.

For the Serbian Orthodox Church, the violence of March 2004 comprised a "pogrom." This term enmeshed that violence in the history of the Second World War, violence against European Jews, genocide, and a perduring history of vicitimization.[47] Precisely what was narrated as retributive violence in Albanian public culture was thus narrated as genocidal violence by the Serbian Orthodox Church; the "pogrom" of March 2004 became an attempt at the "complete annihilation of all traces of Serb and Christian culture in Kosovo and Metohija."[48] Like its Albanian counterpart, that is, Serbian identity was ordered as an identity of victimization by a violent ethnic other. Indeed, five years earlier, Grand Mufti Rexhep Boja of the Islamic Community of Kosovo posed the ruins of Islamic architecture from the 1998–99 war "as a result of the systematic policy of genocide, cultural genocide and urbicide during the last 100 years."[49] Both Kosovar Albanians and Serbs, that is, were figured as "Nazis" by each other and as "Jews" by themselves—testimony to both the violence each projected onto the ethnic other and the victimization each claimed as the center of ethnic identity.

The violence of March 2004, then, was subsumed into one or another symbolic order that already contained a place for that violence; the various names given to violence—event, revolt, pogrom—each rendered that violence in terms of a posited history, simultaneously invoking that history and evoking it in present "actuality." What these histories deferred, then, was a negotiation with alterity: with the appearance of the other and the possibility of difference. Each name for violence enacted a mimesis, a representation of history in the present that both reified history as repetition and denied the present as difference. The identity of the other was itself mimetic, a reflection of the violent others whose actions comprise a history as/of violence. The "event" emerged from an order of progress it could not but continue; the "revolt" emerged from an order of victimization it could only redeem; the "pogrom" emerged from an order of victimization it could only add to. Historicity was here impeded by history. As destruction, architecture confirmed this history—the history of which it was posed as a mere representation, the history that foreclosed on the emergence of the unprecedented or unknown.

I do not have another name for the violence of March 2004, a name to offer as an alternative to the names that its protagonists already gave. There is not—and cannot be—a "proper" name for violence, a name that adequately defines violence across the differentiated space of its authors, victims, witnesses, and audiences; through ongoing time; and to itself in self-presence. Violence is itself a form of nomination, of inscribing names on things, "of revealing by effraction the so-called proper name, the originary violence which severed the proper from its property and its self-sameness."[50] *Event, revolt* and *pogrom* are versions of these names. Subsequent narrations of violence, if only corroborating or replacing those names, are only inflicting their own violence, their own redoubling of mimetic nomination. The narration of the inadequacy of nomination—of the contradictions and remainders attendant upon the subsumption or redemption of violence—perhaps offers no guarantee except that of an interruption and an anticipation—an interruption of received programs of perceiving, interpreting, and remembering violence, and an anticipation of alternatives to those programs. The possibility offered by such a narration is that of preparing for or inviting an unprecedented future; such a future, both solicited and forestalled by violence, requires that a place be made for it. For a future taking place.

Coda:

The End of Preservation

"Preserve it: it's yours!" In Albanian, Serbian, and English, this message—or, more precisely, this command—appeared on billboards throughout Prishtina in the summer of 2004 (Figure C.1). The billboards, which themselves were built in the city a few years earlier, usually advertised cigarettes, perfume, jeans, ice cream novelties, and political candidates: the various goods of the neoliberal political economy whose institution comprised a major component of Kosovo's postwar reconstruction. Considered as an advertisement, the billboard's commanding message made sense: it appealed to the consumer who was addressed by a proliferating array of similar statements, the consumer whose identities and desires emerged in response to multiple exhortations of what to buy, wear, smoke, eat, feel, vote for, and believe in.

The billboards displayed examples of the objects of preservative labor in a series of twelve images, each showing a historical site in Kosovo: the Dečani and Gračanica Monasteries, the Sinan Pasha Mosque, an Ottoman-era *konak*, the Prizren League Building, traditional stone tower houses, the Roman-era Ulpiana archaeological excavations, and so on. References were carefully balanced: Christianity with Islam, Serb with Albanian, high culture with vernacular culture, and the prehistoric with the historic. Looming above all other images was the extraterrestrial form of a neolithic figurine, among the oldest products of human culture in Kosovo. The figurine's size and position on the billboard were easy to understand;

FIGURE C.1   Billboard advertising heritage preservation campaign in former Square of Brotherhood and Unity, Prishtina, 2004. Photograph by author.

as a pre-ethnic artifact, it was the only heritage object whose multiethnic credentials were impeccable, or maybe even believable.

Sponsored by the Ministry of Culture, Youth, and Sports, the billboards appeared to be a response to the "March events." Those events comprised the destruction of what seemed to be the property of a despised ethnic other—but, at least according to the ministry, this property actually belonged to all ethnicities in Kosovo. The ministry's proposition, however, appealed to a subject who did not yet exist: a subject whose cultural identity transcended, even contradicted, other identities—social, political, and also cultural—that were circumscribed primarily by ethnicity for almost all of Kosovo's inhabitants. The ministry's preservation campaign, in other words, posited a multiethnic collective identity, with a posited multicultural heritage as its object, though such an identity had no other collective dimension. What appeared to be a project to *preserve* cultural heritage was, then, a project to *perform* a particular cultural identity using a posited construct of cultural heritage as its referent. The billboard glossed its main message with a sentence that registered this tension between preservation and performance: "Kosovo's cultural heritage is respected as the common patrimony of all of Kosovo's ethnic, religious, and linguistic communities." These otherwise differentiated communities, that is, were supposed to have a singular cultural identity, an identity that united them.

This performance was in service of the multiethnic polity that the Western powers were attempting to institute in Kosovo. Precisely the same object by means of which Albanians and Serbs figured and communicated ethnic difference—architecture—was thereby recruited to figure and communicate nondifference. Thus, whether destroyed in moments of violence or preserved in moments of reconstruction, architecture was apprehended in the same way, as an immediate display of cultural identity and historical truth. In Kosovar Albanian and Serbian discourses, the truth performed in the violence of March 2004 was that of ethnic antagonism, of an Albanian Kosovo in which Serbs had no place. The truth performed by the ministry's preservation campaign was that of a multiethnic polity in which ethnic communities were united by their affiliation with a common cultural heritage. Each of these truths was a fabrication, and each fabrication was supplemented by architecture. Architecture could be destroyed as the property of a despised ethnic other or preserved as the property of a multiethnic polity, but in each case ethnicity did not stand outside of architectural reference as much as it was completed and confirmed by means of that reference.

Preservation, which is to say, nondestruction, continued and extended destruction's extraction of political agency from architecture. It appealed to a political fact in architecture that was performatively constituted by the appeal itself. In the guise of heritage, architecture was polarized between two modes of existence, the first as an object of destruction for self-delegated representatives of antagonistic ethnic communities, and the second as an object of nondestruction for an emerging multiethnic Kosovo state. What was preserved in the ministry's preservation campaign, then, was the architectural supplementation of ethnic identity and political agency. Preservation thereby continued the architecture of the Kosovo conflict and raised the question: preserved for what?

Notes

INTRODUCTION: VIOLENCE TAKING PLACE

1. Andrew Herscher and Andras Riedlmayer, "The Destruction of Cultural Heritage in Kosovo, 1998–1999: A Postwar Survey," prosecution submission, *Prosecutor v. Slobodan Milošević*, case no. IT-02-54-T, International Criminal Tribunal for the Former Yugoslavia, 28 February 2002.

2. In the words of K. Michael Hays, the vocation of architectural theory is to "show the work of architecture as having some autonomous force with which it could also be seen as negating, distorting, repressing, compensating for, and even producing, as well as reproducing, (its) context"; see K. Michael Hays, "Introduction," in *Architectural Theory Since 1968*, ed. K. Michael Hays (Cambridge, MA: MIT Press, 2000), v.

3. Gyanendra Pandey, *Routine Violence: Nations, Histories, Fragments* (Stanford, CA: Stanford University Press, 2006), 17.

4. On violence as inscription, see Anne Norton, *Reflections on Political Identity* (Baltimore: Johns Hopkins University Press, 1988), 145.

5. One of the most detailed discussions to date of architectural destruction is Robert Bevan, *The Destruction of Memory: Architecture at War* (London: Reaktion, 2006). In assuming that architectural destruction can be understood as an attempt at the "erasure of the memories, histories and identities attached to architecture and place" (7), Bevan subsumes destruction under instrumental rationality and thereby leaves unacknowledged its inscriptive complexity and cultural productivity. For an expanded discussion of discourse on destruction, see Andrew Herscher, "Warchitectural Theory," *Journal of Architectural Education* 62:1 (February 2008).

6. Sabrina P. Ramet, "Who's to Blame, and for What? Rival Accounts of the War," in *Thinking About Yugoslavia: Scholarly Debates About the Yugoslav Breakup and the Wars in Bosnia and Kosovo*, ed. Sabrina P. Ramet (Cambridge: Cambridge University Press, 2005).

7. Sabrina Petra Ramet, *Balkan Babel: The Disintegration of Yugoslavia from the Death of Tito to the War for Kosovo* (Boulder, CO: Westview Press, 1999), 287; Florian Bieber, "Approaches to Political Violence and Terrorism in Former Yugoslavia," *Journal of Southern Europe and the Balkans* 5:1 (2003): 43.

8. Michael Sells, "Crosses of Blood: Sacred Space, Religion, and Violence in Bosnia-Hercegovina," *Sociology of Religion* 64:3 (2003): 329.

9. Vjekoslav Perica, *Balkan Idols: Religion and Nationalism in Yugoslav States* (Oxford: Oxford University Press, 2002), 4.

10. Bevan, *Destruction of Memory*, 8.

11. Jacques Derrida, *Of Grammatology*, trans. Gayatri Chakravorty Spivak (Baltimore: Johns Hopkins University Press, 1997), 144.

12. Ibid., 145.

13. Jacques Derrida, "The Theatre of Cruelty and the Closure of Representation," in *Writing and Difference*, trans. Alan Bass (Chicago: University of Chicago Press, 1978), 235, 237.

14. Derrida, *Of Grammatology*, 157.

15. See Jana Howlett and Rod Mengham, eds., *The Violent Muse: Violence and the Artistic Imagination in Europe, 1910–1939* (Manchester, England: Manchester University Press, 1994).

16. See Dario Gamboni, *The Destruction of Art: Iconoclasm and Vandalism Since the French Revolution* (New Haven, CT: Yale University Press, 1997); and Miguel Egana, ed., *Du vandalisme: Art et destruction* (Brussels: La lettre volée, 2005).

17. See Daniel Bertrand Monk, *An Aesthetic Occupation: The Immediacy of Architecture and the Palestine Conflict* (Durham, NC: Duke University Press, 2002); many of the essays in Stephen Graham, ed., *Cities, War, and Terrorism: Towards an Urban Geopolitics* (Oxford: Blackwell, 2004); and Eyal Weizman, *Hollow Land: Israel's Architecture of Occupation* (London: Verso, 2007).

18. The acknowledgement of poststructuralism's relation to modernism has typically been a de facto indictment of the former, as, for example, a mere "recapitulation" of "the basic experience of aesthetic modernity" (Jürgen Habermas, *The Theory of Communicative Action* [London: Beacon Press, 1981], 7), or an "archaeology of modernity" (Andreas Huyssen, *After the Great Divide: Modernism, Mass Culture and Postmodernism* [London: Macmillian, 1988], 209). Such indictments, however, foreclose on, among other things, the poststructuralist opening of the historiography of violence and alterity in and beyond modernity. On poststructuralism and violence, see Beatrice Hanssen, *Critique of Violence: Between Poststructuralism and Critical Theory* (London: Routledge, 2000).

19. Jacques Derrida, "Force and Signification," in *Writing and Difference*, 7.

20. Ibid.

21. See, for example, Derrida's gloss of Francis Fukuyama's *The End of History and the Last Man*, where "all these cataclysms (terror, oppression, repression, extermination, genocide, and so on) . . . would belong to *empiricity* . . . (and) in no way refute the *ideal* orientation of the greater part of humanity towards liberal democracy"—a gloss that, in its relation to the genealogy of violence in *Of Grammatology*'s "Writing Lesson," problematizes the sometimes-drawn distinction between the early "prepolitical" Derrida and the late "political" one. See Jacques

Derrida, *Spectres of Marx: The State of the Debt, the Work of Mourning, and the New International,* trans. Peggy Kamuf (New York: Routledge, 1994), 57.

22. Crucial precedents for this apprehension are Allen Feldman, *Formations of Violence: The Narrative of the Body and Political Terror in Northern Ireland* (Chicago: University of Chicago Press, 1991); and David Campbell, *National Deconstruction: Violence, Identity, and Justice in Bosnia* (Minneapolis: University of Minnesota Press, 1998).

23. Jalal Toufic, *Over-Sensitivity* (Los Angeles: Sun and Moon Press, 1996). For Derrida, the archive's exposure to violence is irreducible; See Jacques Derrida, *Archive Fever: A Freudian Impression,* trans. Eric Prenowitz (Chicago, University of Chicage Press, 1998.)

24. See Bruce Jackson and Wladyslav Stepniak, "General Assessment of the Situation of Archives in Kosovo," UNESCO, 2000, www.unesco.org/webworld/publications/jackson_report.rtf (accessed 17 May 2007).

25. See, for example, Ranajit Guha, "The Prose of Counter-Insurgency," in *Selected Subaltern Studies,* eds. Ranajit Guha and Gayatri Chakravorty Spivak (New York: Oxford University Press, 1988).

26. See, for example, Jay Winter, *Sites of Memory, Sites of Mourning* (Cambridge: Cambridge University Press, 1995); Pierre Nora, *Realms of Memory: Rethinking the French Past,* trans. Arthur Goldhammer (New York: Columbia University Press, 1996); Rudy Koshar, *From Monuments to Traces: The Artifacts of German Memory* (Berkeley: University of California Press, 2000); and Andreas Huyssen, *Present Pasts: Urban Palimpsests and the Politics of Memory* (Stanford, CA: Stanford University Press, 2003).

27. Derrida, *Of Grammatology,* 158.

28. Vladislav Petković Dis, "Spomenik," in *Kosovski boj u srpskoj književnosti,* ed. Vojislav Djurić (Belgrade: Sprska književna zadruga, 1990), 441. All translations are mine unless otherwise stated.

29. Derrida, *Of Grammatology,* 145.

30. Henri Lefebvre, *The Production of Space,* trans. Donald Nicholson-Smith (Oxford: Blackwell, 1991).

31. See, for example, Ramet, *Balkan Babel;* Andrew Baruch Wachtel, *Making a Nation, Breaking a Nation: Literature and Cultural Politics in Yugoslavia* (Stanford, CA: Stanford University Press, 1998); Ivo Zanić, *Prevarena povijest: Guslarska estrada, kult hajduka i rat u Hrvatskoj i Bosni i Hercegovini, 1990–1995* (Zagreb: Durieux, 1998); Eric Gordy, *The Culture of Power in Serbia: Nationalism and the Destruction of Alternatives* (University Park: Pennsylvania State University Press, 1999); Katherine Verdery, *The Political Lives of Dead Bodies: Reburial and Postsocialist Change* (New York: Columbia University Press, 1999); Ivan Čolović, *Bordel ratnika: Foklor, politika i rat* (Belgrade: Čigoja štampa, 2000); and Perica, *Balkan Idols.*

32. This is, also, to maintain, renew, and reinscribe the interpellation of architecture by poststructuralism. To the extent that Derrida's investment in architecture, in

particular, was a reflection of the investment in his work on the part of various architects, the relationship between architecture and poststructuralism was circumscribed by an economy of exchange and a politics of recognition. I have thus eschewed an engagement with Derrida's writing on architecture "as such," of which there are several, in the interest of exploring another sort of relationship between architecture and theory.

33. Timothy Garton Ash, *The Magic Lantern* (New York: Random House, 1990), 21–22.

34. Key precedents for this reflection are Denis Hollier's *Against Architecture*, in which Bataille's theory of architecture as violence is deployed to deconstruct Hegel's architectural representation of history as the manifestation of freedom and Daniel Bertrand Monk's *An Aesthetic Occupation*, in which the architectural mediation of political claims in the Palestine conflict is theorized as a negative dialectic in which failed attempts to manifest history in architecture preserve the ideology of historical manifestation. See Denis Hollier, *Against Architecture: The Writings of George Bataille*, trans. Betsy Wing (Cambridge, MA: MIT Press, 1989); and Monk, *Aesthetic Occupation*.

35. The conception of history as a simple repression of alterity and difference characterizes some poststructuralist accounts. Derrida's notion of history is more complicated:

It has happened that I have spoken very quickly of (history as) a "metaphysical concept." But I have never believed that there were metaphysical concepts in and of themselves. No concept is, by itself, and consequently in and of itself, metaphysical, outside all the textual work in which it is inscribed. This explains why, although I have formulated many reservations about the "metaphysical" concept of history, I very often use the word "history" in order to reinscribe its force and in order to produce another concept or conceptual chain of "history": in effect, a "monumental, stratified, contradictory" history; a history that also implies a new logic of repetition and the trace.

See Jacques Derrida, *Positions*, trans. Alan Bass (Chicago: University of Chicago Press, 1981), 57.

36. Dominick LaCapra, *Writing History, Writing Trauma* (Baltimore: Johns Hopkins University Press, 2001), 41.

37. Ibid., 40.

CHAPTER I: A RELIC OF THE PAST, FAST DISAPPEARING

1. Stanoje Aksić, ed., *Kosovo i Methohija, 1943–1963* (Priština: Skupština Autonomne pokrajine Kosova i Metohije, 1963). The year 1963 was the twentieth anniversary of the Partisans' establishment of a provisional government of Yugoslavia in Jajce, Bosnia; the documentation of Kosovo's modernization between 1943 and 1963 thereby included the Second World War as part of modernization's initial phase.

2. Jacques Derrida, "Force and Signification," in *Writing and Difference*, trans. Alan Bass (Chicago: University of Chicago Press, 1978), 289.

3. Walter Benjamin, "The Paris of the Second Empire in Baudelaire," in *Charles Baudelaire: A Lyric Poet in the Era of High Capitalism*, trans. Harry Zohn (London: Verso, 1983), 86.

4. Benjamin, "Paris: Capital of the Nineteenth Century," in *Charles Baude-laire*, 174.

5. For Benjamin's apprehension of the workers' uprising as the source of social transformation, see Walter Benjamin, "Critique of Violence," in *Selected Writings, 1913–1926*, ed. Marcus Bullock and Michael Jennings (Cambridge, MA: Harvard University Press, 1996).

6. Benjamin, "Paris: Capital of the Nineteenth Century," 176.

7. Walter Benjamin, *Gesammelte Schriften*, vol. 5 (Frankfurt: Suhrkamp Verlag, 1978), 208, in Susan Buck-Morss, *The Dialectics of Seeing* (Cambridge, MA: MIT Press, 1989), 317.

8. Benjamin, "Paris: Capital of the Nineteenth Century," 174.

9. For a critical account of histories of modernization in Yugoslavia, see John B. Allcock, *Explaining Yugoslavia* (London: Hurst, 2000).

10. On the history of historic preservation in Kosovo, see Milan Ivanović, "Spomenici kulture Kosova i Metohije i problematika njihove zaštite i egzistencije," in *Problemi zaštite i egzistencije spomenika kulture i prirodnih objekata i rezervata na Kosovu i Metohiji*, ed. Milan Ivanović (Priština-Belgrade: Savetovanje konzervatora Jugoslavije, 1968). On the work of Kosovo's Institute for the Protection and Study of Cultural Monuments, see Ratomir Karakušević, "Rad Zavoda za zaštitu i proučavanje spomenika kulture AKMO od svog osnivanja do danas," in *Glasnik Muzeja Kosova i Metohije* 1 (1956).

11. See, for example, Esat Kamberi, *Etnokultorocidi në Kosovë* (Tetovo: Çabej, 1999).

12. In Julia Kristeva's formulation, the abjected object functions much like a supplement to the social order it is formulated in and expelled from: "The abject appears in order to uphold 'I' within the Other." See Julia Kristeva, *Powers of Horror: An Essay on Abjection* (New York: Columbia University Press, 1984).

13. In an urban planning report, the destruction of the bazaar is described as "the destruction [*rušenje*] of the 'covered market'"; see Municipal Archive of Prishtina, Prishtina urbanizm fonds, Bogoljub Jovanović, "Dosadašnja urbanistička aktivnost u Prištini" (1965).

14. Dijana Alić and Maryam Gusheh, "Reconciling National Narratives in Socialist Bosnia and Herzegovina: The Baščaršija Project, 1948–1953," *Journal of the Society of Architectural Historians* 58:1 (March 1999).

15. After World War II, both the Baščaršija and Prishtina's bazaar more or less retained a centuries-old street pattern and block structure, but were composed of buildings that had been rebuilt many times. In Prishtina, for example, parts of the bazaar were burned down twice in the nineteenth century, so that many of its buildings dated from that period.

16. On the morphology of Old Prishtina, see Flamur Doli, *Arkitektura tradicionale-popullore e Kosovës*, Prishtina: Flamur Doli, 2001.

17. On the Popular Fronts in early socialist Yugoslavia, see Ljubodrag Dimić, *Agitprop kultura: Agitpropovska faza kulturne politike u Srbiji, 1945–1952* (Belgrade: Rad, 1988); and Carol S. Lilly, *Power and Persuasion: Ideology and Rhetoric in Communist Yugoslavia, 1944–1953* (Boulder, CO: Westview Press, 2001).

18. Both *Rilindja* and *Jedinstvo* were published in 1947 in short editions of only a few pages; the destruction of Prishtina's bazaar may have also escaped reportage due to the newspapers' primary status as transmitters of national and provincial news. For a general report on the activities of the Popular Fronts in Kosovo in the three years after the war, see "Kontributi i organizatave te Frontit ne punen per plotesimin e detyravet te vitit te pare te planit," *Rilindja*, 8 January 1948, 4.

19. The coercive activities of the Popular Fronts are discussed by Dimić and Lilly.

20. Interviews with former Popular Front workers, Prishtina, October 2003 and February 2004.

21. Borislav Stojkov, "Odredni održivog urbanog razvoja Prištine," in *Obnova Prištine*, ed. Borislav Stojkov (Belgrade: Institut za arhitekturu i urbanizam Srbije, 1996), 10; Nikola Dobrović, "Perspektivni izgled gradskog centra" and "Detalj glavnog gradskog centra," Municipal Archive of Prishtina, Prishtina urbanizm fonds, Prishtina.

22. In Prague, Dobrović worked for Bohumíl Hübschmann and then Antonín Engel after he graduated from the Technical University; both of his employers had been students of Otto Wagner in Vienna. On the career of Dobrović, see Miloš R. Perović, "Stvaralaštvo Nikole Dobrovića: Misaone Pritoke," in *Nikola Dobrović: Eseji, projekti, kritike*, ed. Miloš R. Perović and Spasoje Krunić (Belgrade: Arhitektonski fakultet univerziteta u Beogradu and Muzej arhitekture, 1998).

23. Nikola Dobrović, *Urbanizam kroz vekove*, vol. 1, Jugoslavija (Belgrade: Naučna knjiga, 1950).

24. Ibid., unpaginated.

25. Nikola Dobrović, "Urbanistička razmatranja o čuvanju istorijskih spomenika," *Zbornik Zaštite Spomenika Kulture* 2:1 (1951), reprinted in *Urbanizam Beograda* 12:58 (1980): 126.

26. "Prishtina po shendrrohet ne nji qytet te madh modern," *Rilindja*, 24 August 1952, 5. A version of Dobrović's plan, from 1954, is published in *Obnova Prištine*, ed. Stojkov, 29.

27. These buildings and spaces were eventually realized, though not in the form envisioned in Dobrović's plan.

28. Ger Duijzings, *Religion and the Politics of Identity in Kosovo* (New York: Columbia University Press, 2000).

29. Benedict Anderson, *Imagined Communities: Reflections on the Origins and Spread of Nationalism* (London: Verso, 1983).

30. Esad Mekuli and Dragan Čukić, eds., *Prishtina* (Belgrade: Beogradski grafički zavod, 1965).

31. The description continues,

The industry in Prishtina and its surroundings until 1945 consisted of a small coal mine, a tiny thermoelectric power plant for meeting the minimum needs of the town, and three flour mills, while the land was cultivated extensively. Since the Liberation, big resources of lignite running to some 6.5 billion tons, have been discovered . . . very convenient for exploitation by means of the open pit method. The "Kosovo" mining power plant and chemical combined works has established two open pits with an annual capacity of 3.2 million tons of lignite and has constructed corresponding separation plants, the thermoelectric power plants "Kosovo I" and "Kosovo II," the lignite drying plant and semicoke producing plant. . . . Plants for the generation of industrial gas and nitrogen fertilizer are under construction. Two lead-zinc mines have been established . . .

See Mekuli and Čukić, *Prishtina*, unpaginated (English in original).

32. Ivan Vučković, ed., *Yugoslav Cities* (Belgrade: Turistička štampa, 1965).

33. Zoran Petrović, "Arhitektonsko-urbanističko nasleđe u gradovima Srbije," *Arhitektura Urbanizam* 8:48 (1967): 6.

34. Ibid.

35. Ibid.

36. Jacques Derrida, *Of Grammatology*, trans. Gayatri Chakravorty Spivak (Baltimore: Johns Hopkins University Press, 1997), 144.

CHAPTER 2: IT IS NOT ONLY VANDALISM

1. Slavko Bozić, "Paljevina konaka Pećke Patrijaršije," *Pravoslavlje*, 1 April 1981, 8.

2. The fire, usually preceded by the descriptor "mysterious," is often noted in passing in histories of the Kosovo conflict. The questions discussed here have been drawn from Atanasije Jevtić, *Stradanja Srba na Kosovu i Metohiji od 1941 do 1990* (Priština: Jedinstvo, 1990); and Milorad Tomanić, *Srpska crkva u ratu i ratovi u njoj* (Belgrade: Medijska knjižara krug, 2001).

3. The magazine cover played upon the traditional figure of the *vojvod* (guardian), an Albanian family entrusted with protecting an Orthodox church or monastery. The patriarchate, along with the other important Orthodox buildings in Kosovo, had such an guardian; the magazine alleged that this guardian did not return his *besa* (oath) to guard the site.

4. Derrida poses iterability as constitutive of the event: "The time and place of the *other time* (is) already at work, altering from the start the start itself, the *first time*, the at once"; see Jacques Derrida, *Limited Inc.*, trans. Jeffrey Mehlman and Samuel Weber (Chicago: Northwestern University Press, 1988), 200.

5. Svetislav Spasojević, "Odupiranje zaboravu," *NIN*, 6 March 1988, 29.

6. See Paul Shoup, *Communism and the Yugoslav National Question* (New York: Columbia University Press, 1968); Sabrina P. Ramet, *Nationalism and Federalism in Yugoslavia, 1962–1991* (Bloomington: Indiana University Press,

1992); Dejan Djokić, ed., *Yugoslavism: Histories of a Failed Idea* (London: Hurst, 2003).

7. On these demonstrations, see Mary Motes, *Kosova Kosovo: Prelude to War, 1966–1999* (Homestead, FL: Redlands Press, 1998), 101–10; and Miranda Vickers, *Between Serb and Albanian: A History of Kosovo* (New York: Columbia University Press, 1998), 167.

8. It is important to note here the equivocation between what seem like "political" demands (republican status for Kosovo) and "symbolic" demands (freedom to fly the Albanian flag and renaming the province). This equivocation shows that the capacity to symbolize was itself a focus of political action and that symbolic representation was at once political practice. No line can be drawn, then, between the putative "objective reality" of politics and the symbolization of this reality through other systems of representation. Of course this line, a key instrument of knowledge and power, is constantly drawn—but this drawing occludes the fact that, as in Kosovo, conflict and violence took place over both symbolic forms and the issues explicitly being symbolized. On the politics of symbolization, see Allen Feldman, *Formations of Violence: The Narrative of the Body and Political Terror in Northern Ireland* (Chicago: University of Chicago Press, 1991), 165–66.

9. Jevtić, *Stradanja Srba*, 43.

10. See, for example, the documents collected in Atanasije Jevtić, ed., *Zadužbine Kosova: Spomenici i znamenja srpskog naroda* (Prizren-Belgrade: Eparhija Raško-prizrenska, 1987), 798–817. With regard to vandalism, Church leaders reported that state authorities "refuse to seek out those responsible and instead demand that the church administration seek them out"; see Archive of the Serbian Orthodox Eparchy of Raško-Prizren, Peć, no. 7/1951; reprinted in *Zadužbine Kosova*, 804.

11. Vjekoslav Perica, *Balkan Idols: Religion and Nationalism in the Yugoslav States* (Oxford: Oxford University Press, 2002), 45.

12. A report on the Holy Council meeting was published in "Saopštenje o radu svetog arhijerejskog sabora," *Pravoslavlje*, 22 May 1969, 6.

13. The petition is quoted in Slobodan Reljić, "Šta je German pisao Titu," *NIN*, 21 September 1990, 64.

14. This letter is quoted in ibid., 64.

15. Perica, *Balkan Idols*, 45; Reljić, "Šta je German pisao Titu," 64.

16. Alex N. Dragnich and Slavko Todorovich, *The Saga of Kosovo: Focus on Serbian-Albanian Relations* (Boulder, CO: East European Monographs, 1984), 167.

17. Archive of the Eparchy of Raško-Prizren, no. 2731/1968; reprinted in Jevtić, *Stradanja Srba*, 44–45, and Jevtić, ed., *Zadužbine Kosova*, 817.

18. Archive of the Eparchy of Raško-Prizren, no. 204 (18 August 1972); reprinted in Jevtić, *Stradanja Srba*, 45–46.

19. Archive of the Eparchy of Raško-Prizren, no. 1670/1969; reprinted in Jevtić, ed., *Zadužbine Kosova*, 820.

20. Roland Barthes, "The Discourse of History," in *The Rustle of Language*, trans. Richard Howard (Berkeley: University of California Press, 1989, 137.

21. Indeed, Barthes himself would make the same argument after his post-structuralist turn; see, for example, Roland Barthes, *Le Neutre: Notes de cours au Collège de France, 1977–1978* (Paris: Éditions du Seuil, 2002).

22. See, for example, Zdravko Petrović, "Pola s plačem a pola s pevačem," *Pravoslavlje*, 27 February 1969, 5.

23. On the events of 1981, see Julie A. Mertus, *Kosovo: How Myths and Truths Started a War* (Berkeley: University of California Press, 1999), 17–93.

24. See Pedro Ramet, "The Yugoslav Press in Flux," in *Yugoslavia in the 1980s*, ed. Pedro Ramet (Boulder, CO: Westview Press, 1985); Sabrina P. Ramet, "The Role of the Press in Yugoslavia," in John B. Allcock et al., eds., *Yugoslavia in Transition: Choices and Constraints* (New York: St. Martin's Press, 1992).

25. Slavoljub Djukić, "Nije za štampu," *Politika*, 19 April 1981, 7.

26. Ramet, "Yugoslav Press in Flux," 116.

27. D.V., "Strategija posrednog nastupanja: Igra na nacionalističku kartu," *Narodna Armija*, 28 May 1981, 16.

28. "Political Platform for Action by the League of Communists of Yugoslavia in Regard to the Development of Socialist Self-Management, Brotherhood, Unity, and Community Spirit in Kosovo," *Yugoslav Survey* 23:1 (February 1982): 32.

29. *Rilindja*, 7 May 1981.

30. J. M., "Oskvrnuti nadgrobni spomenici," *Borba*, 1 December 1982, 4.

31. R. Kljajić, "Nije samo vandalizam," *Politika*, 11 July 1985.

32. Mirko Čupić and Nikola Sarić, "Nočne reprise iredente," *NIN*, 17 June 1984, 18.

33. On post-1981 public culture in Yugoslavia, see Pedro Ramet, "Apocalypse Culture and Social Change in Yugoslavia," in *Yugoslavia in the 1980s*, ed. Ramet; and Harold Lydall, *Yugoslavia in Crisis* (Oxford: Clarendon Press, 1989).

34. Svetislav Spasojević, *The Communists and I: The Serbian Patriarch German and the Communists* (Grayslake, IL: Free Serbian Orthodox Diocese of the United States of America and Canada, 1991), 90.

35. Jevtić, *Stradanja Srba*, 49. As accounts discussed in the following show, the fire was also narrated as destroying "the patriarchate" itself, as it still is in Church narratives and in some historical accounts.

36. Since 1974, the presidency of Yugoslavia was a committee, composed of the leaders of the Communist Party from each republic and the Serbian provinces of Kosovo and Vojvodina, chaired by Tito. Tito died in May 1980 and the committee continued, with one of its members annually elected chairman. On German's meeting with Kraigher, see "Srpska crkva traži zaštitu svetinja i vernih na Kosovu," *Pravoslavlje*, 15 July 1981, 1.

37. "Pobuna savesti u srpskoj pravoslavnoj crkvi," *Naša Reč* (June–July 1982): 15–16.

38. "Apel za zaštitu srpskog življa i njegovih svetinja na Kosovu," *Pravoslavlje,* 15 May 1982, 1–4; "An Appeal for the Protection of the Serbian Population and Their Sacred Monuments in Kosovo," *Diocesan Observer,* 30 June 1982, republished in *South Slav Journal* 5:3 (Autumn 1982): 49–54. The "Appeal" is discussed in Jasna Dragović-Soso, *Saviours of the Nation: Serbia's Intellectual Opposition and the Revival of Nationalism* (Montreal: McGill-Queen's University Press, 2002), 125–26; and Perica, *Balkan Idols,* 124.

39. "Appeal for the Protection of the Serbian Population," 49.

40. Ibid., 52.

41. Barthes, "Discourse of History," 128.

42. Ibid., 129.

43. "Appeal for the Protection of the Serbian Population," 52.

44. A genealogy of the term *ethnic cleansing* (*etničko čišćenje*) has yet to be written; however, the term *cleansing* was used in Yugoslavia during the Second World War in both Ustaša and Četnik contexts to describe the creation of monoethnic territories. See, for example, Dragoljub Todorović, "The Moljević Memorandum," *Bosnia Report* 47–48 (September–November 2005).

45. Wolfgang Höpken, "War, Memory, and Education in a Fragmented Society: The Case of Yugoslavia," *East European Politics and Society* 13:1 (Winter 1999).

46. Dragović-Soso, *Saviours of the Nation,* 100–114; Bette Denich, "Dismembering Yugoslavia: Nationalist Ideologies and the Symbolic Revival of Genocide," *American Ethnologist* 21:2 (May 1994); Robert Hayden, "Recounting the Dead: The Discovery and Redefinition of Wartime Massacres in Late- and Post-Communist Yugoslavia," in *Memory, History, and Opposition Under State Socialism,* ed. R. S. Watson (Santa Fe: School of American Research Press, 1994).

47. Thus, while some observers, commenting on the use of the term *ethnic cleansing* in the post-Yugoslav wars in Bosnia and Croatia, have criticized the term as a euphemism for the violence it described, in the early 1980s in Kosovo the term was mobilized to hyperbolize violence, not to minimize it.

48. "Napadi na srpske svetinje i pravoslavne vernike na Kosovu," *Glasnik Srpske Pravoslavne Crkve* (July 1982), and *Pravoslavlje,* 15 November 1982; republished in Jevtić, ed., *Zadužbine Kosova,* 833–35.

49. These photographs also began to circulate through popular media; see, for example, the photographs of vandalized graves illustrating articles on Serb migration from Kosovo, such as "Kuča na prodaju," *Ilustrovana Politika* (19 May 1981).

50. See Marko Živković, "Kosovo Is the Most Expensive Serbian Word: Political Enchantment and Milošević's Rise to Power," *Anthropology of East Europe Review* 19:1 (Spring 2001).

51. See Atanasije Jevtić, "Sa Kosova i oko Kosova," *Pravoslavlje,* 15 June 1982; reprinted in Atanasije Jevtić, *Od Kosova do Jadovna: Putni zapisi* (Belgrade: Glas crkve, 1987), 23.

52. Atanasije Jevtić, "Od Kosova do Jadovna," *Pravoslavlje*, 15 November 1983, 10 January 1984, 24 January 1984; reprinted in *Od Kosova do Jadovna.*

53. Radović, introduction to Jevtić, *Od Kosova do Jadovna*, 4.

54. Jevtić, *Stradanja Srba*, 11; emphasis in original.

55. Matija Bećković, "Kosovo Polje," in Jevtić, *Stradanja Srba*, 469.

56. Danko Popović, *Božuri i trnje: Monografija o Đelatovićima* (Belgrade: Inter Ju Press, 1995), 187.

57. For a genealogy of this refraction, see Tomislav Longinović, "The Perpetual Resurrection of the Past: The Kosovo Legacy and Serbian Nationalist Discourse," *Belgrade Circle* 3–4 (1996) and 1–2 (1997).

58. Rajko Đurđević, "Pale, siluju, tuku, kamenuju, ruše, lome, skrnave," *Duga* (17–30 September 1988).

59. The rededication is described in "Svečano osvećen konak u Pećkoj patriaršiji," *Pravoslavlje*, 1 November 1983.

60. *Rilindja*, 13 November 1983; see also Louis Zanga, "The Nationality Dilemma in Kosovo," *RAD Background Report* 279, 28 December 1983.

61. Tanjug press release, 19 September 1983.

62. This did not imply that the Church itself became a supporter of the Milošević regime; on Church-regime relations, see Radmila Radić, "The Church and the 'Serbian Question,'" in *The Road to War in Serbia: Trauma and Catharsis*, ed. Nebojša Popov (New York: Central University Press, 2000).

63. On the speeches of the Kosovar Serbs at meetings with the Federal Assembly in Belgrade in February 1986, see "Šta su Kosovci rekli u Skupštini," *NIN* (23 March 1986, 30 March 1986, 6 April 1986, 13 April 1986); on the meetings of Kosovar Serbs with Milošević and Kosovo officials in Kosovo Polje in April 1987, see "Šta je ko rekao u Kosovu Polju," *Borba*, 8, 9–10 (11 April 1987). See also Nebojša Vladisovljević, "Nationalism, Social Movement Theory, and the Grass Roots Movement of Kosovo Serbs, 1985–1988," *Europe-Asia Studies* 54:5 (2002).

64. "Peticija 2016 građana Kosova," *Književne Novine* (15 December 1985), republished in Jevtić, ed., *Zadužbine Kosova*, 840–41.

65. Dragović-Sosa points out that "it was the increasing assertiveness and mobilization of the Kosovo Serbs from 1983 onward and their search for support in Belgrade that pushed the intelligentsia into adopting a more active role in the 'defense of the people'"; see Dragović-Sosa, *Saviours of the Nation*, 135.

66. *Književne Novine* (15 December 1985); *NIN* (16 March 1986); "To the Assembly of the Socialist Federal Republic of Yugoslavia," *South Slav Journal* 9:1 (Spring–Summer 1986); and "Petition by Belgrade Intellectuals," in Branka Magaš, *The Destruction of Yugoslavia: Tracking the Break-Up, 1980–1992* (London: Verso, 1993), 49–50.

67. Zoran Avramović, *Drugo lice demokratije: Srbija, Jugoslavija, svet, 1980–1994* (Belgrade: Visnjić, 1998), 45.

68. "To the Assembly of the Socialist Federal Republic of Yugoslavia," *South Slav Journal*, 108.

69. Ibid.

70. On the memorandum, see Aleksander Pavković, "From Yugoslavism to Serbism: The Serb National Idea, 1986–1996," *Nations and Nationalism* 4:4 (1998); and Audrey Budding Helfant, "Systemic Crisis and National Mobilization: The Case of the 'Memorandum of the Serbian Academy,'" in *Cultures and Nations of Central and Eastern Europe: Essays in Honor of Roman Szporluk*, ed. Zvi Gitelman et al. (Cambridge, MA: Harvard Ukranian Research Institute, 2000).

71. Kosta Mihailović and Vasilije Krestić, *Memorandum of the Serbian Academy of Sciences and Arts: Answers to Criticisms* (Belgrade: Serbian Academy of Sciences and Arts, 1995).

72. On nationalism in Milošević's rise to authority, see Lenard J. Cohen, *Serpent in the Bosom: The Rise and Fall of Slobodan Milošević* (Boulder, CO: Westview Press, 2001); and Robert Thomas, *Serbia Under Milošević: Politics in the 1990s* (London: Hurst, 1999).

73. See Slobodan Milošević, *Godine raspleta* (Belgrade: Beogradksi izdavačko-grafički zavod, 1989).

74. "Kosovo is sacred Serbian ground"; "The field of Kosovo is our bleeding wound"; "The peonies in Kosovo are withering, mourning Serbs who had to move away"; "Kosovo is the soul of the Serbs, their unhealed wound, their blood and their prayer, their memory and their cradle." See Mile Nedeljković, "Kosovo i Metohija u svesti i na usnama naroda," in *Kosovo u pamćenju i stvaralastvu*, ed. Nenad Ljubinković (Belgrade: Raskovnik, 1989), 266–78.

75. See, for example, the analysis of the popular magazine *Duga*, in Snježana Milivojević, "The Nationalization of Everyday Life," in *Road to War in Serbia*, ed. Popov.

76. "Religious mythology cannot actualize itself. It needs to be instrumentalized. . . . The list of crimes that Serb religious nationalists had falsely claimed were being carried out against Serbs became a blueprint for Serb nationalist programs of ethnic cleansing: the Serb Orthodox nationalists who had alleged that Albanians were systematically destroying Serb heritage in Kosovo enacted precisely the same kind of program against others": see Michael Sells, "Crosses of Blood: Sacred Space, Religion, and Violence in Bosnia-Hercegovina," *Sociology of Religion* 64:3 (2003): 314.

77. On protests by Kosovar Albanians in 1988 and 1989, see Blerim Shala, *Kosovo: Krv i suze* (Ljubljana: ZAT, 1990); and Howard Clark, *Civil Resistance in Kosovo* (London: Pluto Press, 2000).

78. Momčilo Petrović, "Besa za grljavi rat," *Ilustrovana Politika* (4 April 1989).

79. Sami Repishti, "Human Rights and the Albanian Nationality," in *Human Rights in Yugoslavia*, ed. Oskar Gruenwald and Karen Rosenblum-Cale (New

York: Irvington, 1986); and Vladan A. Vasilijević, "Kosovo: Exercise and Protection of Human Rights," in *Conflict or Dialogue: Serbian-Albanian Relations and the Integration of the Balkans*, ed. Dušan Janjić and Shkelzen Maliqi (Subotica, Serbia: Open University Press, 1994).

80. Barthes, "Discourse of History," 138–39.

81. Ibid., 139.

82. Ibid., 140.

CHAPTER 3: WARCHITECTURE

Epigraph from Chris Bird, "How Spring Was Killed in Kosovo," *The Guardian*, 17 April 1999, www.guardian.co.uk/world/1999/apr/17/5 (accessed 23 October 2008).

1. Operation Allied Force press briefing, 14 May 1999, http://ftp.fas.org/irp/imint/990514–view.htm (accessed 17 August 2007).

2. Ibid.

3. See Rogers Brubaker, "Ethnic and Nationalist Violence," in *Ethnicity Without Groups* (Cambridge, MA: Harvard University Press, 2004).

4. With regard to violence in the former Yugoslavia, for a sophisticated version of the thesis of top-down manipulation, see V. P. Gagnon, Jr., *The Myth of Ethnic War: Serbia and Croatia in the 1990s* (Ithaca, NY: Cornell University Press, 2004); for sophisticated versions of the thesis of bottom-up mobilization, see Mart Bax, "Warlords, Priests, and the Politics of Ethnic Cleansing: A Case-Study from Rural Bosnia-Herzegovina," *Ethnic and Racial Studies* 23:1 (January 2000); and Mattijs van de Port, *Gypsies, Wars, and Other Instances of the Wild: Civilization and Its Discontents in a Serbian Town* (Amsterdam: Amsterdam University Press, 1998); and for the thesis of primordial antagonism, see Warren Zimmerman, *Origins of a Catastrophe: Yugoslavia and Its Destroyers* (New York: Random House, 1997).

5. Jacques Derrida, *Of Grammatology*, trans. Gayatri Chakravorty Spivak (Baltimore: Johns Hopkins University Press, 1997), 157.

6. Ibid., 163.

7. Jacques Derrida, "The Theatre of Cruelty and the Closure of Representation," in *Writing and Difference*, trans. Alan Bass (Chicago: University of Chicago Press, 1978), 237.

8. Asocijacija arhitekta DAS-SABIH, *Warchitecture: Urbicide Sarajevo* (Sarajevo: Asocijacija arhitekta DAS-SABIH, 1994).

9. International Crisis Group, *Kosovo's Long Hot Summer: Briefing on Military, Humanitarian, and Political Developments in Kosovo*, 2 September 1998, www.crisisgroup.org/home/index.cfm?id=1597&l=3 (accessed 8 September 2007).

10. Filipović interviewed members of Serb forces in Kosovo in 2000; see Miroslav Filipović, "Serb Officers Relive Killing," *Balkan Crisis Report* 130 (4 April 2000), http://iwpr.net/?p=bcr&s=f&o=247641&apc_state=henibcr2000 (accessed

15 August 2007). The publication of the preceding article occasioned Filipović's arrest; see Anthony Border, "The Filipović Story," *Balkan Crisis Report* 231, 30 March 2001, http://iwpr.net/?p=bcr&s=f&o=157955&apc_state=henibcr200103 (accessed 15 August 2007). Transcripts of some of Filipović's interviews, such as the ones I quote from here, were published online by Public Broadcasting Service (PBS), *War in Europe: NATO's 1999 War Against Serbia over Kosovo*, www.pbs.org/wgbh/pages/frontline/shows/kosovo/interviews/serbs.html (accessed 15 August 2007).

11. PBS, *War in Europe: NATO's 1999 War Against Serbia over Kosovo*.

12. The prosecutor of the tribunal against Slobodan Milošević et al., transcripts, case no. IT-02-54, 21 and 25 February 2002, www.ictytranscripts.org/trial transcripts/html/transe54/02-02-25-IT.html (accessed 8 August 2007).

13. This does not mean, however, that Morina's testimony was unmediated. Rather, it emerged in a stuttering series of overlapping, meandering, and at times discrepant observations. Morina's testimony was conditioned at once by the questions of the prosecutor, focused on ascertaining the identity of the Serb protagonists in his story, the better to situate them in a chain of command leading to Milošević, and the questions of Milošević himself, who, acting as his own defense attorney, focused on Morina's frequently imprecise or fluctuating recollection of dates and times on the days and times when his life and world became unrecognizable.

14. Postwar documentation revealed that the undamaged homes in Landovica belonged to Roma families in the village; see United Nations High Commission on Refugees, "Kosovo Emergency," United States Information Agency, 19 July 1999, www.ess.uwe.ac.uk/kosovo/Kosovo-Refugees93.htm (accessed 25 September 2007).

15. On Račak, see Human Rights Watch, *Report on the Massacre in Račak*, January 1999, www.hrw.org/campaigns/kosovo98/racak.shtml (accessed 14 October 2007).

16. As of 1993, there were 607 mosques in Kosovo, 528 congregational mosques (*xhamia*), of which 498 were in active use, and 79 smaller neighborhood mosques (*masxhid*), of which 70 were in active use. This and the following data are drawn from Andrew Herscher and Andras Riedlmayer, "The Destruction of Cultural Heritage in Kosovo, 1998–1999: A Postwar Survey," prosecution submission, *Prosecutor v. Slobodan Milošević*, case no. IT-02-54-T, International Criminal Tribunal for the Former Yugoslavia, 28 February 2002. See also Sabri Bajgora, ed., *Barbaria Serbe ndaj monumenteve Islame në Kosovë* (Prishtina: Dituria Islame, 2000).

17. Jacques Derrida, "Signature Event Context," in *Margins of Philosophy*, trans. Alan Bass (Chicago: University of Chicago Press, 1982), 322.

18. Physicians for Human Rights, *War Crimes in Kosovo: A Population-Based Assessment of Human Rights Violations Against Kosovar Albanians* (Boston: Physicians for Human Rights, 1999). The question posed to refugees in interviews was

"In the past year, while you were in Kosovo, did you see places of worship that had been destroyed?"

19. International Crisis Group, *Reality Demands: Documenting Violations of International Humanitarian Law in Kosovo 1999* (Brussels: International Crisis Group, 2000); and Human Rights Watch, *Under Orders: War Crimes in Kosovo*, 2001, www.hrw.org/reports/2001/kosovo/ (accessed 22 November 2007).

20. James Gow, for example, discusses the targeting of architecture in "ethnic cleansing" as aiming at the "complete destruction of property"; see *The Serbian Project and Its Adversaries: A Strategy of War Crimes* (London: Hurst, 2003), 118.

21. Florian Bieber, "Approaches to Political Violence and Terrorism in Former Yugoslavia," *Journal of Southern Europe and the Balkans* 5:1 (2003): 43.

22. During the counterinsurgency, Serb forces vandalized approximately sixty-nine mosques; burned ninety-three mosques; shelled nineteen mosques; set off explosions in forty-five mosques; and bulldozed the sites of five mosques.

23. The four Cyrillic *C*'s are an acronym of the sentence "Samo sloga Srbina spasava" (Only unity saves the Serbs). The cross was also used by Serbs in ethnically mixed areas in Bosnia and Croatia during the wars of the 1990s to identify their homes to Serb forces.

24. In one of Miroslav Filipović's interviews with a Yugoslav Army reservist active in Kosovo, the reservist mentioned that "we were all masked and protected, so that we couldn't be identified, in case anyone, for any reason, wanted to record something."

25. Some of the photographs, as well as the story of their collection, are published in Fred Abrahams, ed., *A Village Destroyed: May 14, 1999*, photographs by Gilles Peress (Berkeley: University of California Press, 2002).

26. In one testimonial, for example, an Albanian imprisoned in a police station reported that prisoners were forced to sing the traditional Serbian song "Ko to kaže Srbija je mala?" (Who Says That Serbia Is Small?) while being abused: see Human Rights Watch, *A Week of Terror in Drenica: Humanitarian Law Violations in Kosovo*, February 1999, www.hrw.org/reports/1999/kosovo/ (accessed 7 January 2008), 46–47. In the Milošević trial, a number of Albanian witnesses testified that they and other Albanian prisoners were forced to make the "three-fingered salute" while marching, shout Serbian nationalist slogans, or sing various Serbian nationalist songs.

27. See Physicians for Human Rights, *War Crimes in Kosovo*, as well as testimony at the International Criminal Tribunal for the Former Yugoslavia.

28. The prosecutor of the tribunal against Slobodan Milošević, et al., transcripts, case no. IT-02-54, 1 March 2002, www.ictytranscripts.org/trialtranscripts/html/transe54/02-03-01-CR.html (accessed 14 January 2008).

29. On the desexualization of violence, see Katherine M. Franke, "Putting Sex to Work," in *Left Legalism/Left Critique*, ed. Wendy Brown and Janet Halley (Durham, NC: Duke University Press, 2002).

CHAPTER 4: THE RIGHT PLACE

Epigraph from Operation Allied Force press briefing, 26 March 1999, www.nato
.int/kosovo/press/p9903262.htm (accessed 17 November 2007).

1. On "humanitarian war," see Susan Woodward, "Humanitarian War: A New
Consensus," *Disasters* 25:4 (December 2001); on "humane warfare," see Christopher
Coker, *Humane Warfare* (New York: Routledge, 2001); on "military humanism,"
see Ulrich Beck, *Cosmopolitan Vision* (London: Polity, 2005); on the "cosmopolitan state," see Jürgen Habermas, "Bestiality and Humanity: A War on the Border Between Law and Morality," www.theglobalsite.ac.uk/press/011habermas.htm
(accessed 3 December 2007).

2. As late as 1919, the U.S. secretary of war, Newton D. Baker, argued for a prohibition on aerial bombing on ethical grounds; on the development of aerial bombing, see Sven Lindqvist, *The History of Bombing* (New York: W. W. Norton, 2003).

3. Paul Virilio, *Strategy of Deception* (New York: Verso, 2000), 71.

4. Ibid., 53.

5. Bruce R. Nardulli et al., *Disjointed War: Military Operations in Kosovo* (Santa
Monica, CA: RAND, 2002), 27. In this quotation, as in others that follow, the
term *Yugoslav* is used for Serb forces, as Serbia was, along with Montenegro, still
nominally a part of Yugoslavia.

6. In the words of Jacques Rancière, aesthetics "is a delimitation of spaces and
times, of the visible and the invisible, of speech and noise, that simultaneously
determines the place and the stakes of politics as a form of experience"; see *The
Politics of Aesthetics*, trans. Gabriel Rockhill (London: Continuum, 2004), 13.

7. The application of aerial bombing to the large-scale and indiscriminate
destruction of civilian environments—"area bombing" or "strategic bombing"—
was an innovation of the British and U.S. air forces; on its development, see
Michael S. Sherry, *The Rise of American Air Power: The Creation of Armaged-
don* (New Haven, CT: Yale University Press, 1989); Hermann Knell, *To Destroy a
City: Strategic Bombing and Its Human Consequences in World War II* (New York:
Da Capo, 2003); and A. C. Grayling, *Among the Dead Cities: The History and
Moral Legacy of the WWII Bombing of Civilians in Germany and Japan* (New York:
Walker, 2006). On the American visual culture of World War II aerial bombing,
see George H. Roeder, Jr., *The Uncensored War: American Visual Experience During
World War Two* (New Haven, CT: Yale University Press, 1993).

8. See, for example, Douglas Kellner, *Media Spectacle and the Crisis of Democracy: Terrorism, War, and Election Battles* (New York: Palgrave, 2005).

9. See, for example, Piers Robinson, *The CNN Effect: The Myth of News, Foreign Policy, and Intervention* (New York: Routledge, 2002).

10. Walter Benjamin, "The Work of Art in the Age of Mechanical Reproduction," in *Illuminations*, trans. Harry Zohn (New York: Schocken, 1968).

11. The "Contact Group" consists of France, Germany, Italy, Russia, the United

Kingdom, and the United States; it was formed during the early 1990s in the context of negotiating diplomatic and military responses to the war in Bosnia-Herzegovina. On diplomacy in the Kosovo War, see Ivo H. Daalder and Michael E. O'Hanlon, *Winning Ugly: NATO's War to Save Kosovo* (Washington, DC: Brookings Institution, 2000).

12. NATO spokesman Jamie Shea, Operation Allied Force press briefing, 27 March 1999, NATO, www.nato.int/kosovo/press/p990327a.htm (accessed 11 December 2007).

13. General Wesley Clark, Operation Allied Force press briefing, 25 March 1999, NATO, www.nato.int/kosovo/press/p990325a.htm (accessed 12 December 2007).

14. Dennis M. Drew, *Basic Aerospace Doctrine of the United States*, vol. 1 (Washington, DC: United States Department of the Air Force, 1992), 11.

15. General Wesley Clark, United States Department of Defense special press briefing, "Kosovo Strike Assessment," 16 September 1999, NATO, www.nato.int/kosovo/press/ p990916a.htm (accessed 9 December 2007).

16. United States Department of Defense, *Kosovo/Operation Allied Force After Action Report*, 31 January 2000, www.defenselink.mil/pubs/kaar02072000.pdf/, 7–8 (accessed 9 December 2007).

17. Anthony Cordesman, *The Lessons and Non-Lessons of the Air and Missile War in Kosovo* (Washington, DC: Center for Strategic and International Studies, 1999); U.S. Department of Defense, *Kosovo/Operation Allied Force After Action Report*, 55–56; 60; 86–87.

18. U.S. Department of Defense, *Kosovo/Operation Allied Force After Action Report*, 8–9.

19. Colonel Konrad Freytag, Operation Allied Force press briefing, 23 April 1999, NATO, www.nato.int/kosovo/press/p990423a.htm (accessed 13 December 2007).

20. Ibid.

21. Ibid.

22. Amnesty International, *"Collateral Damage" or Unlawful Killings? Violations of the Laws of War by NATO During Operation Allied Force* (New York: Amnesty International, 2000), 41.

23. Ibid.; and Human Rights Watch, *Civilian Deaths in the NATO Air Campaign*, February 2000, www.hrw.org/reports/2000/nato/index.htm (accessed 11 December 2007). The most complete statement of the rules governing armed conflict is Protocol 1 to the Geneva Conventions of 1949; article 52 (2) of this protocol defines military objectives as "those objects which by their nature, purpose or use make an effective contribution to military action and whose total or partial destruction, capture or neutralization, in the circumstances ruling at the time, offers a definite military advantage." Human rights organizations contested the classification of the RTS building as a military target on the basis of this definition. This contestation was challenged by, among other factors, the fact that the

United States, the key actor in the Kosovo War, has never ratified Protocol 1 and by the fact that NATO, as an alliance, is not party to any convention on the rules of armed conflict.

24. Bryan Bender, "Tomahawk Achieves New Effects in Kosovo," *Jane's Defense Weekly*, 18 July 2000.

25. About eighty-five hundred or 34–37 percent of the twenty-three thousand to twenty-five thousand bombs and missiles launched by NATO were precision guided; see U.S. Department of Defense, *Kosovo / Operation Allied Force After Action Report*. NATO's "strict rules of engagement" were never either specified nor related to existing conventions on the rules of war and so remain impossible to evaluate, except insofar as their invocation testified to the adequacy, for NATO, of the nominal or performative existence of many of the war's "humanitarian" dimensions.

26. General Wesley Clark, Operation Allied Force press briefing, 25 March 1999.

27. That NATO officials knew before the attack that the interruption to state television broadcasting would be brief was testified to by General Clark, who stated that "we knew when we struck that there would be alternate means of getting out the Serb television. There's no single switch to turn off everything." See interview with General Wesley Clark, in *Moral Combat: NATO at War*, BBC2, 12 March 2000, transcript at http://news.bbc.co.uk/hi/english/static/events/panorama/transcripts/transcript_12_03_00.txt (accessed 19 December 2007).

28. Whether there was a causal relation between the NATO bombing and the course of the violence it was intended to stop was a much debated topic during the bombing campaign and has remained so afterward. Almost all positions agree, however, on the intensification of Serb violence against Kosovar Albanians during this campaign.

29. BBC2, *Moral Combat: NATO at War*.

30. On April 12, 1999, NATO bombed a civilian passenger train crossing a bridge in Grdelica, Serbia, killing at least twelve people; on May 1, 1999, NATO bombed a bus crossing a bridge in Lužane, Kosovo, killing at least forty people.

31. Colonel Konrad Freytag, Operation Allied Force press briefing, 2 May 1999, NATO, www.nato.int/kosovo/press/p990502a.htm (accessed 12 December 2007).

32. William Arkin, "Operation Allied Force: 'The Most Precise Application of Air Power in History,'" in *War over Kosovo: Politics and Strategy in a Global Age*, ed. Andrew J. Bacevich and Eliot A. Cohen (New York: Columbia University Press, 2001), 11.

33. Operation Allied Force press briefing, 30 March 1999, NATO, www.nato.int/kosovo/press/p990330a.htm (accessed 10 December 2007).

34. Judith Butler, "Contingent Foundations: Feminism and the Question of 'Postmodernism,'" in *Feminists Theorize the Political*, ed. Judith Butler and Joan Scott (New York: Routledge, 1992), 11.

35. United States Department of Defense press briefing, 2 June 1999, United States Department of Defense, www.defenselink.mil/transcripts/transcripts.aspx ?transcriptsid=470 (accessed 15 December 2007).

36. Clark, "Kosovo Strike Assessment," 16 September 1999.

37. Jacques Derrida, *Writing and Difference*, trans. Alan Bass (Chicago: University of Chicago Press, 1978), 91.

38. On Serb civilian casualties, see Human Rights Watch, *Civilian Deaths in the NATO Air Campaign*; for official government figures on Serb military casualties, see *Politika*, 11 June 1999, and "Dnevnik," *Ilustrovana Politika* (19 June 1999); and for an assessment of these figures, see Marija Vidić and Jasmina Lazić, "Srpska strana rata: mrtvi po potrebi," *Vreme* (8 September 2005).

39. Dubravka Ugrešić, *The Culture of Lies: Antipolitical Essays*, trans. Celia Hawkesworth (University Park: Pennsylvania State University Press, 1998), 153.

40. Udruženje ljubitelja Avalskog tornja, www.avalskitoranj.com (accessed 11 January 2008).

41. Dragan Klaic, "Letter from Amsterdam," Nettime, www.nettime.org/ Lists-Archives/nettime-l-9904/msg00074.html (accessed 12 January 2008).

42. Srdjan Jovanović Weiss, "NATO as Architectural Critic," *Cabinet* 1 (Winter 2000–2001). For a predestruction elegy to the building, see Vladimir Kulić, "Architectural Guide to the Ruins of Belgrade," 3 April 1999, Ctheory, www .ctheory.net/articles.aspx?id=210 (accessed 12 January 2008).

43. Weiss, "NATO as Architectural Critic," 88.

44. For narratives in the popular press, see, for example, "I mrtve bombarduju," *Ilustrovana Politika* (24 April 1999), 9; for the state narrative, see *NATO Crimes in Yugoslavia: Documentary Evidence*, vols. 1 and 2 (Belgrade: Savezno Ministarstvo za inostrane posleve, 1999).

CHAPTER 5: RECONSTRUCTION/REDESTRUCTION

1. Bill Clinton, "Remarks by the President to the Troops and Officers of U.S. Task Force Falcon, Including Troops of the 1st Infantry, 'The Big Red One,'" 23 November 1999, www.clintonpresidentialcenter.org/legacy/112399-speech-by -president-to-us-troops-in-kosovo.htm (accessed 10 February 2008).

2. René Girard, *Violence and the Sacred*, trans. Patrick Gregory (Baltimore: Johns Hopkins University Press, 1977), 149.

3. Veton Surroi, "Fashizmi ne Kosove, turpi i Shqiptareve" *Koha Ditore*, 25 August 1999, 1. This editorial was published in English translation as "Victims of the Victims," *New York Review of Books*, 7 October 1999.

4. Kosovapress press release, "Mendjet e robëruara në Kosovën e lirë," 2 October 1999.

5. Merxhan Avdyli, "Mendjet e robëruara në Kosovën e lirë," *Koha Ditore*, 4 October 1999, 11.

6. Girard, *Violence and the Sacred*, 26, 14.

7. Ibid., 49.

8. Ibid., 69.

9. Human Rights Watch, *Abuses Against Serbs and Roma in the New Kosovo*, August 1999, www.hrw.org/reports/1999/kosov2/#_1_15 (accessed 4 February 2008); and Organization for Security and Cooperation in Europe (OSCE) Mission in Kosovo, *Human Rights in Kosovo: As Seen, as Told*, vol. 2 (5 November 1999), www.osce .org/odihr/item_11_17755.html (accessed 4 February 2008).

10. On the authorship of postwar violence, see Human Rights Watch, *Under Orders: War Crimes in Kosovo*, 2001, www.hrw.org/reports/2001/kosovo, especially chapter 17; and OSCE Mission in Kosovo, *Human Rights in Kosovo*.

11. See Zoran Stefanović, ed., *Raspeto Kosovo*, 1–3 (Belgrade: Glas Kosova i Metohije, 1999, 2000, 2001).

12. Kosovapress press release, "Kisha Serbe ishte vënë tërësisht në shërbim të politikës së shfarosjes së shqiptarëve dhe të serbizimit të Kosovës," 28 July 1999.

13. Shkelzen Maliqi, "Mbi fajin kolektiv serb," *Zëri Ditor*, 17 July 1999, 7.

14. See, for example, Kosovapress press release, "Serb Priests Help Sneak Out Arkan's Men from Kosova," 6 July 1999. After 2001, many news reports focused on Dečani Monastery, after it was granted a large "protection zone" by the United Nations Interim Administration Mission in Kosovo (UNMIK); see Ibrahim Kelmendi, "Manastiri i Deçanit gjithmonë ka qenë çerdhe e fashizmit serb," *Koha Ditore*, 5 September 2001, 9; E. Ulaj, "Manastiri i Deçanit gjithmonë ka qënë çerdhe e formacioneve serbe që terrorizuan shqiptarët," *Zëri Ditor*, 5 September 2001, 10.

15. Naser Ferri, "Përpjekje për denigrim të shqiptarëve në sy të botës," *Zëri Ditor*, 12 March 2003, 19.

16. Mehmet Kraja, "Ujku, gomari dhe ëndrra," *Koha Ditore: Koha për Kulturë*, 15 February 2003, 1.

17. United Nations Interim Administration Mission in Kosovo (UNMIK), fact sheet, 2 July 1999, Albanian News and Information Network, http://listserv.acsu. buffalo.edu/cgi-bin/wa?A2=ind9907a&L=albanews&T=0&P=11104 (accessed 15 February 2008).

18. Kosovapress press release, "Albanians of Kosova, Serbs Seek to End Violence," 3 July 1999.

19. OSCE Mission in Kosovo, *Preliminary Assessment of the Situation of Ethnic Minorities in Kosovo*, 26 July 1999, OSCE, www.osce.org/item/1295.html (accessed 15 February 2008).

20. Human Rights Watch, *Under Orders: War Crimes in Kosovo*.

21. Bernard Kouchner, foreword to OSCE Mission in Kosovo, *Human Rights in Kosovo*.

22. KFOR press statement, 7 July 1999, www.nato.int/kosovo/press/jnt-grdn .htm (accessed 18 February 2008).

23. KFOR press statement, 12 July 1999, www.nato.int/kosovo/press/jnt-grdn .htm (accessed 13 February 2008).

24. United Nations Resolution 1244 (1999), annex 2, para. 6.

25. NATO, "Human Rights Violations in the Kosovo Area and KFOR Assistance for Humanitarian Causes," *NATO Handbook*, 2002, www.nato.int/docu/handbook/2001/hb050305.htm (accessed 18 February 2008).

26. Reuters press release, "Orthodox Church on Post-War Kosovo Firing Line," 13 June 2000, Albanian News and Information Network, http://listserv.buffalo.edu/cgi-bin/wa?A2=ind0006&L=twatch-l&D=1&O=D&F=P&P=39211 (accessed 16 February 2008).

27. Stefanović, ed., *Raspeto Kosovo*, 3rd ed., 16.

28. See, for example, ANSA press release, "KFOR: We Will Only Protect Historic Churches," 18 November 2002.

29. The following account is drawn from United Nations Interim Administration Mission in Kosovo (UNMIK), Ministry of Culture, Youth, and Sports, "Report on Two Serbian Orthodox Churches in Istog/k Municipality Damaged by Explosives" (19 November 2002), collection of author.

30. UNMIK press release, "SRSG Michael Steiner Flies to the Scene of Damaged Serbian Churches, Announced Quick Action" (17 November 2002), UNMIK, www.unmikonline.org/press/2002/pressr/pr868.htm (accessed 8 February 2008).

31. Serbian Orthodox Eparchy of Raško-Prizren Information Service, "Church Strongly Protests Because of KFOR Decision," 20 November 2002, www.kosovo.net/rep201102.html (accessed 8 February 2008).

32. Forum 18 News Service, "Kosovo: Further Attacks on Orthodox Sites," 30 June 2003, www.forum18.org/Archive.php?article_id=94&pdf=Y (accessed 16 November 2008).

33. These reports were circulated, in Serbian and English, by the Eparchy's news service at www.kosovo.net.

34. UNESCO, *Cultural Heritage in South-East Europe: Kosovo* (Venice: UNESCO Office in Venice, 2003), 8.

35. UNMIK, Ministry of Culture, Youth, and Sports, "UNESCO Mission Report: Comments of the Minister of Culture" (17 October 2003), collection of author.

36. UNMIK police spokesperson Dmitry Pryakhin, UNMIK press briefing, 16 December 2003, www.unmikonline.org/press/2003/trans/tr161203.pdf (accessed 12 February 2008).

37. Girard, *Violence and the Sacred*, 151.

38. See Amnesty International, *The March Violence: KFOR and UNMIK's Failure to Protect the Rights of the Minority Communities*, 8 July 2004, http://web.amnesty.org/library/print/ENGEUR700162004 (accessed 2 February 2008).

39. Renate Flottau et al., "Deutsche Soldaten: Die Hasen vom Amselfeld," *Der Spiegel* (3 May 2004).

40. Gazmend Syla, "Parlamentarët ndërpresin punën, akuzojnë ndërkomëtarët për dhunën në Kosovë," *Koha Ditore*, 18 March 2004, 2.

41. KTV news report, 17 March 2004, in OSCE Mission in Kosovo, *The Role of the Media in the March 2004 Events in Kosovo*, 2004, www.osce.org/documents/rfm/2004/04/2695_en.pdf (accessed 12 February 2008).

42. From a private conversation with the author, Prizren, June 2004. The Web site, www.besimi.com, was subsequently mirrored on the Web site of the Serbian Orthodox Eparchy of Raško-Prizren, at www.kosovo.net/www.besimi.com/prizreni/default.htm (accessed 4 December 2007).

43. Rrahman Rexhaj, "U shkatërrua një pjesë e trashëgimisë kombëtare," *Bota Sot*, 20 March 2004, 22.

44. Reshat Sahitaj, "Raporti i policisë së UNMIK-ut është i njëanshëm," *Epoka e Re*, 4 May 2004, 9.

45. Sh. Krasniqi, "Shqiptarët që duan të bëhen agjentë të Beogradit," *Epoka e Re*, 7 May 2004, 2.

46. UNMIK Press Office, "SRSG Holkeri Visits Sites Damaged by Recent Rioting," 22 March 2004, www.unmikonline.org/press/2004/pressr/pr1144.pdf (accessed 9 December 2007).

47. Branko B. Jokić, ed., *Martovski Pogrom* (*The March Pogrom*) (Belgrade: Ministry of Culture of the Republic of Serbia, Museum of Priština, 2004).

48. Rev. Sava (Janjić), foreword to *Raspeto Kosovo*, ed. Stefanović, 2nd ed., 6 (English in original).

49. Dr. Rexhep Boja, "The Serbian Genocide, Culturocide and Urbicide in Kosova," in *Barbaria Serbe ndaj Monumenteve Islame në Kosovë*, ed. Sabri Bajgora (Prishtina: Dituria Islame, 2000), 6.

50. Jacques Derrida, *Of Grammatology*, trans. Gayatri Chakravorty Spivak (Baltimore: Johns Hopkins University Press, 1997), 112.

Bibliography

REPORTS AND TRANSCRIPTS

Amnesty International. *The March Violence: KFOR and UNMIK's Failure to Protect the Rights of the Minority Communities.* 8 July 2004. http://web.amnesty .org/library/print/ENGEUR700162004 (accessed 2 February 2008).

———. *"Collateral Damage" or Unlawful Killings? Violations of the Laws of War by NATO During Operation Allied Force.* New York: Amnesty International, 2000.

BBC2. *Moral Combat: NATO at War.* 12 March 2000. http://news.bbc.co.uk/hi/ english/static/events/panorama/transcripts/transcript_12_03_00.txt (accessed 19 December 2007).

Clinton, Bill. "Remarks by the President to the Troops and Officers of U.S. Task Force Falcon, Including Troops of the 1st Infantry, 'The Big Red One.'" 23 November 1999. www.clintonpresidentialcenter.org/legacy/112399-speech-by -president -to-us-troops-in-kosovo.htm (accessed 10 February 2008).

Herscher, Andrew, and Andras Riedlmayer. "The Destruction of Cultural Heritage in Kosovo, 1998–1999: A Postwar Survey." Prosecution submission, *Prosecutor v. Slobodan Milošević,* case no. IT-02-54-T, International Criminal Tribunal for the Former Yugoslavia, 28 February 2002.

Human Rights Watch. *Abuses Against Serbs and Roma in the New Kosovo.* August 1999. www.hrw.org/reports/1999/kosov2/#_1_15 (accessed 4 February 2008).

———. *Civilian Deaths in the NATO Air Campaign.* February 2000. www.hrw .org/reports/2000/nato/index.htm (accessed 11 December 2007).

———. *Report on the Massacre in Račak.* January 1999. www.hrw.org/campaigns/ kosovo98/racak.shtml (accessed 14 October 2007).

———. *Under Orders: War Crimes in Kosovo.* 2001. www.hrw.org/reports/2001/ kosovo/ (accessed 22 November 2007).

———. *A Week of Terror in Drenica: Humanitarian Law Violations in Kosovo.* February 1999. www.hrw.org/reports/1999/kosovo/ (accessed 7 January 2008).

International Crisis Group. *Kosovo's Long Hot Summer: Briefing on Military, Humanitarian, and Political Developments in Kosovo.* 2 September 1998. www.crisis group.org/home/index.cfm?id=1597&l=3 (accessed 8 September 2007).

————. *Reality Demands: Documenting Violations of International Humanitarian Law in Kosovo 1999*. Brussels: International Crisis Group, 2000.

Jackson, Bruce, and Wladyslav Stepniak, "General Assessment of the Situation of Archives in Kosovo." UNESCO, 2000. www.unesco.org/webworld/publications /jackson_report.rtf (accessed 17 May 2007).

KFOR press statements. 11 June–31 December 1999. NATO. www.nato.int/jnt-grdn .htm (accessed 13 December 2007).

Klaic, Dragan. "Letter from Amsterdam." 4 April 1999. Nettime. www.nettime.org /Lists-Archives/nettime-l-9904/msg00074.html (accessed 12 January 2008).

NATO, "Human Rights Violations in the Kosovo Area and KFOR Assistance for Humanitarian Causes," *NATO Handbook*, 2002. www.nato.int/docu/handbook /2001/hb050305.htm (accessed 18 February 2008).

————. *Kosovo/Operation Allied Force After Action Report*. 31 January 2000. NATO. www.afsouth.nato.int/archives/transcripts/alliedforce.pdf (accessed 9 December 2007).

No Peace Without Justice. *Report on Serious Violations of International Humanitarian Law in Kosovo in 1998*. February 1999. www.ess.uwe.ac.uk/kosovo/Kosovo -Background12_Main.html (accessed 16 September 2007).

Operation Allied Force press briefings. 23 March–10 June 1999. NATO. www .nato.int/kosovo/all-frce.htm.

OSCE (Organization for Security and Cooperation in Europe) Mission in Kosovo. *Human Rights in Kosovo: As Seen, as Told*. Vol. 2. 5 November 1999. www .osce.org/odihr/item-11_17755.html (accessed 4 February 2008).

————. *Preliminary Assessment of the Situation of Ethnic Minorities in Kosovo*, 26 July 1999. www.osce.org/item/1295.html (accessed 15 February 2008).

————. *The Role of the Media in the March 2004 Events in Kosovo*. 2004. www .osce.org/documents/rfm/2004/04/2695_en.pdf (accessed 13 January 2008).

Prosecutor of the tribunal against Slobodan Milošević, et al. Transcripts, case no. IT-02-54. 21 and 25 February 2002. www.ictytranscripts.org/trialtranscripts/ html/transe54/02-02-21-IT.html and www.ictytranscripts.org/trialtranscripts/ html/transe54/02-02-25-IT.html (accessed 8 August 2007).

————. Transcripts, case no. IT-02-54. 1 March 2002. www.ictytranscripts.org/ trialtranscripts/html/transe54/02-03-01-ED.html (accessed 14 January 2008).

Public Broadcasting Service. "War in Europe: NATO's 1999 War Against Serbia over Kosovo." 1999. www.pbs.org/wgbh/pages/frontline/shows/kosovo/ (accessed 15 August 2007).

Udruženje ljubitelja Avalskog tornja. www.avalskitoranj.com (accessed 11 January 2008).

United Nations High Commission on Refugees. "Kosovo Emergency." United States Information Agency, 19 July 1999. www.ess.uwe.ac.uk/kosovo/Kosovo -Refugees93.htm (accessed 25 September 2007).

United Nations Interim Administration Mission in Kosovo (UNMIK). Fact sheet. 2 July 1999. Albanian News and Information Network. http://listserv.acsu .buffalo.edu/cgi-bin/wa?A2=ind9907a&L=albanews&T=0&P=11104 (accessed 15 February 2008).

United Nations Interim Administration Mission in Kosovo (UNMIK), Ministry of Culture, Youth, and Sports. "Report on Two Serbian Orthodox Churches in Istog/k Municipality Damaged by Explosives." 19 November 2002. Collection of author.

————. "UNESCO Mission Report: Comments of the Minister of Culture." 17 October 2003. Collection of author.

United States Department of Defense. Press briefing. 2 June 1999. United States Department of Defense. www.defenselink.mil/transcripts/transcript.aspx ?transcriptid=470 (accessed 2 December 2008).

————. Special press briefing. 20 September 1999. NATO. www.nato.int/kosovo/ press/p990916a.htm (accessed 9 December 2007).

NEWSPAPERS, PERIODICALS, AND PRESS AGENCIES

ANSA (Rome).
Arhitektura Urbanizam (Belgrade).
Borba (Belgrade).
Bota Sot (Prishtina).
Diocesan Observer (Grayslake, IL).
Duga (Belgrade).
Epoka e Re (Prishtina).
Forum 18 News Service (Oslo).
Glasnik Muzeja Kosova i Metohije (Prishtina).
Glasnik Srpske Pravoslavne Crkve (Belgrade).
The Guardian (London).
Ilustrovana Politika (Belgrade).
Književne Novine (Belgrade).
Književna Reč (Belgrade).
Koha Ditore (Prishtina).
Kosovapress (Prishtina).
Narodna Armija (Belgrade).
Naša Reč (Belgrade).
NIN (*Nedjelne Informativne Novine*) (Belgrade).
Politika (Belgrade).
Pravoslavlje (Belgrade).
RAD Background Report (Washington, DC).
Reuters (London).

Rilindja (Prishtina).
Serbian Orthodox Eparchy of Raško-Prizren Information Service (Peć).
Tanjug (Belgrade).
United Nations Interim Administration Mission in Kosovo Press Office
    (UNMIK) (Prishtina).
Urbanizam Beograda (Belgrade).
Vreme (Belgrade).
Yugoslav Survey (Belgrade).
Zëri Ditor (Prishtina).

BOOKS AND ARTICLES

"An Appeal for the Protection of the Serbian Population and their Sacred Monu-
    ments in Kosovo." *South Slav Journal* 5:3 (Autumn 1982).
Abrahams, Fred, ed. *A Village Destroyed: May 14, 1999.* Photographs by Gilles
    Peress. Berkeley: University of California Press, 2002.
Aksić, Stanoje, ed. *Kosovo i Methohija, 1943–1963* (Kosovo and Metohija, 1943–
    1963). Prishtina: Skupština Autonomne pokrajine Kosova i Metohije, 1963.
Alić, Dijana, and Maryam Gusheh. "Reconciling National Narratives in Social-
    ist Bosnia and Herzegovina: The Baščaršija Project, 1948–1953." *Journal of the
    Society of Architectural Historians* 58:1 (March 1999).
Allcock, John B. *Explaining Yugoslavia.* London: Hurst, 2000.
Allcock, John B., et al., eds. *Yugoslavia in Transition: Choices and Constraints.* New
    York: St. Martin's Press, 1992.
Anderson, Benedict. *Imagined Communities: Reflections on the Origins and Spread
    of Nationalism.* London: Verso, 1983.
Appaduraj, Arjun. "Dead Certainty: Ethnic Violence in the Era of Globalization."
    Public Culture 10:2 (Winter 1998).
———. *Fear of Small Numbers: An Essay on the Geography of Anger.* Durham, NC:
    Duke University Press, 2006.
Arkin, William. "Operation Allied Force: 'The Most Precise Application of Air Power
    in History.'" In *War over Kosovo: Politics and Strategy in a Global Age,* ed. Andrew
    J. Bacevich and Eliot A. Cohen. New York: Columbia University Press, 2001.
Asocijacija arhitekta DAS-SABIH. *Warchitecture: Urbicide Sarajevo.* Sarajevo:
    Asocijacija arhitekta DAS-SABIH, 1994.
Avramović, Zoran. *Drugo lice demokratije: Srbija, Jugoslavija, svet, 1980–1994* (The
    Other Face of Democracy: Serbia, Yugoslavia, the World, 1980–1994). Bel-
    grade: Visnjić, 1998.
Bajgora, Sabri, ed. *Barbaria Serbe ndaj monumenteve Islame në Kosovë* (Serbian
    Barbarities Against the Islamic Monuments of Kosovo). Prishtina: Dituria
    Islame, 2000.

Barthes, Roland. "The Discourse of History." In *The Rustle of Language*, trans. Richard Howard. Berkeley: University of California Press, 1989.

———. *Le Neutre: Notes de cours au Collège de France, 1977–1978*. Paris: Éditions du Seuil, 2002.

Bax, Mart. "Warlords, Priests, and the Politics of Ethnic Cleansing: A Case-Study from Rural Bosnia-Herzegovina." *Ethnic and Racial Studies* 23:1 (January 2000).

Beck, Ulrich. *Cosmopolitan Vision*. London: Polity, 2005.

Bećković, Matija. "Kosovo Polje" (Kosovo Field). In Atanasije Jevtić, *Stradanja Srba na Kosovu i Metohije of 1941 do 1990*. Priština: Jedinstvo, 1990.

Bender, Bryan. "Tomahawk Achieves New Effects in Kosovo." *Jane's Defense Weekly* (18 July 2000).

Benjamin, Walter. "Critique of Violence." In *Selected Writings, 1913–1926*, ed. Marcus Bullock and Michael Jennings. Cambridge, MA: Harvard University Press, 1996.

———. "Paris: Capital of the Nineteenth Century." In *Charles Baudelaire: A Lyric Poet in the Era of High Capitalism*, trans. Harry Zohn. London: Verso, 1983.

———. "The Paris of the Second Empire in Baudelaire." In *Charles Baudelaire: A Lyric Poet in the Era of High Capitalism*, trans. Harry Zohn. London: Verso, 1983.

———. "The Work of Art in the Age of Mechanical Reproduction." In *Illuminations*, trans. Harry Zohn. New York: Schocken, 1968.

Berman, Marshall. *All That Is Solid Melts into Air: The Experience of Modernity*. New York: Penguin Books, 1982.

Bevan, Robert. *The Destruction of Memory: Architecture at War*. London: Reaktion, 2006.

Bičanić, Rudolf. *Economic Policy of Socialist Yugoslavia*. Cambridge: Cambridge University Press, 1972.

Bieber, Florian. "Approaches to Political Violence and Terrorism in Former Yugoslavia." *Journal of Southern Europe and the Balkans* 5:1 (2003).

Border, Anthony. "The Filipović Story." *Balkan Crisis Report* 231. 30 March 2001. http://iwpr.net/?p=bcr&s=f&o=157955&apc_state=henibcr200103 (accessed 15 August 2007).

Boya, Dr. Rexhep. "The Serbian Genocide, Culturcide, and Urbicide in Kosovo." In *Barbaria Serb ndaj monumenteve Islame në Kosovë*, ed. Sabri Bajgora. Prishtina: Dituria Islame, 2000.

Bracewell, Wendy. "Rape in Kosovo: Masculinity and Serb Nationalism." *Nations and Nationalism* 6:4 (2000).

Brubaker, Rogers. *Ethnicity Without Groups*. Cambridge, MA: Harvard University Press, 2004.

Buck-Morss, Susan. *The Dialectics of Seeing*. Cambridge, MA: MIT Press, 1989.

Burton, Richard P., John W. Dyckman, and Jack C. Fisher. "Toward a System of Social Planning in Yugoslavia." *Papers in Regional Science* 18:1 (1967).

Butler, Judith. "Contingent Foundations: Feminism and the Question of 'Postmodernism.'" In *Feminists Theorize the Political*, ed. Judith Butler and Joan Scott. New York: Routledge, 1992.

Campbell, David. *National Deconstruction: Violence, Identity, and Justice in Bosnia*. Minneapolis: University of Minnesota Press, 1998.

Clark, Howard. *Civil Resistance in Kosovo*. London: Pluto Press, 2000.

Cohen, Lenard J. *Serpent in the Bosom: The Rise and Fall of Slobodan Milošević*. Boulder, CO: Westview Press, 2001.

Coker, Christopher. *Humane Warfare*. New York: Routledge, 2001.

Čolović, Ivan. *Bordel ratnika: Foklor, politika i rat* (The Warrior's Bordello: Folklore, Politics, and War). Belgrade: Čigoja štampa, 2000.

———. *The Politics of Symbols in Serbia: Essays in Political Anthropology*. London: Hurst, 2002.

———. "The Renewal of the Past: Time and Space in Contemporary Political Mythology." *Other Voices* 2:1 (February 2000).

Cordesman, Anthony. *The Lessons and Non-Lessons of the Air and Missile War in Kosovo*. Washington, DC: Center for Strategic and International Studies, 1999.

Daalder, Ivo H., and Michael E. O'Hanlon. *Winning Ugly: NATO's War to Save Kosovo*. Washington, DC: Brookings Institution, 2000.

Daniel, E. Valentine. *Charred Lullabies: Chapters in an Anthropography of Violence*. Princeton, NJ: Princeton University Press, 1996.

Denich, Bette. "Dismembering Yugoslavia: Nationalist Ideologies and the Symbolic Revival of Genocide." *American Ethnologist* 21:2 (May 1994).

Derrida, Jacques. *Archive Fever: A Freudian Impression*. Trans. Eric Prenowitz. Chicago: University of Chicago Press, 1998.

———. *Limited Inc.* Trans. Jeffrey Mehlman and Samuel Weber. Chicago: Northwestern University Press, 1988.

———. *Margins of Philosophy*. Trans. Alan Bass. Chicago: University of Chicago Press, 1982.

———. *Of Grammatology*. Trans. Gayatri Chakravorty Spivak. Baltimore: Johns Hopkins University Press, 1997.

———. *Positions*. Trans. Alan Bass. Chicago: University of Chicago Press, 1981.

———. "Sending: On Representation." Trans. Peter and Mary Ann Caws. *Social Research* 49:2 (Summer 1982).

———. *Spectres of Marx: The State of the Debt, the Work of Mourning, and the New International*. Trans. Peggy Kamuf. New York: Routledge, 1994.

———. *Writing and Difference*. Trans. Alan Bass. Chicago: University of Chicago Press, 1978.

Dimić, Ljubodrag. *Agitprop kultura: Agitpropovska faza kulturne politike u Srbiji, 1945–1952* (Agitprop Culture: The Agitprop Period of Cultural Politics in Serbia, 1945–1952). Belgrade: Rad, 1988.

Djokić, Dejan, ed. *Yugoslavism: Histories of a Failed Idea*. London: Hurst, 2003.

Djurić, Vojislav, ed. *Kosovski boj u srpskoj književnosti* (The Kosovo Battle in Serbian Literature). Belgrade: Sprska književna zadruga, 1990.

Dobrović, Nikola. "Urbanistička razmatranja o čuvanju istorijskih spomenika" (Urbanistic Considerations in the Preservation of Historic Monuments). *Zbornik Zaštite Spomenika Kulture* 2:1 (1951). Reprinted in *Urbanizam Beograda* 12:58 (1980): 126.

———. *Urbanizam kroz vekove*, vol. 1: Jugoslavija (Urbanism Through the Centuries, vol. 1: Yugoslavia). Belgrade: Naučna knjiga, 1950.

Doli, Flamur. *Arkitektura tradicionale-popullore e Kosovës* (Traditional-Popular Architecture of Kosovo). Prishtina: Flamur Doli, 2001.

Dragnich, Alex N., and Slavko Todorovich. *The Saga of Kosovo: Focus on Serbian-Albanian Relations*. Boulder, CO: East European Monographs, 1984.

Dragović-Soso, Jasna. *Saviours of the Nation: Serbia's Intellectual Opposition and the Revival of Nationalism*. Montreal: McGill-Queen's University Press, 2002.

Drançolli, Fejaz, ed. *Monumentet e Kosovës, 1998–1999* (Monuments of Kosovo, 1998–1999). Prishtina: Institut i Mbrojtjes së Monumenteve të Kosovës, 1999.

———, ed. *Kulla Shqiptare, 1979–1999* (The Albanian Kulla, 1979–1999). Prishtina: Institut i Mbrojtjes së Monumenteve të Kosovës, 1999.

Drew, Dennis M. *Basic Aerospace Doctrine of the United States*. Vol. 1. Washington, DC: United States Department of the Air Force, 1992.

Duijzings, Ger. *Religion and the Politics of Identity in Kosovo*. New York: Columbia University Press, 2000.

Egana, Miguel, ed. *Du vandalisme: Art et destruction*. Brussels: La lettre volée, 2005.

Feldman, Allen. *Formations of Violence: The Narrative of the Body and Political Terror in Northern Ireland*. Chicago: University of Chicago Press, 1991.

Filipović, Miroslav. "Serb Officers Relive Killing." *Balkan Crisis Report* 130. 4 April 2000. http://iwpr.net/?p=bcr&s=f&o=247641&apc_state=henibcr2000 (accessed 15 August 2007).

Fisher, Jack C. "Urban and Regional Planning." In *Yugoslavia: Proceedings of a Conference on Yugoslavia's Social, Economic, and Urban Planning Policies*, ed. George M. Raymond. New York: Pratt Institute, 1972.

Flottau, Renate, et al. "Deutsche Soldaten: Die Hasen vom Amselfeld." *Der Spiegel* (3 May 2004).

Franke, Katherine M. "Putting Sex to Work." In *Left Legalism/Left Critique*, ed. Wendy Brown and Janet Halley. Durham, NC: Duke University Press, 2002.

Gagnon, V. P., Jr. *The Myth of Ethnic War: Serbia and Croatia in the 1990s*. Ithaca, NY: Cornell University Press, 2004.

Gamboni, Dario. *The Destruction of Art: Iconoclasm and Vandalism Since the French Revolution*. New Haven, CT: Yale University Press, 1997.

Garton Ash, Timothy. *The Magic Lantern*. New York: Random House, 1990.

Gasché, Rodolphe. *The Tain of the Mirror: Derrida and the Philosophy of Reflection*. Cambridge, MA: Harvard University Press, 1996.

Girard, René. *Violence and the Sacred*. Trans. Patrick Gregory. Baltimore: Johns Hopkins University Press, 1977.

Gordy, Eric. *The Culture of Power in Serbia: Nationalism and the Destruction of Alternatives*. University Park: Pennsylvania State University Press, 1999.

Gow, James. *The Serbian Project and Its Adversaries: A Strategy of War Crimes*. London: Hurst, 2003.

Graham, Stephen, ed. *Cities, War, and Terrorism: Towards an Urban Geopolitics*. Oxford: Blackwell, 2004.

Grayling, A. C. *Among the Dead Cities: The History and Moral Legacy of the WWII Bombing of Civilians in Germany and Japan*. New York: Walker, 2006.

Guha, Ranajit. "The Prose of Counter-Insurgency." In *Selected Subaltern Studies*, ed. Ranajit Guha and Gayatri Chakravorty Spivak. New York: Oxford University Press, 1988.

Habermas, Jürgen. "Bestiality and Humanity: A War on the Border Between Law and Morality." www.theglobalsite.ac.uk/press/011habermas.htm (accessed 3 December 2007).

———. *The Theory of Communicative Action*. London: Beacon Press, 1981.

Hanssen, Beatrice. *Critique of Violence: Between Poststructuralism and Critical Theory*. London: Routledge, 2000.

Hayden, Robert. "Intolerant Sovereignties and 'Multi-Multi' Protectorates: Competition over Religious Sites and (In)tolerance in the Balkans." In *Postsocialism: Ideals, Ideologies, and Practices in Eurasia*, ed. C. M. Hann. Routledge: London, 2002.

———. "Recounting the Dead: The Discovery and Redefinition of Wartime Massacres in Late- and Post-Communist Yugoslavia." In *Memory, History, and Opposition Under State Socialism*, ed. R. S. Watson. Santa Fe: School of American Research Press, 1994.

Hays, K. Michael. "Introduction." In *Architectural Theory Since 1968*, ed. K. Michael Hays. Cambridge, MA: MIT Press, 2000.

Helfant, Audrey Budding. "Systemic Crisis and National Mobilization: The Case of the 'Memorandum of the Serbian Academy.'" In *Cultures and Na-*

tions of Central and Eastern Europe: Essays in Honor of Roman Szporluk, ed. Zvi Gitelman et al. Cambridge, MA: Harvard Ukranian Research Institute, 2000.

Herscher, Andrew. "Warchitectural Theory." *Journal of Architectural Education* 62:1 (February 2008).

Hollier, Denis. *Against Architecture: The Writings of George Bataille.* Trans. Betsy Wing. Cambridge, MA: MIT Press, 1989.

Höpken, Wolfgang. "War, Memory, and Education in a Fragmented Society: The Case of Yugoslavia." *East European Politics and Society* 13:1 (Winter 1999).

Horvat, Branko. *The Yugoslav Economic System.* White Plains, NY: M. E. Sharpe, 1976.

Howlett, Jana, and Rod Mengham, eds. *The Violent Muse: Violence and the Artistic Imagination in Europe, 1910–1939.* Manchester, England: Manchester University Press, 1994.

Huyssen, Andreas. *Present Pasts: Urban Palimpsests and the Politics of Memory.* Stanford, CA: Stanford University Press, 2003.

———. *After the Great Divide: Modernism, Mass Culture and Postmodernism.* London: Macmillian, 1988.

Ivanović, Milan. "Spomenici kulture Kosova i Metohije i problematika njihove zaštite i egzistencije" (Cultural Monuments of Kosovo and Metohija and the Problematic of Their Protection and Existence). In *Problemi zaštite i egzistencije spomenika kulture i prirodnih objekata i rezervata na Kosovu i Metohiji*, ed. Milan Ivanović. Priština-Belgrade: Savetovanje konzervatora Jugoslavije, 1968.

Jevtić, Atanasije. *Od Kosova do Jadovna: Putni zapisi* (From Kosovo to Jadovno: Travel Notes). Belgrade: Glas crkve, 1987.

———. *Stradanja Srba na Kosovu i Metohiji od 1941 do 1990* (The Sufferings of Serbs in Kosovo and Metohija from 1941 to 1990). Pristettina: Jedinstvo, 1990.

———, ed. *Zadužbine Kosova: Spomenici i znamenja srpskog naroda* (Endowments of Kosovo: Monuments and Symbols of the Serb Nation). Prizren-Belgrade: Eparhija Raško-prizrenska, 1987.

Jokić, Branko B., ed. *Martovski Pogrom* (The March Pogrom). Belgrade: Ministry of Culture of the Republic of Serbia, Museum of Priština, 2004.

Kamberi, Esat. *Etnokultorocidi në Kosovë* (Ethnoculturcide in Kosovo). Tetovo: Çabej, 1999.

Karakušević, Ratomir. "Rad Zavoda za zaštitu i proučavanje spomenika kulture AKMO od svog osnivanja do danas" (The Work of the Institute for the Protection and Study of Cultural Monuments AKMO from Its Founding to Today). *Glasnik Muzeja Kosova i Metohije* 1 (1956).

Kellner, Douglas. *Media Spectacle and the Crisis of Democracy: Terrorism, War, and Election Battles.* New York: Palgrave, 2005.

Kiel, Machiel. *Studies on the Ottoman Architecture of the Balkans.* Aldershot, England: Variorum, 1990.

Knell, Hermann. *To Destroy a City: Strategic Bombing and Its Human Consequences in World War II.* New York: Da Capo, 2003.

Kojadinović, Dragan. "The Fate of Cultural Heritage in Kosovo and Metohija." In *Martovski Pogrom* (The March Pogrom). Belgrade: Ministry of Culture of the Republic of Serbia, Museum of Priština, 2004.

Koshar, Rudy. *From Monuments to Traces: The Artifacts of German Memory.* Berkeley: University of California Press, 2000.

Kristeva, Julia. *Powers of Horror: An Essay on Abjection.* New York: Columbia University Press, 1984.

Krstić, Djordje. *Kolonizacija u južnoj Srbiji* (Colonization in Southern Serbia). Sarajevo: Štamparija bosanska pošta, 1928.

Kulić, Vladimir. "Architectural Guide to the Ruins of Belgrade." Ctheory. www.ctheory.net/articles.aspx?id=210 (accessed 12 January 2008).

LaCapra, Dominick. *Writing History, Writing Trauma.* Baltimore: Johns Hopkins University Press, 2001.

Lang, Nicholas R. "The Dialectics of Decentralization: Economic Reform and Regional Inequality in Yugoslavia." *World Politics* 27:3 (1975).

The Law on the Five-Year Plan for the Development of the National Economy of the Federative People's Republic of Yugoslavia in the Period from 1947–1951. Belgrade: Office of Information, 1947.

Lefebvre, Henri. *The Production of Space.* Trans. Donald Nicholson-Smith. Oxford: Blackwell, 1990.

Lilly, Carol S. *Power and Persuasion: Ideology and Rhetoric in Communist Yugoslavia, 1944–1953.* Boulder, CO: Westview Press, 2001.

Lindqvist, Sven. *The History of Bombing.* New York: W. W. Norton, 2003.

Longinović, Tomislav. "The Perpetual Resurrection of the Past: The Kosovo Legacy and Serbian Nationalist Discourse." *Belgrade Circle,* 3–4 (1996) and 1–2 (1997).

Lydall, Harold. *Yugoslavia in Crisis.* Oxford: Clarendon Press, 1989.

Magaš, Branka. *The Destruction of Yugoslavia: Tracking the Break-Up, 1980–1992.* London: Verso, 1993.

Malcolm, Noel. *Kosovo: A Short History.* New York: New York University Press, 1999.

Malkki, Liisa. *Purity and Exile: Violence, Memory, and National Cosmology Among Hutu Refugees in Tanzania.* Chicago: University of Chicago Press, 1995.

Mekuli, Esad, and Dragan Čukić, eds. *Prishtina.* Belgrade: Beogradski grafički zavod, 1965.

Mertus, Julie A. *Kosovo: How Myths and Truths Started a War.* Berkeley: University of California Press, 1999.

Mihailović, Kosta, and Vasilije Krestić. *Memorandum of the Serbian Academy of*

Sciences and Arts: Answers to Criticisms. Belgrade: Serbian Academy of Sciences and Arts, 1995.

Milivojević, Snježana. "The Nationalization of Everyday Life." In *The Road to War in Serbia: Trauma and Catharsis,* ed. Nebojša Popov. New York: Central University Press, 2000.

Milošević, Slobodan. *Godine raspleta* (The Years of Solution). Belgrade: Beogradski izdavačko-grafički zavod, 1989.

Monk, Daniel Bertrand. *An Aesthetic Occupation: The Immediacy of Architecture and the Palestine Conflict.* Durham, NC: Duke University Press, 2002.

Moore, J. H., Fred Singleton, and B. Carter. *The Economy of Yugoslavia.* London: Croom Helm, 1982.

Motes, Mary. *Kosova Kosovo: Prelude to War, 1966–1999.* Homestead, FL: Redlands Press, 1998.

Mueller, John. "The Banality of 'Ethnic War.'" *International Security* 25:11 (Summer 2000).

Nardulli, Bruce R., et al. *Disjointed War: Military Operations in Kosovo.* Santa Monica, CA: RAND, 2002.

NATO Crimes in Yugoslavia: Documentary Evidence. Vols. 1–2. Belgrade: Savezno Ministarstvo za inostrane posleve, 1999.

Nedeljković, Mile. "Kosovo i Metohija u svesti i na usnama naroda" (Kosovo and Metohija in Consciousness and on the Lips of the Nation). In *Kosovo u pamćenju i stvaralaštvu,* ed. Nenad Ljubinković. Belgrade: Raskovnik, 1989.

Nora, Pierre. *Realms of Memory: Rethinking the French Past.* Trans. Arthur Goldhammer. New York: Columbia University Press, 1996.

Norton, Anne. *Reflections on Political Identity.* Baltimore: Johns Hopkins University Press, 1988.

Palairet, Michael. "Ramiz Sadiku: A Case Study in the Industrialization of Kosovo." *Soviet Studies* 44:5 (1992).

Pandey, Gyanendra. *Routine Violence: Nations, Histories, Fragments.* Stanford, CA: Stanford University Press, 2006.

Pavković, Aleksander. "From Yugoslavism to Serbism: The Serb National Idea, 1986–1996." *Nations and Nationalism* 4:4 (1998).

Perica, Vjekoslav. *Balkan Idols: Religion and Nationalism in the Yugoslav States.* Oxford: Oxford University Press, 2002.

Perović, Miloš R. "Stvaralaštvo Nikole Dobrovića: Misaone pritoke" (The Creativity of Nikola Dobrović: Thoughtful Tributaries). In *Nikola Dobrović: Eseji, projekti, kritike,* ed. Miloš R. Perović and Spasoje Krunić. Belgrade: Arhitektonski fakultet univerziteta u Beogradu and Muzej arhitekture, 1998.

Pesić, Vesna. "O krivičnom delu silovanja: Uporedna analiza sa SFRJ, užu Srbiju, Kosovo i Vojvodinu" (On the Criminal Action of Rape: A Comparative Analysis

From SFRJ, Central Serbia, Kosovo and Metohija). In *Kosovski čvor: Dresiti ili seči*, ed. Srdja Popović et al. Belgrade: Chronos, 1990.

Petrović, Ruža, and Marina Blagojević. *Seobe Srba i Crnogorca sa Kosova i iz Metohije* (The Migration of Serbs and Montenegrins from Kosovo and Metohija). Belgrade: Srpska akademija nauka i umetnosti, 1989.

Petrović, Zoran. "Arhitektonsko-urbanističko nasleđe u gradovima Srbije" (Architectural-Urbanistic Heritage in the Cities of Serbia). *Arhitektura Urbanizam* 8:48 (1967).

Petković Dis, Vladislav. "Spomenik" (Monument). In *Kosovski boj u srpskoj književnosti*, ed. Vojislav Djurić. Belgrade: Srpska književna zadruga, 1990.

Physicians for Human Rights. *War Crimes in Kosovo: A Population-Based Assessment of Human Rights Violations Against Kosovar Albanians*. Boston: Physicians for Human Rights, 1999.

Pleština, Dijana. "From 'Democratic Centralism' to Decentralized Democracy? Trials and Tribulations of Yugoslavia's Development." In *Yugoslavia in Transition: Choices and Constraints*, ed. John B. Allcock, John J. Horton, and Marko Milivojević. New York: Berg, 1992.

Popović, Danko. *Božuri i trnje: Monografija o Đelatovićima* (Peonies and Thorns: A Monograph About the Đelatovići). Belgrade: Inter Ju Press, 1995.

Radić, Radmila. "The Church and the 'Serbian Question.'" In *The Road to War in Serbia: Trauma and Catharsis*, ed. Nebojša Popov. New York: Central University Press, 2000.

Ramet, Pedro. "Apocalypse Culture and Social Change in Yugoslavia." In *Yugoslavia in the 1980s*, ed. Pedro Ramet. Boulder, CO: Westview Press, 1985.

———. "The Yugoslav Press in Flux." In *Yugoslavia in the 1980s*, ed. Pedro Ramet. Boulder, CO: Westview Press, 1985.

Ramet, Sabrina P. *Balkan Babel: The Disintegration of Yugoslavia from the Death of Tito to the War for Kosovo*. Boulder, CO: Westview Press, 1999.

———. *Nationalism and Federalism in Yugoslavia, 1962–1991*. Bloomington: Indiana University Press, 1992.

———. "Who's to Blame, and for What? Rival Accounts of the War." In *Thinking About Yugoslavia: Scholarly Debates About the Yugoslav Breakup and the Wars in Bosnia and Kosovo*, ed. Sabrina P. Ramet. Cambridge: Cambridge University Press, 2005.

Rancière, Jacques. *The Politics of Aesthetics*. Trans. Gabriel Rockhill. London: Continuum, 2004.

Repishti, Sami. "Human Rights and the Albanian Nationality." In *Human Rights in Yugoslavia*, ed. Oskar Gruenwald and Karen Rosenblum-Cale. New York: Irvington, 1986.

Robinson, Piers. *The CNN Effect: The Myth of News, Foreign Policy, and Intervention.* New York: Routledge, 2002.

Roeder, George H., Jr. *The Uncensored War: American Visual Experience During World War Two.* New Haven, CT: Yale University Press, 1993.

Roux, Michel. *Les Albanais en Yougoslavie: Minorité nationale territoire et développement.* Paris: Éditions de la Maison des sciences de l'homme, 1992.

Rusinow, Dennison. *The Yugoslav Experiment, 1948–1974.* Berkeley: University of California Press, 1977.

Sells, Michael. "Crosses of Blood: Sacred Space, Religion, and Violence in Bosnia-Hercegovina." *Sociology of Religion* 64:3 (2003).

Shala, Blerim. *Kosovo: Krv i suze* (Kosovo: Blood and Tears). Ljubljana: ZAT, 1990.

Sherry, Michael S. *The Rise of American Air Power: The Creation of Armageddon.* New Haven, CT: Yale University Press, 1989.

Shoup, Paul. *Communism and the Yugoslav National Question.* New York: Columbia University Press, 1968.

Smith, Anthony D. *Myths and Memories of the Nation.* Oxford: Oxford University Press, 1999.

Spasojević, Svetislav. *The Communists and I: The Serbian Patriarch German and the Communists.* Grayslake, IL: Free Serbian Orthodox Diocese of the United States of America and Canada, 1991.

Stefanović, Zoran, ed. *Raspeto Kosovo* (Crucified Kosovo). Eds. 1–3. Belgrade: Glas Kosova i Metohije, 1999, 2000, 2001.

Stojadinović, Miloslav. *Kosovska trilogija* (Kosovo Trilogy). Belgrade: Srboštampa, 1970.

Stojkov, Borislav. "Odrednice održivog urbanog razvoja Prištine" (Determinants of Sustainable Urban Development in Priština). In *Obnova Prištine,* ed. Borislav Stojkov. Belgrade: Institut za arhitekturu i urbanizam Srbije, 1996.

Surroi, Veton. "Victims of the Victims." *New York Review of Books,* 7 October 1999.

Thomas, Robert. *Serbia Under Milošević: Politics in the 1990s.* London: Hurst, 1999.

"To the Assembly of the Socialist Federal Republic of Yugoslavia." *South Slav Journal* 9:1 (Spring–Summer 1986).

Todorović, Dragoljub. "The Moljević Memorandum." *Bosnia Report* 47–48 (September–November 2005).

Tomanić, Milorad. *Srpska crkva u ratu i ratovi u njoj* (The Serbian Church in War and the Wars in It). Belgrade: Medijska knjižara krug, 2001.

Toufic, Jalal. *Over-Sensitivity.* Los Angeles: Sun and Moon Press, 1996.

Ugrešić, Dubravka. *The Culture of Lies: Antipolitical Essays.* Trans. Celia Hawkesworth. University Park: Pennsylvania State University Press, 1998.

UNESCO. *Cultural Heritage in South-East Europe: Kosovo.* Venice: UNESCO Office in Venice, 2003.

van de Port, Mattijs. *Gypsies, Wars, and Other Instances of the Wild: Civilization and Its Discontents in a Serbian Town*. Amsterdam: Amsterdam University Press, 1998.

Vasilijević, Vladan A. "Kosovo: Exercise and Protection of Human Rights." In *Conflict or Dialogue: Serbian-Albanian Relations and the Integration of the Balkans*, ed. Dušan Janjić and Shkelzen Maliqi. Subotica, Serbia: Open University Press, 1994.

Verdery, Katherine. *The Political Lives of Dead Bodies: Reburial and Postsocialist Change*. New York: Columbia University Press, 1999.

Vickers, Miranda. *Between Serb and Albanian: A History of Kosovo*. New York: Columbia University Press, 1998.

Virilio, Paul. *Speed and Politics: An Essay on Dromology*. Trans. Mark Polizzotti. New York: Semiotext(e), 1986.

―――. *Strategy of Deception*. New York: Verso, 2000.

Vladisovljević, Nebojsa. "Nationalism, Social Movement Theory, and the Grass Roots Movement of Kosovo Serbs, 1985–1988." *Europe-Asia Studies* 54:5 (2002).

Vučković, Ivan, ed. *Yugoslav Cities*. Belgrade: Turistička štampa, 1965.

Wachtel, Andrew Baruch. *Making a Nation, Breaking a Nation: Literature and Cultural Politics in Yugoslavia*. Stanford, CA: Stanford University Press, 1998.

Weiss, Srdjan Jovanović. "NATO as Architectural Critic." *Cabinet* 1 (Winter 2000–2001).

Weizman, Eyal. *Hollow Land: Israel's Architecture of Occupation*. London: Verso, 2007.

Winter, Jay. *Sites of Memory, Sites of Mourning*. Cambridge: Cambridge University Press, 1995.

Woodward, Susan. "Humanitarian War: A New Consensus." *Disasters* 25:4 (December 2001).

Zanić, Ivo. *Prevarena povijest: Guslarska estrada, kult hajduka i rat u Hrvatskoj i Bosni i Hercegovini, 1990–1995* (The Swindled Past: Guslar Entertainment, the Hajduk Cult, and the War in Croatia and Bosnia and Herzegovina). Zagreb: Durieux, 1998.

Zimmerman, Warren. *Origins of a Catastrophe: Yugoslavia and Its Destroyers*. New York: Random House, 1997.

Živković, Marko. "Kosovo Is the Most Expensive Serbian Word: Political Enchantment and Milošević's Rise to Power." *Anthropology of East Europe Review* 19:1 (Spring 2001).

INTERVIEWS

Interviews by Andrew Herscher with former Popular Front members, Prishtina, October 2003 and February 2004.

ARCHIVAL AND MANUSCRIPT SOURCES

Archive of the Serbian Orthodox Eparchy of Raško-Prizren, Peć.
Municipal Archive of Prishtina, Prishtina.
Open Society Archive, Central European University, Budapest.

Index

Note: Place names are alphabetized according to their Albanian form, with the Serbian form following (Prishtina/Priština).

Aerial bombing, 100; architectural representation of, 101–3; concept of dual use in, 108; in Kosovo War, 103–9; in Kosovo War, architectural representation of, 109–15; in World War II, architectural representation of, 102. *See also* Collateral damage; Strategic bombing; Tactical bombing

Agency: as response to architectural interpellation, 52–53; solicitation of, in indicative narrative, 58; solicitation of, in discourse of desecration, 70

Amnesty International, 106

Anderson, Benedict, 38

Architectural heritage: abjection of, 13, 29–33; in postwar Kosovo, preservation of, 149–51; sacralization of in ethnic violence, 65; in socialist modernization, definition of, 28–33; in socialist modernization, destruction of, 13, 42–43; in socialist modernization, preservation of, 29–30; as supplement of ethnic identity, 13, 51, 150–51. *See also* Architecture; Historic preservation

Architecture: empirical historiography of, 17; historicization of, 16–18; as mimetic, 16–17; as patrimony, 13; as representation of alterity, 12; as sign or symbol, 5–6, 82, 88; in strategic bombing, 104–9; as supplement, 17; as supplement of ethnic identity, 52, 81, 82, 150–51; as supplement of history, 43, 64–65; as supplement of humanitarian violence, 101–3; as supplement of modernization, 24–25; theorization of, 3–4; as trace, 120. *See also* Architectural heritage; Supplement

Archive: as object of violence, 10–11; as construction of state, 11

Arkin, William, 109

Artaud, Antonin, 8, 9

Artemije (Radosavljević), Bishop, 140

Ash, Timothy Garton, 16

Atanasije (Jevtić), Bishop, 68–69

Avala Tower Fans Association, 116. *See also* Belgrade, destruction of Avala Tower in

Bahtiu, Enver, 144

Barthes, Roland, 47, 57–58, 64, 73–74. *See also* Narrative

Battle of Kosovo (1389), 63–64, 68–69

Bataille, George, 8, 9

Bećković, Matija, 47, 69, 70

Belgrade: destruction of Avala Tower in, 116, 117; destruction of RTS building in, 106–8, 109; destruction of Yugoslav Army headquarters in, 118, 119. *See also* Avala Tower Fans Association

Benjamin, Walter, 8, 9, 23; on architecture as object of distracted perception, 102; on Haussmann's Paris, 26–27. *See also* Haussmannization
Bergson, Henri, 118
Bevan, Robert, 155n5
Blair, Prime Minister Tony, 109
Bogdanović, Bogdan, 33
Boya, Grand Mufti Rexhep, 123, 147
Buck-Morss, Susan, 27
Butler, Judith, 112

du Camp, Maxime, 26
Cernicë/Cernica, 90
Clark, General Wesley, 103–4, 108, 124
von Clausewitz, Karl, 104
Clinton, President Bill, 124
Collateral damage: in humanitarian war, 101; in Kosovo War, 108–15. *See also* Aerial bombing
Committee for the Defense of Freedom of Thought and Expression, 71–72
Counterinsurgency (1998–1999), 83–87; destruction of Islamic architecture in, 87–91; destruction of archives in, 11; ethnicization of violence in, 91–98; representation of, 82. *See also* Yugoslav Army, in counterinsurgency
Creative destruction, 26. *See also* Destruction
Čukić, Dragan, 23

Democratic League of Kosovo, 128
Derrida, Jacques, 6–7, 9, 11, 81, 156n21, 157n32, 158n34, 161n4. *See also* Iterability; Performativity; Poststructuralism; Representation; Supplement
Desecration: destruction of Serbian Orthodox architecture as, 47–53; in discourse of Milošević regime, 72–73; human rights abuses and civil rights violations as, 70–72; in 1986 "Memorandum," 72
Destruction: in counterinsurgency (1998–1999), 82, 87–91; in counterinsurgency (1998–1999), as displace-

ment of embodied violence, 92–94; as cultural production, 8; and ethnicization of violence, 77–81, 86–87, 87–91, 92; historiography of, 5–6; in humanitarian war, as displacement of embodied violence, 101–3, 108–15; in Kosovo War, 103–9; in Kosovo War, countermemories of, 115–20; in Milošević trial, 3, 5; as mimetic, 16; in modernization, 26; multiple modes of, 115; as retributive violence, 127–33; in socialist modernization, of abjected heritage, 30–33; in socialist modernization, representation of, 39–42; as supplement of ethnic identity, 7, 91; as supplement of modernization, 25–27, 43; as supplement of retributive violence, 143; theorization of, 3–5; as vandalism of Serbian Orthodox architecture, 65–69. *See also* Creative destruction; Desecration; Haussmannization; Islamic architecture, as target of violence in counterinsurgency; Redestruction; Serbian Orthodox architecture, as target of violence in socialism; Vandalism
Dis, Vladislav Petković, 12
Djukić, Slavoljub, 59
Dobrović, Nikola, 33–37; conceptualization of heritage, 37; Prishtina, analysis of, 35–37; Prishtina, urban plan for, 36–38; Yugoslav Army headquarters, author of, 118. *See also* Belgrade, destruction of Yugoslav Army headquarters in; Prishtina, New Prishtina in, construction of
Dresnik/Drsnik, 130

Ethnic cleansing, 65, 164n44, 164n47; in discourse of Serbian Orthodox Church, 65; in discourse of NATO, 77–82. *See also* Ethnic violence; Genocide
Ethnic identity: architectural mediation of, 13, 51–52, 81–82; and ethnic violence, 58–62, 81; Serbian performance

Cultural Memory | *in the Present*

René Girard, *Mimesis and Theory: Essays on Literature and Criticism, 1959-2005*

Richard Baxstrom, *Houses in Motion: The Experience of Place and the Problem of Belief in Urban Malaysia*

Jennifer L. Culbert, *Dead Certainty: The Death Penalty and the Problem of Judgment*

Samantha Frost, *Lessons from a Materialist Thinker: Hobbesian Reflections on Ethics and Politics*

Regina Mara Schwartz, *Sacramental Poetics at the Dawn of Secularism: When God Left the World*

Gil Anidjar, *Semites: Race, Religion, Literature*

Ranjana Khanna, *Algeria Cuts: Women and Representation, 1830 to the Present*

Esther Peeren, *Intersubjectivities and Popular Culture: Bakhtin and Beyond*

Eyal Peretz, *Becoming Visionary: Brian De Palma's Cinematic Education of the Senses*

Diana Sorensen, *A Turbulent Decade Remembered: Scenes from the Latin American Sixties*

Hubert Damisch, *A Childhood Memory by Piero della Francesca*

José van Dijck, *Mediated Memories in the Digital Age*

Dana Hollander, *Exemplarity and Chosenness: Rosenzweig and Derrida on the Nation of Philosophy*

Asja Szafraniec, *Beckett, Derrida, and the Event of Literature*

Sara Guyer, *Romanticism After Auschwitz*

Alison Ross, *The Aesthetic Paths of Philosophy: Presentation in Kant, Heidegger, Lacoue-Labarthe, and Nancy*

Gerhard Richter, *Thought-Images: Frankfurt School Writers' Reflections from Damaged Life*

Bella Brodzki, *Can These Bones Live? Translation, Survival, and Cultural Memory*

Rodolphe Gasché, *The Honor of Thinking: Critique, Theory, Philosophy*

Brigitte Peucker, *The Material Image: Art and the Real in Film*

Natalie Melas, *All the Difference in the World: Postcoloniality and the Ends of Comparison*

Jonathan Culler, *The Literary in Theory*

Emmanuel Levinas, *On Escape*

Dan Zahavi, *Husserl's Phenomenology*

Rodolphe Gasché, *The Idea of Form: Rethinking Kant's Aesthetics*

Michael Naas, *Taking on the Tradition: Jacques Derrida and the Legacies of Deconstruction*

Herlinde Pauer-Studer, ed., *Constructions of Practical Reason: Interviews on Moral and Political Philosophy*

Jean-Luc Marion, *Being Given That: Toward a Phenomenology of Givenness*

Theodor W. Adorno and Max Horkheimer, *Dialectic of Enlightenment*

Ian Balfour, *The Rhetoric of Romantic Prophecy*

Martin Stokhof, *World and Life as One: Ethics and Ontology in Wittgenstein's Early Thought*

Gianni Vattimo, *Nietzsche: An Introduction*

Jacques Derrida, *Negotiations: Interventions and Interviews, 1971-1998*, ed. Elizabeth Rottenberg

Brett Levinson, *The Ends of Literature: The Latin American "Boom" in the Neoliberal Marketplace*

Timothy J. Reiss, *Against Autonomy: Cultural Instruments, Mutualities, a nd the Fictive Imagination*

Hent de Vries and Samuel Weber, eds., *Religion and Media*

Niklas Luhmann, *Theories of Distinction: Re-Describing the Descriptions of Modernity*, ed. and introd. William Rasch

Johannes Fabian, *Anthropology with an Attitude: Critical Essays*

Michel Henry, *I Am the Truth: Toward a Philosophy of Christianity*

Gil Anidjar, *"Our Place in Al-Andalus": Kabbalah, Philosophy, Literature in Arab-Jewish Letters*

Hélène Cixous and Jacques Derrida, *Veils*

F. R. Ankersmit, *Historical Representation*

F. R. Ankersmit, *Political Representation*

Elissa Marder, *Dead Time: Temporal Disorders in the Wake of Modernity (Baudelaire and Flaubert)*

Didier Maleuvre, *Museum Memories: History, Technology, Art*

Jacques Derrida, *Monolingualism of the Other; or, The Prosthesis of Origin*

Andrew Baruch Wachtel, *Making a Nation, Breaking a Nation: Literature and Cultural Politics in Yugoslavia*

Niklas Luhmann, *Love as Passion: The Codification of Intimacy*

Mieke Bal, ed., *The Practice of Cultural Analysis: Exposing Interdisciplinary Interpretation*

Jacques Derrida and Gianni Vattimo, eds., *Religion*